in
Mothers and Babies

HIV and AIDS
in
Mothers and Babies

A Guide to Counselling

Lorraine Sherr
BA Hons, Dip Clin Psychol, PhD
Principal Clinical Psychologist, St Mary's Hospital, Paddington

OXFORD
BLACKWELL SCIENTIFIC PUBLICATIONS
LONDON EDINBURGH BOSTON
MELBOURNE PARIS BERLIN VIENNA

© Lorraine Sherr 1991

Blackwell Scientific Publications
Editorial offices:
Osney Mead, Oxford OX2 0EL
25 John Street, London WC1N 2BL
23 Ainslie Place, Edinburgh EH3 6AJ
3 Cambridge Center, Cambridge,
    Massachusetts 02142, USA
54 University Street, Carlton,
    Victoria 3053, Australia

Other Editorial Offices:
Arnette SA
2, rue Casimir-Delavigne
75006 Paris
France

Blackwell Wissenschaft
Meinekestrasse 4
D-1000 Berlin 15
Germany

Blackwell MZV
Feldgasse 13
A-1238 Wien
Austria

First published 1991

Set by Best-Set Typesetter Ltd. H.K.
Printed and bound in Great Britain by
Hartnolls Ltd, Bodmin, Cornwall

DISTRIBUTORS
Marston Book Services Ltd
PO Box 87
Oxford OX2 0DT
(*Orders:* Tel: 0865 791155
       Fax: 0865 791927
       Telex: 837515)

USA
Mosby-Year Book, Inc.
11830 Westline Industrial Drive
St Louis, Missouri 63146
(*Orders:* Tel: 800 633-6699)

Canada
Mosby-Year Book, Inc.
5240 Finch Avenue East
Scarborough, Ontario
(*Orders*: Tel: 416 298-1588)

Australia
Blackwell Scientific Publications
(Australia) Pty Ltd
54 University Street,
Carlton, Victoria 3053
(*Orders*: Tel: 03 347-0300)

British Library
Cataloguing in Publication Data

British Library Cataloguing in
Publication Data
Sherr, Lorraine
    HIV and AIDS in mothers and
    babies: a guide to counselling.
    1. Humans. AIDS. Patients.
    Counselling
    I. Title
    362.198929792

ISBN 0-632-02834-3

To
Avrom
Ari, Ilan, Yonatan,
Natalie, Gregory, Stacey, Lisa, Tanya, Shula,
Benjamin, Jonathan, Dan, Joshua
Cassy, Danni, Gina, Matthew & Clifford.
The children in my life.

Contents

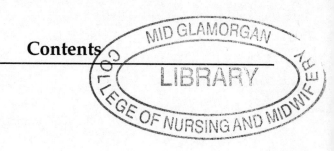

Preface

Childbirth usually brings with it the notion of life and new beginnings. AIDS on the other hand signifies illness, fear, death and uncertainty. When the two notions are held together they can set up competing emotions which contradict each other to such an extent that workers may not acknowledge their coexistence. Yet one in three of those with HIV are women, most people infected with HIV are in their child-bearing years, HIV can cross the placenta and infect the fetus, and mothers and babies, all over the world, are dying from AIDS.

Despite the enormous growth in research on HIV and AIDS infection, containment is still elusive. Women and children seem to have taken a low level in priority and thus many questions for these groups remain unanswered. Despite the fact that the client group may be small, the problems raised are enormous.

The individual chapters of this book present an overview of the current literature together with an integrated counselling approach to such clients and their problems. There is no way that this insight can be totally comprehensive, but it is hoped that the lessons that emerge will guide the practitioner. When faced with a new challenge, it is important not to abandon the lessons we have already learned: research towards a better understanding of the problems raised by HIV and AIDS has to incorporate the knowledge of counselling which we already have. Practitioners need to acknowledge their limitations and to know where to turn when they face uncertainty. HIV has set challenges which can humble all. If we are to move forward we have to place our preconceived notions and our prejudices on one side, take a fresh new look and be prepared to listen, especially to the voices of the women and children themselves.

Acknowledgements

A book like this is never easily written. It is usually the culmination of many years of work and there are always silent helpful people along the way without whom the path would never have been opened in the first place.

Thanks must always be given to the few outstanding individuals who make the final attempt possible. Insightful obstetricians and paediatricians play their role, people in overworked clinics all over the world who give of their time and open their arms in welcome. Funding agencies such as the Winston Churchill Memorial Fellowship who encourage one to travel in the first place and without whom the seeds of this work would never have been planted.

I would like to mention some special people who helped on the way. Thanks first to Avrom who did not comment on any drafts at all and thereby ensured a peace treaty which allowed for progress. Ester Whine gave interminable light relief from writing. Ari, Ilan and Yoni built boats, went camping, watched television, climbed trees and fences to Paul and Keith so that I could be given time and silence. Tanya has a talent that leaves me in awe. Her drawings are gratefully received. Lottie and Louis did their usual. Chaya and David Lewi once again were conspicuous by their absence. Books on women and motherhood can only have relevance if one looks at one's own family and Lilian and Ceymon Isaacs provided the perfect family for me to look back on, as well as Gogo Dolly and my sad lost Granny Sally. No secretary would type my manuscript, no friend would proofread it and colleagues nodded me on in encouragement.

Chapter 1

Introduction

A twentieth-century dean of Harvard Medical School wrote, 'In a hundred years we will realise that half of what we do today will be wrong – but which half?'. This wise statement is especially true when we consider new areas such as AIDS (Acquired Immune Deficiency Syndrome) and HIV (Human Immunodeficiency Virus) infection. At the beginning of the 1980s HIV was not fully identified. A decade later a wealth of information has been built up. Yet this only serves as a stark reminder of how ignorant we really are. Furthermore, despite the fact that it has long been known that HIV affects women and children as well as men, there is a comparative dearth of written information on the impact of AIDS and HIV on the first two groups. This is now being addressed – although somewhat late in the day – as the wide-ranging impact of the virus reveals itself.

This book will examine the full range of psychological factors associated with HIV and AIDS in mothers and babies. Fathers, grandparents and siblings are also touched by AIDS or the threat of AIDS and should be incorporated and included in the counselling process. It is also true that motherhood is not a woman's only role in life. She has many others. Yet motherhood does constitute a unique and special role. As such it affects many women, and it is in the context of woman as a mother that this book is designed. Other roles of women, while being acknowledged, will be mentioned only briefly.

AIDS – a world view

Griscelli (1989) noted that by the end of the 1980s, the decade in which we learned about AIDS, 6 million people worldwide had been found to be HIV positive; one third (2 million) of them were female. In terms of numbers, there are sharp contrasts between countries in the West and in Africa. The ratio of male to female in the West is 9 to 1 but reaches 2 males to every 1 female in Africa. This epidemic in women closely parallels the spread in children. The direct and indirect effects of AIDS and women on children are widespread, covering the ability of parents to raise their children as well as having wide social, economic and financial ramifications.

By the end of the present century, up to 500 000 children will lose one or both parents from AIDS – the problem of AIDS orphans is one that concerns the whole international community. By the year 2000, 10% of those under 15 years of age in ten African countries will be orphaned. AIDS orphans are not an exclusively African problem. In New York, between 50 000 and 100 000 children will lose one parent to AIDS by the end of the century.

Mann (1989) proposed seven ways in which women and children with HIV infection could be assisted. These are:

(1) Prevent infection;
(2) Support those who are HIV positive;
(3) Link with existing services;
(4) Increase number of women representatives on national and inter-national bodies;
(5) Ensure safe blood supplies and injections. Childbirth may represent a major transfusion risk to many women. Childbirth is a hazard for women in many parts of the world. In the third world, there is a risk of death during childbirth that ranges between one in 15 to one in 50;
(6) Provide information and support for the decisions of women;
(7) Provide special health and welfare support for women who are HIV positive and pregnant. This should extend to their newborns, the family and orphans.

The number of women with HIV infection is closely indicative of the number of children who will become HIV infected. In Europe it is mostly women associated with drug use who become infected with HIV. This happens either directly through their own sharing behaviour, or indirectly through sexual partners. Not only is this a worrying factor in itself, but mathematical predictions indicate a rapid rise in HIV infection through the intravenous drug use route which will exceed infection in the gay community by the beginning of the 1990s. Indeed, the latter mode of transmission has slowed down in the United States of America compared to the increase among heterosexuals. For the period of 1980–84, for example, infection rates within the gay community were 62% compared to 9% in intravenous drug users (IVDUs). The corresponding figures for 1989 are 42% in the gay community (a drop of 20%) and 17% in the IVDU community (an increase of 8%). The problem extends to children. For the period 1980–88, the ninth leading cause of death in the 1–4 year old group for the USA was AIDS. As has been mentioned, prevalence rates among women give a direct indication of childhood mortality and transmission from mother to infant accounts directly for an increase in the prevalence of paediatric AIDS.

Now that all blood products are screened, transmission via contaminated blood will decrease. However, centres still exist where screening is not yet routine. Furthermore, screening is not a perfect solution since the window of infection may allow for blood from a newly infected HIV donor to enter the blood bank undetected. The level of background infection can be assumed to determine the statistical risk of such a factor within a blood bank.

The main routes of transmission in the case of young children are:

- Non sterile needles;
- Blood transfusion;
- Mother to child transmission.

Infection can occur before, during, or after birth. HIV has been isolated in fetal tissue from as early as 15 weeks gestation (Sprecher *et al.* 1986; Joviasas & Koch 1985). Illness mostly occurs in the first year of life (Mok 1989; Scott 1989; Goedert *et al.* 1989). There are many problems of HIV diagnosis in children. Disease in young children also seems more severe than in adults.

The clinical signs and symptoms of AIDS have been described in numerous studies (Mok *et al.* 1989; Goedert *et al.* 1989; Peckham 1989). The definitions currently used in many studies are drawn from the US Centers for Disease Control (CDC) classification. These include:

ONE of the following:

- Lymphocytic interstitial pneumonitis (LIP);
- Persistent oral candida;
- Progressive encephalopathy.

Together with TWO or more of the following:

- Persistent generalized lymphadenopathy;
- Parotid swelling;

- Unexplained fever;
- Loss of developmental milestones;
- Hepatomegaly;
- Splenomegaly;
- Chronic recurrent diarrhoea;
- Failure to thrive.

In some centres, where diagnostic tools and facilities are limited, criteria are sometimes simplified.

In some studies, neurological signs in infants have been reported as severe (Belman 1989; Hopkins *et al.* 1989; Hittleman 1989). They report an early onset and express themselves in terms of progressive loss of developmental milestones. Belman summarizes the neurological problems for paediatric patients with AIDS:

- Acquired microcephaly;
- Pyramidal symptoms;
- Brain-cortical atrophy and calcification;
- Motor problems are greater than cognitive decline;
- Changes in gait have been recorded;
- IQ levels between 68 and 70 have been recorded. Although there are many problems with measurement of interpretation of intelligence quotients, it clearly indicates a group with special needs;
- Two out of three children show spinal cord differences on examination.

There seem to be two patterns of HIV expression in paediatrics. A group of approximately 30% children appear to have severe onset of symptoms. A second group – roughly 70% – seem to have a more slowly progressing disease. It is unclear what the reasons for this may be. One can postulate that a different strain of the virus may be involved; it may be related to host factors; it may be as a result of co-infection with other agents such as cytomegalo virus (CMV) or herpes, or it may be associated with the time of transmission of HIV to the fetus. All this is unknown at present. Critical periods have been isolated with other viral infections such as rubella yet with HIV it is unclear whether such critical periods exist and if so when these occur.

Pregnancy

AIDS presents a particular challenge in pregnancy (Forbes 1987). Since HIV can cross the placenta and infect the baby, the mantle of infection may spread. Knowledge about AIDS is in its infancy and, with time and research, data banks will expand. Insight will also increase and some ideas accepted as accurate now will be found to be wrong.

In Africa, where heterosexual transmission of the HIV virus is the norm, the number of infected women is roughly equal to that of men. Variation in ratio is often accounted for by socio/economic and demographic factors. In the West, the ratio of male to female HIV rates is about 9:1. However, such figures are misleading since they may obscure the wide range of problems associated with HIV and overlook the level of problems faced by women. Pregnancy is achieved by the self-same route by which HIV can be transmitted. Pregnancy also brings with it the increased likelihood of exposure to other potential HIV transmission routes. These include exposure to blood transfusions and skin piercing.

In the UK, 1100 women had tested positive to HIV by the beginning of the 1990s. Surveys of a comprehensive cohort of obstetric units (Peckham 1989) revealed just over 400 HIV-positive pregnancies in the UK. In the United States, the figures are greatly increased and in Africa particularly high numbers have been identified (see Chapter 3).

Overall, prevalence data are always limited. They reflect minima rather than the complete epidemiological picture. The rule of thumb should be to treat such figures as invariably representing an under-estimate of prevalence.

Defining HIV

HIV is an acronym for Human Immunodeficiency Virus – the virus associated with AIDS. This virus is a newly discovered entity. It was first isolated by French and American workers who named it LAV and HTLV-III respectively. HIV is now the internationally accepted term for the virus, but earlier published studies may use the older names when referring to the same virus.

All viruses have a site of action. HIV attacks T4 (CD4) helper cells which normally play a central role in the human immune response. HIV belongs to the family of viruses known as retroviruses. Essentially, this means that they are made of RNA (a precursor of DNA). The mode of action seems to involve penetration of the gene. The virus integrates with the gene which it can then 'hijack' and use for its own replication. The difficulties of creating a specific vaccine for such a virus are therefore enormous. The virus is known to operate in the presence of a specific enzyme – reverse transcriptase. Efforts to combat the virus have been focused on interfering with the enzyme action.

Once infected with HIV, an individual is infected for life and can also transmit the virus to others. Current data point to two peaks in infectivity. These are times when the individual is viraemic: at the point of infection, and when viral replication occurs at the time of disease progression. These facts have particular relevance in pregnancy and indeed they may interact with the likelihood of materno–fetal transmission and disease in the baby.

The test used to diagnose HIV exposure is essentially an antibody test. On exposure to HIV, the body reacts by producing antibodies. The HIV test can detect such antibodies in the bloodstream. As a diagnostic tool, therefore, it has widespread uses. However, the nature of the test carries its own limitations. Since it is an antibody test, it can only tell that the person has been exposed to HIV and produced antibodies. It can not tell how the person was exposed, when they were exposed, nor whether they will progress to a state of immune compromise, susceptible to opportunistic infections – and thereby be classified as having 'AIDS'.

The test cannot pick up the presence of antibodies for some time after infection – often as long as three months. This means that a person may test negative yet may have been exposed to the virus. A repeat test after a further three months may be needed to confirm this. This raises the difficulty of a period of time known as the 'window period'. This refers to a window when someone has been exposed to the virus – and may well transmit the virus – yet will test negative.

A virus test for widespread public use has not yet been perfected and the limitations of the antibody test must be remembered at all times. The polymerase chain reaction (PCR) test, however, which is undergoing research testing at the moment, does hold out some promise for the future.

Defining AIDS

AIDS refers to the medical syndrome known in full as the 'Acquired Immune Deficiency Syndrome'. This condition is often the end point of HIV infection. A weakened immune system becomes susceptible to opportunistic infections. These may express themselves with particular severity in someone with a compromised immune system. In addition, some conditions which a healthy individual could cope with easily become severe in someone with a depleted immune system. AIDS is a serious condition. In the UK, since 1981 when the condition was first noted, half of those diagnosed with AIDS have now died. The picture is similar in other countries.

The World Health Organization (WHO) maintain that about half of those infected with HIV will develop AIDS within ten years. They further maintain that the majority of those infected are expected to develop disease eventually. Effective drug treatments may hinder or prolong this progression. There are no data at present to identify the people who will progress to disease quickly and those who will become the longer term survivors. Furthermore, as facts about the disease progression are only in their infancy (10 years of data) the full picture is limited – and perhaps even inaccurate.

Women and HIV

HIV can be passed from men to women and from women to men during sex. The virus has been found in both vaginal and seminal fluid. The virus can also cross the placenta during pregnancy and infect the fetus. The interpretation of data concerning the mechanisms, timing, and impact of transmission, is still in its early stages.

Since women pass on antibodies to their babies across the placenta, a baby may test positive for HIV antibody but be virus free. It is the passive maternal antibody which is being picked up. This has profound implications for neonatal and infant care. Essentially true HIV status cannot yet be established in young babies for a long period – up to 2 years in some cases. This means that the infant will require constant testing and/or monitoring and the family will have to live with a period of uncertainty and apprehension. Psychologically, this may represent a severe and protracted crisis period for a family already facing maternal and sometimes paternal infection. This is one clear example of the interrelationship that exists between psychological care and medical advances. The demands for support may alter if technological advances allow for early clarification of infection or HIV status in the neonate. Until such time, the emotional burden that must be carried by parents over a considerable length of time is profound.

Cultural factors

HIV in women and children does not occur in a vacuum but occurs within a culture and within a society. Within such societies and cultures, the decision pathways open to women may be bound up with their lifestyles, life opportunities and expectations. These may challenge women and present them with many dilemmas. In essence, a woman with HIV must face the option of a possibly sick child or childlessness. Such choices are never straightforward. It must be remembered that for many women, their life role and fertility are intricately bound together.

The psychological consequences of HIV are as profound for women as for any other group, given that HIV not only affects their body but may indirectly implicate their life role. Mortality for women in Africa is high: one in twenty mothers die and one in five reach menopause. The increasing presence of HIV in the female population may dramatically alter these figures for the worse.

Despite the fact that HIV is a disease of individuals, it encroaches on the lives and continuity of families. It may change the roles and structures within a family. Grandparents, for example, may now be brought in as primary child carers on the death of a mother or parents. The death of a father may necessitate a change in roles for a woman. Some women may suddenly need to become breadwinners, others will become the sole breadwinner when previously this role may have been shared. Siblings too may need to take on parenting roles.

The diagnosis of HIV infection may herald conflicts within the family and thereby reduce its ability to provide welfare. Marital stress in the presence of HIV is not uncommon. Within the different sub-groups of AIDS-affected people many other life problems will come to the fore.

With gay or bisexual men, sexual orientation may previously have been kept secret and is difficult for other family members to deal with. With haemophilia, the onset of HIV infection heralds the need to live in the face of two life-threatening conditions and this may overburden coping mechanisms. HIV represents a dramatic turnaround in someone like a haemophiliac where hope for 'normal' life has been given by the advent of the very treatment which led to HIV.

The notion of what constitutes a 'family' may need to be made much wider. Roles may alter and this may in turn filter through to all structures within a defined society. HIV not only brings with it new challenges, but often also serves as a vehicle to address many of the old-established problems in society. Some examples of these include the role of women, social, medical, and legal rights, poverty, and discrimination.

Counselling provision may need to be widely available. It is wrong to think that procreation is the domain of women alone. In a study of 92 HIV-positive clients, Sherr and Hedge (1989) recorded a number of

themes common to heterosexual men and women as well as homosexual and bisexual men. These included:

- Desire for a child;
- Reproductive decision making;
- Termination counselling;
- Coming to terms with childlessness;
- Informing children about HIV;
- Support during pregnancy;
- Death of a child;
- Infection control issues.

Thus workers need to be ready to deal with a wide range of clients,
for all of whom counselling may be relevant. HIV counselling and
pregnancy may be targeted at:

- Those contemplating pregnancy;
- All those faced with HIV testing during pregnancy;
- Those who are pregnant with unknown HIV status;
- Those who are pregnant and find out they are HIV-positive;
- Those who are known to be HIV-positive and become pregnant;
- Those with AIDS who are pregnant;
- Those who are sexually active.

HIV counselling in relation to babies and children is relevant for:

- The families of HIV infected babies;
- HIV-positive mothers with babies of unknown status;
- HIV-negative parents with HIV-positive children;
- The wider family and carers of HIV-positive children;
- The wider family and carers of AIDS orphans (be they HIV-positive
  or HIV-negative).

In addition, these categories ought to be extended to include staff
caring for the above.

HIV screening for those identified as 'High Risk' in countries where
such behaviours can be identified, brings with it a need for counselling,
particularly for all pregnant mothers who may be offered HIV screening. Seroprevalence surveys may raise anxieties in otherwise well
women and this should not be overlooked. It seems that pregnant
women provide a ready group for such studies. Chapter 4 describes in
some detail a number of studies worldwide where seroprevalence has

been studied in groups of pregnant women. This raises concerns not only for the numbers of women infected with the virus but also for the number of pregnant women who are subjected to HIV testing. Few studies report on pre- and post-test counselling for these groups.

Counselling during pregnancy is essentially an ongoing process. Although long-term support may be necessary, there are certain stages during pregnancy which need particular attention. Furthermore, if counselling resources are limited or even absent, these may constitute vital input points. They include:

- The decision to conceive;
- HIV testing;
- Decisions to continue or terminate a pregnancy;
- The birth of the baby;
- Illness during the neonatal period.

How to obtain a full understanding of the facts and of current up-to-date knowledge is perhaps the first stumbling block for anyone dealing with AIDS. The size and extent of the problem is essentially unknown at present. Numerous studies have looked at the outcome of seropre-valence studies and monitored the numbers of women infected with HIV in order to predict future problems more accurately. It is clear that the situation varies from country to country and region to region. In Africa, where HIV is essentially a heterosexual disease, male to female ratios are closer than in the West. Many of those infected worldwide fall into the reproductive age groups, hence the number of babies infected is high and is increasing. In the West, the majority of children identified to date have a drug-using parent as a risk factor for infection. Many of the HIV positive drug users are both sexually active and in the reproductive age groups. As the number of babies infected correlates fairly highly with the numbers of women infected, increases in infection within drug-using adults will mark projected infection in their children in the future. In Eastern Europe, pockets of paediatric infection have come to light as a result of nosocomial spread via microtransfusions after birth or the use of unsterilized injecting equipment.

The problems arising from HIV and AIDS and their management are complex. This book sets out some of the many psychological hurdles that may be encountered and describes some of the skills which can be summoned up to meet the challenges. It includes a detailed account of the general counselling approach and its components and then goes on to describe pre- and post-test counselling, termination, pregnancy and labour in the presence of HIV. It adheres to no individual school of thought but gathers together many useful methodologies in an attempt to provide a useful working model for frontline carers. The special needs of children are examined, together with a general chapter on death and bereavement. Finally, education and training on the care of mothers and babies are touched upon as the future challenges come to be faced.

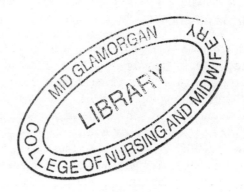

Chapter 2

Counselling and
Basic Counselling Skills

This chapter sets out very briefly what is meant by the term 'counselling' and describes a variety of approaches to counselling types of intervention and the fundamental principles underlying them. It describes some of the tools such as listening skills, helping strategies, problem solving, and the provision of support. Subsequent chapters will look at some of the applied counselling issues, and the ideas covered here will form the backdrop against which these are set.

What is counselling?

In health care, the professional will already have a wide range of experience in interacting with clients and will also have a unique range of technical expertise in their area of speciality. Counselling should supplement and complement this.

All human interaction can be seen as communication. Professionals working in health care have often gone beyond social communication as they identify individuals at times of stress, trauma, pain, anxiety, grief, uncertainty or joy. The key notion about counselling is that it is an active skill rather than a passive theoretical exercise. Thus all the book learning one can acquire is only part of counselling. It may be easy to know what ought to be done or to recognize good 'counselling' when it has occurred, but it is often very difficult, when faced with a situation, to provide that good counselling and have the necessary skills at one's fingertips.

This means that most people will come to counselling with a good bit of practice under their belt. They will already have experienced person to person interaction. They may have helped people solve their problems or deal with their pain or simply have supported them. A good working knowledge of counselling can help them to improve on these skills, avoid errors, and draw the distinction between taking over for people in trouble, and helping people to help themselves.

Counselling can be seen as a process which uses dialogue and inter-action to help people understand, clarify and respond to their life events. The skills involved are essentially those which help people to put their problems into words, which highlight the areas of need and then provide a safe and non-judgemental atmosphere in which people can think through their problems, perhaps understand their reactions to them, evaluate why they respond in particular ways, perhaps look back at their life experience, and finally to think through and sub-sequently try out solutions. Counselling, therefore, cannot be imposed on someone like a cough linctus. It requires the skilled input of the counsellor and the agreement, commitment and participation of the counsellee.

There are a wide range of counselling philosophies or approaches. These supply theoretical understanding and working frameworks. Ap-proaches include the psychodynamic, behavioural interventions, cog-nitive, humanistic, transactional analysis, personal construct or gestalt or, alternatively, an eclectic approach which does not aspire to one model but adapts approach to circumstance and individuals.

Some of the above models differ greatly, but many have certain threads in common. Counselling operates by addressing the mental processes which intervene between an outside occurrence and an in-dividual reaction.

The skills of counselling can be broken down into different areas. Often the totality of a counselling approach is more than the sum of the individual skills. However, preparation and learning with subse-quent practice is made easier if people can divide out the individual skills, examine these and understand their own behaviour.

First and foremost counselling is an active process. All the reading in the world is no substitute for actually doing it. Practice is an important component of counselling. Initially counselling must have an aim or a goal. This can include:

(1) Counselling for support
This is a common and commonly used form of counselling. Here the client needs to sound out their problem and the necessary skills require many listening and empathizing abilities.

(2) The provision of factual information
Much counselling is involved with the passage of factual information. Very often this forms a basis of counselling sessions in health care.

Some professionals may underestimate their roles as providers of accurate, unambiguous, relevant and clear information. In some areas, if the counsellor simply carries out the informational component of their interview efficiently they will have done an excellent job of counselling. Thus, even those who are untrained in counselling approaches, or wary of entering into a counselling role, may utilize counselling techniques to get across basic factual information. This is a key issue as many psychologists have shown that seemingly simple information is often misunderstood or poorly recalled by the uninformed (Ley 1990) and that if some simple behavioural changes are incorporated, understanding and recall can be altered.

Most people need some form of basic knowledge in order to evaluate stressful situations and to make sensible and appropriate decisions about a course of action. However, the necessary information is often lacking, incomplete or not recalled.

People also find it enormously helpful if they are given a clear statement about the frequency and commonness of a reaction and forewarning of possible outcomes and reactions.

The world of one individual may be difficult to explain to another and very soon the skilled counsellor will learn that the passage of information which appeared simple to start off with is a complex process affected by the listener, the speaker, the messages themselves, and the context in which they occur.

Information transfer may appear to be straightforward. Yet in practice it is never that simple. People are rarely passive receptors of information. They approach a situation with preconceptions, beliefs and notions which may affect what they hear, how they take it in, and indeed how they act upon it. In a medical setting, information may be laden with emotion and in such circumstances understanding, focus, recall, and attention may vary considerably.

Variability occurs among counsellors as well. Ley (1989) has shown how difficult it is for professionals (including nurses, doctors, dentists, psychologists and physiotherapists among others) to comply with instructions and to provide uniform sets of information.

(3) Counselling for judgements
Basic information is the tool on which judgements are made. However judgements are often illogical, made on limited information, and not well thought out. The process of reaching a decision is complicated and judgements are not infallible.

Thus judgements and decision making are not events but processes. At each stage they are open to influence, misjudgement and error. Furthermore each stage may be interdependent on previous stages. The kinds of factors which influence these processes should be known and understood by the counsellor. A counselling session may allow the counsellor to draw these out and examine them so that the subject can address decisions without the untoward influence of previous limitations. For example, when people are faced with large amounts of information and complex or emotion-ridden facts, they often do not weigh up the factors equally or spend an enormous amount of time on each possible pathway. Instead they may make very quick judgements based on simple rules or heuristics. Factors which may not be useful – such as expectations – can also often affect decision making (Nisbett and Ross 1980).

At times, consciousness may not have achieved full insight into the factors that contribute to decisions. Some judgements are inaccurate.

(4) Counselling for decision making
Many workers have found cognitive psychology a useful tool to approach decision making, especially when making life decisions and plans of action in the presence of depressed or anxious mood states. These are, it should be pointed out here, common situations faced by people with HIV or AIDS.

There are mental or cognitive processes which intervene between an event in the external world and an individual's reaction to it. Input into this phase can allow for a reinterpretation of the environmental event and the attributions or thoughts prompted by the event, and thereby perhaps change the reaction.

If one has an understanding of how people perceive information, process it, attend selectively to the information, code and store it, recall it and subsequently utilize it in their decision making processes, then counselling can be used to intervene in the process and perhaps ensure a clearer and better thought-out decision or action.

These ideas form the basis of some of the major models in clinical psychology. For example Ellis and Beck (1962; 1967) have set out the way in which dysfunctional moods (such as depression or anxiety) may arise more from perceptions and evaluations of events than from the event itself. Challenges to these assumptions may alter these and thereby alter the mood state or approach to the problem.

(5) Counselling and major life stresses and vulnerability

AIDS and HIV infection can be categorized as major life stresses. As such, one can look at the literature on life stress to see if it has important lessons to provide. The psychological problems associated with life stress have been widely reported (Brown & Harris 1978). However, prospective studies have shown that not all people who experience such stress also experience psychological problems. What emerges from the literature is the potential psychological problems associated with stress, and also, of perhaps equal importance, the wide range of individual variation in emotional expression in reaction to such stress.

The literature on stress goes on to explore the possibility of vulnerable individuals who are more prone to the ill effects of stress. In AIDS and HIV infection this line of thinking has been tentatively explored, looking at whether there is a link between coping and immune competence (Temoshok, 1989). It seems unclear from the literature to date whether there is validation for the vulnerability theory, but from the counselling angle it can certainly do no harm to increase self-esteem which may in itself be a protective factor. Brown and Harris (1978), for example, found that women who lost their mothers early in life who were without a current intimate relationship were more likely to become depressed. If such an example is used to examine reactions to HIV diagnosis, it would seem useful to examine ways of working on intimate relationships (which perhaps provide support and counterbalance some of the ill effects of the stressor).

The most common theme to emerge from the literature on vulnerability is that if social support is missing or inadequate, physical and psychological disorders are more common. This may form part of a complicated spiral where someone is unable to obtain social support due to negative self esteem. Counselling input may reduce vulnerability indirectly by helping someone increase their self-esteem and then be more able (and hopefully more successful) to create supportive relationships.

(6) Counselling and recovery

The interaction of cognitive factors and recovery may be extensive. Perhaps the question of whether cognitive factors can precipitate or in any way cause an adverse or stressful situation may never be resolved. Yet there certainly does seem to be some evidence that cognitive factors may well determine an individual's reaction to a problem and how they subsequently cope with it. People choose coping strategies from a limited set of options

(7) Crisis intervention
The need for counselling often arises suddenly and unexpectedly in situations where an individual is thrown into a crisis. The needs for counselling at such times depend on many factors such as accessibility and prompt reaction (as crises are often of limited duration). The aim of such counselling is to mobilize the individual as soon as possible. It is often difficult to predict 'crisis situations'. People respond in very different ways to events and although some situations are clearly more likely to provoke a crisis in many individuals, there are always those who will cope admirably in overwhelming circumstances and those who find a seemingly everyday event the prelude to an individual crisis.

A crisis can thus be typified by an individual's reaction to an un-anticipated circumstance. It includes:

Anxiety. Expressed as psychological disarray or physical symptoms such as heart palpitations, dry mouth, sweating, stomach churning, shaking knees (or body), increase in body heat.
Panic/terror. The situation is overwhelming and the person feels immo-bilized, unable to act or react, and frozen into their panic without recourse to action or relief
Depression. Depression is a common reaction to crises. For example Weinman (1987) notes that between 20–30 per cent of inpatients suffer from depression symptoms.
Need. The individual is torn between their feelings of helplessness and their desire to overcome these uncomfortable feelings and relieve their acute anxiety.
Focus. The situation is all-consuming and may impede other areas of the individual's existence.

Interventions for crises are often determined (or limited) by the amount of access the counsellor has at the key points. Some crisis intervention groups run very successfully. Other methods of interven-tion come from crisis help lines which provide telephone access. This has the advantage of immediacy, availability, and convenience, but has limitations in the realm of person to person interaction, loss of control and, in some cases, limited follow-up.

Crisis intervention should have the following aims:

Address the problem face on
Divide and conquer. The enormity of some crisis situations may lead to paralysis. There is always some small avenue of input and the counsellor can help to identify this and start the process of reactivation.

Honesty. The counsellor needs to be the person who acknowledges the crisis and the full extent of its impact on the individual rather than denying it or providing meaningless platitudes.

Listen. The person may need to talk the crisis through. They may have a full and long story which needs to be heard. The counsellor ought to listen to the story as told by the affected person as it is their experience of the situation (rather than the counsellor's imagined or personal reaction to a similar situations) which will determine how they cope.

Help people to make their own decisions. Do not impose your individual solutions onto the situation. Although they may seem obvious to you (and for you) they may not suit your client. Indeed, if the obvious solutions and the ones that everyone will tell them actually worked, they probably would not turn to you.

Activation. Ensure that people can be moved to action. This can be done by agreement, contracts or pacing. This shows the individual one of the pathways out of paralysis.

Follow-up. Survival of a crisis must not only imply that an individual has handled the situation to the end, but ideally it should also provide them with insight into the processes they adopted so that in a subsequent similar situation they can adopt these themselves.

Prevention is better than cure. Crisis intervention may be appropriate as an access point to counselling, but often a situation could have been avoided or handled better in the first place if counselling strategies had been adopted.

(8) Counselling to ease distress and promote recovery
Another common role of counselling is to provide psychological expression at times of emotional distress. This can either be the aim of intervention or emerge in the process of intervention. The skills involved in counselling in these situations are often in sharp contrast to those perfected in social interactions. In the latter, one tries to gloss over problems, see the bright side or dismiss them. In counselling it is important for people to express their pain. The process of counselling is to allow for the expression of the distress in the first instance and subsequently to make it easier to live with such distress.

This means that the counsellor needs to help the person find a place for their pain, find a way of dealing with their pain, and continue with their life in a way that is meaningful for them. Distress may necessitate life change and counselling may facilitate decision making and coming to terms with new situations, insights or goals.

(9) Counselling for emotional expression

One way to ease distress is the provision of a method for a client to vent bottled up emotion. Although this may often present a welcome avenue of release for clients, there are occasions where it may not be appropriate either in terms of timing or the clients' willingness to express their emotions.

(10) Counselling to resolve problems

Life is often beset with problems which present themselves as impeding hurdles. Counselling is one way of addressing these problems in a controlled and helpful setting. Such problems concern, for example, relationships, interactions, life decisions. In such circumstances the counsellor may want to involve all the parties involved in the problem (as, for example, in family therapy), a single key individual, or perhaps a couple (in psychosexual counselling, for example).

(11) Counselling to acquire skills

Although many counselling interventions are aimed in part at promoting or acquiring life skills, some counselling interventions are specifically set up to focus on just this aspect. This may occur in settings where individuals feel unable to meet the demands of society, family, or even themselves, and thus may need to examine their own skill base. Such examples include social skill training or some group work.

(12) Counselling as intervention

This may be the form of counselling that health care workers are most familiar with. It may take the form of direct advice (e.g. to take iron tablets in pregnancy). These interventions run the risk of becoming directives rather than advice. Another form of advice can arise from pre-warning or alerting interventions. This may relate to, for example, the ways in which a woman is told labour can commence. Here, a midwife may issue instructions on the different ways in which labour can commence and how the woman may react. The difficulty with such information transfer often rests in the fact that the health care worker, who is in possession of the information base, may become over-powerful and take control.

(13) Counselling to face the unfaceable

Counselling interventions teach that the fear of something is often greater than the problem itself. Based on this notion, much relief can be generated if people can face up to issues which were so enormous that they were deemed unthinkable. With HIV, this can often be issues such as telling loved ones, fear of rejection, becoming ill. Counselling can allow clients to verbalize their fears, think through all the possible outcomes without experiencing their ramifications, and plan strategies for these. This process often allows subjects to deal with reality rather than fantasy and can bring relief either because denial and avoidance can end, or because (as is often the case) the dreaded outcomes do not in fact materialize, or, if they do, they are not as terrible as feared.

(14) Reducing or increasing specific client behaviour

Individual expression is a complex mixture of behavioural repertoires. Some behaviours within this repertoire may be maladaptive or may reduce the competence of an individual in a situation. They may previously have been effective, but now become useless or even a hindrance yet the client may still revert to them. Essentially, people possess some behaviours which may render them vulnerable and others which are particular strengths. One role of counselling is to highlight such strengths and at the same time to provide a client with an opportunity to see limitations or weaknesses, practise alternatives, and have support carrying them out in reality.

(15) Counselling to restructure client perceptions

It is not uncommon for clients to feel emotional pain as a result of their own thought processes. Perhaps these arise from demanding (even unreasonable) internal standards, or reflections on themselves which are negative, critical and discouraging. Cognitive interventions are often aimed at identifying these, and assisting clients to identify these and work through a process to restructure their thoughts (Beck 1976).

Counselling tools

Effective intervention is reliant on practice and skilled proficiency with a number of techniques. Counsellors also need to understand the limits of their role and where their expertise ends.

(1) Listening skills

Although everyone believes they know what listening involves, it can often be quite disturbing to appreciate how difficult this skill is in reality. Try, for example, to listen to someone for two minutes without interrupting them. Most people find they interrupt within seconds. If they do manage to listen for the entire period, their concentration has often lapsed and they cannot remember the content of the dialogue or forget chunks from the middle. Listening can involve hearing the words and phrases that a client uses without having much insight into the overall message, mood and experience that the client conveys. Listening skills can, with practice, free the counsellor to attend to the message the client conveys without necessarily recalling every word or factual item. The goals of listening should include:

- Show interest in what the client is saying;
- Allow clients to tell the story in their own way;
- Pick up both the content and the mood of the dialogue;
- Concentrate sufficiently to focus on the client's dialogue and mood and do not waft into fantasy;
- Limit interruptions and focussed questioning which may result in clients saying what they think the counsellor wants to hear or what they 'ought' to be saying, rather than fully expounding their problem;
- Let the client finish.

Listening does not only refer to the words and content of the dialogue. There is much in the conversation that can provide insight into the client. The listener needs to concentrate on pitch, volume, timing, hesitations and flow. At the same time there may be a host of non-verbal aspects to the communication process which may interact with the dialogue and at times even run counter to it. These include body position, facial expression, eye contact and gestures. If the listening process is designed to put the client at ease and facilitate expression, the counsellor should face the client with good eye contact in a relaxed and comfortable manner. Counsellors will find difficulty listening when they themselves have personal problems or are suffering from anxiety which intrudes into the session. They may also experience difficulty if they are seated badly, especially behind barriers such as desks or high chairs, if they are eager to interrupt, if they have limited time, or if they are impatient.

(2) Questioning

Questions form a major theme in all dialogue. Counsellors need to be aware of the number of questions they use and the type of questioning style they adopt. These may often determine the style of answering and may dictate the course of the conversation. Generally, questions fall into open and closed categories.

Closed questions
These are often used in health care settings. They are usually questions which result in one-word answers. They have a place but this may be limited at times. Examples of closed questions are:

- Are you happy with your pregnancy?
- Are you married?
- What is your full name?

The advantages of closed questions are:

- They are necessary for clarification;
- They allow for careful opening up with a wary, cautious or shy person;
- They allow confidence building (this occurs when a patient can answer a question and has no problem with the response; (all patients, for example, know their names and where they live);
- They may allow for dialogue at a time of stress.

The disadvantages of closed questions are often better known:

- They are very controlling;
- They limit the response and may hide a myriad of facts;
- It may pre-set the response (a classic example of this is the question 'do you have any questions' – very often clients take this to mean

'the interview has now ended, I am busy and if you have any questions make them short and few');

- The person posing the questions is usually in charge of the dialogue;
- The counsellor may be able to predict either the nature of the response or even the content prior to reply;
- They may funnel the conversation according to a plan or structure which the counsellor imposes on the dialogue, rather than reflect the story as it seems to the client. This may emphasize some aspects of the problem which the client may then concentrate on.

Counsellors should be aware of the impact of closed questions and use them where appropriate.

Open questions
The task of open questions is to encourage the client to talk, to tell their story, and to do so in their own way. Examples of open questions are:

- Tell me about your pregnancy;
- How does your husband feel about all this?
- What outcomes do you foresee for all this?

Within counselling, open questions often form the bulk of the interview and indeed some of the skill of a counsellor is to phrase a question in an open and encouraging way to allow for a free and comfortable flow of information from the client.

The disadvantages of these questions are:

- They may take up considerable time;
- They may be threatening to clients who do not want to divulge their circumstances;
- The answers are rarely predictable.

Advantages include:

- They allow for the client's story to take precedence over the counsellor's view of the story;
- They are less prone to value judgements;
- They may encourage dialogue and may reassure the client that the counsellor is sympathetic, interested, and willing to give time (perhaps the major components of empathy);

- Replies may be long enough for the counsellor to focus on other aspects such as non-verbal communication, tone, interruptions, body position. These may provide the counsellor with much extra information.

Silence
This can be seen as a form of questioning. In everyday conversations, silences rarely occur, they create embarrassment and are often filled rapidly. A counsellor needs to check their usual social reaction to silence and examine the purpose of silence. Essentially silence allows space. It may allow the client time to gather their thoughts. It may challenge the client to contemplate the previous comment and enlarge upon it, expand it or clarify it. Often silence can trigger movement onto a deeper plane of disclosure and dialogue. An excess of silence is threatening. Counsellors ought to use silence carefully.

Focussing
Focussing questions are often helpful in sifting through large chunks of information. This is a strategy which may utilize open or closed questions and which moves the conversation from the general to the specific and may highlight the nub of a problem. For example:

CLIENT: I hate the whole issue of HIV.
COUNSELLOR: What is it that you hate about it?
CLIENT: Well what am I going to tell my husband?
COUNSELLOR: What does your husband think about the pregnancy?
CLIENT: Well, he may want me to have an abortion.

Here, the counsellor allowed the client to express emotion, and then proceeded to move on to a problem which could be tackled.

Judgemental questions
It is often very hard to remain non-judgemental in an interaction. Many of the counselling skills centre around the ability to change habitual social dialogue to eliminate or minimize questions which show bias, judgement, opinion, castigation or disdain. For example:

- In retrospect should you have used contraception?
- Do you feel guilty about your sex life?
- Have you taken up safe sex?

These questions may alienate the client and may also provide answers to those questions which were inevitable and as such have little bearing on the client's inner thoughts and feelings. The questions may generate discomfort and alienation in the client who may well be reluctant to discuss problems with a counsellor; the obvious outcome of such reluctance is a limited ability to provide help.

(3) Statements

Some part of counselling comprises statements which make sense, gather the client's thoughts, reflect or clarify the issues for a client, or bring problems into focus. The simple repetition of the client's statements may be overdoing reflection. It should be used selectively.

There are many para-verbal statements that can be interjected into conversation to highlight issues, to show clients that concentration has been maintained even in a long and complicated tale, or to encourage them to continue. These are the 'um' and 'ahha' type of statements.

(4) Help

There are many possible avenues of help. This section will only serve as a summary. Bear in mind that counselling approaches can be incorporated easily into the provision of care on the one hand, but competent counselling therapy cannot be learned overnight and often takes considerable time to perfect. Possibilities for help include:

Anxiety. Anxiety is an unpleasant emotion. Clients need to be aware of the link between their minds and their bodies and to understand the flight/fright reaction. They may benefit from anxiety reduction, amelioration, or simply understanding their bodily reactions and gathering reassurance from the fact that it is 'normal'.

Problem solving. Emotional trauma often renders decision-making difficult, impossible or non-fruitful. People do not make logical decisions and many decisions are made based on simple availability of information without much contemplation of the consequences and implications of the decision. In everyday life this often does not matter. However in crisis times, problem-solving and decision-making may be key elements in adjustment. Help with thinking through options, imagining positive and negative outcomes, and planning strategies to deal with these may allow clients to mobilize in the first place and to ensure optimum decisions even in difficult or limited situations.

It is wrong to think that counselling deals with strange and rare problems. Very often it is the everyday problems which take up most time. At any given time, a client under pressure may have difficulties coping. Help with problem-solving strategies may provide a lifeline for someone who is in such difficulty or one who is overwhelmed by the enormity of their problems. Such a person cannot distinguish between linked problems which create chain reactions, those which can be easily tackled, and those which appear insurmountable. Most people possess their own individual problem-solving capabilities which they have often used in the past. The counsellor can examine how they have reacted to past problems and try to help them see which strategies they adopted to help them through at that time. They can examine whether these strategies will work again, if not why not, and what other possibilities they can try.

Pain. Pain phenomena are not fully understood. Wherever pain comes from (and that is often a useless question when there is no relief for the pain despite its origins), the experience of pain is essentially a psychological event. Clients can be helped to minimize pain, to dull pain experience, to distract from pain and perhaps to incorporate some physical measures (such as posture, stance or muscle tone) to lessen pain or prevent the development of secondary pain. Relaxation techniques can facilitate pain relief.

Perspective. When people face problems they may seem overwhelming or present an aspect that makes them difficult to counter. One method of helping is for the counsellor to assess the problems objectively and to help the patient see other sides, or different sides to the problem.

Emotion. Emotions can overwhelm people. Heron (1977) differentiates anger, fear, grief and embarrassment. When overwhelmed by these emotions understanding is necessary to eliminate fear and to allow for unrestricted choices. Extreme emotional experiences can affect a client's self-image, can engender feelings of helplessness and hopelessness, can lead to constant failure when unattainable (or unrealistic) goals are set, or can impede full functioning by misattributions of causality. In such circumstances people may constantly attribute events to internal causes and thereupon feel helpless to exert control over their lives. Help can be given by allowing people to express their emotions, by working on the self-image, and by altering attributions. Sometimes people simply need emotional expression.

Reachable goals. For counselling to be productive, the counsellor needs to set objectives clearly and attempt to limit these to numerous attainable goals rather than feeling a sense of overwhelming enormity. Within such goals, the counsellor can create manageable components.

This must be one of the initial aims of counselling where the counsellor should clarify the problem to be dealt with, the goals and aims based on clear understanding with the client.

(5) Environment

The counselling environment plays a crucial role and may dramatically affect the course of the intervention. There are a wide range of environmental factors.

(a) Physical environment: the counsellor should ensure that there is a quiet and private place where there will be no interruptions. These include telephones ringing, other people wandering in, noise or distractions.
(b) Emotional environment: ensure that the client is ready to talk, consents and desires the dialogue, and understands the role of a counsellor.
(c) Preparation: optimum counselling must come from individuals who have received training, have skills and insight, and have recourse to their own back-up, support and expression. Counselling can be draining and counsellors need to be well prepared.
(d) Cultural environment: counsellors should be aware of background cultural factors related to the client, the context in which they are operating and the social norms of the society. These may be key factors in determining the success of the intervention, the pressures and expectations that the client may hold, and the support that may be available.

(6) Pitfalls

Finally, counselling brings with it some problems. These can be avoided if the counsellor takes care not to become trapped. A few golden rules are:

* Do not take things personally;
* Do not see the clients' problems from your own point of view;

- Do not take control;
- When things are so overwhelming you feel like leaving the room – do not. That is exactly how the client feels and they cannot get up and walk away;
- Do not give copious advice. There are many other places for clients to go to for this (and they probably have been there already);
- If you get a sense of something happening in the interview do not dismiss it with thoughts that you must be crazy! You may well be, but the chances are that you are feeling something real;
- Do not be false;
- Be available;
- Do not solve all problems – dependency is counterproductive in the long term;
- Have sufficient time available to complete the task;
- Make sure you are in a private place or one where there can be confidentiality;
- Do not impose counselling on an unwilling client;
- Set limits and boundaries.

Mucchielli (1983) gives clear guidance on what the counselling interview should not be:

(a) It is not a conversation: in a social conversation there is dialogue and exchange of views. Although elements of the counselling interview may initially resemble a 'conversation' it must go beyond this.

(b) It is not a discussion: in a social argument people put forward opposing or differing views which they defend. This may limit the ability to understand the other as one is concentrating on one's own point of view. A counselling interview needs to be more objective.

(c) It is not a newspaper interview: such an interview, although seemingly designed to elicit the story of a client, has an ulterior motive of seeking interest, intrigue or fascination for the public. Undue emphasis may be placed on elements which are not necessarily the key features for the client. This is almost the opposite of the goals of the counselling interview.

(d) It is not an interrogation. It is important not to focus on the questions the interrogator wants to ask (which would be the case with a judge or policeman). Counselling is more concerned with the questions the client wants to address;

(e) It is not a discourse by the interviewer. This is not the time for the interviewer to conduct a monologue of his/her own views;

(f) It is not a confession. Confessions invoke moral standards. The

counsellor is not concerned with pardon, but with understanding;
(g) It is not a diagnostic interview. Problems may have themes in common but diagnosis and stereotyping may not be helpful to understand the personal and individual needs and reactions of a client.

Impediments to counselling

There are many impediments that hinder the provision of good counselling. These are:

(1) Training

Counselling is a skill that needs training. Many professionals believe that counselling comes naturally and if they only had some extra time and motivation they could easily provide this commodity. Although time and motivation can greatly enhance the quality of medical care, they do not constitute the totality of counselling training. This belief may be based on the fact that the tools of counselling (namely verbal interaction) are tools that are readily available to most (unlike, say, chemistry which needs a laboratory, or space flight which requires a rocket!). Furthermore, when outsiders observe counselling they may conclude that it is 'common sense' and 'child's play'. However, common sense is only obvious in retrospect, and child's play is often very much more sophisticated than it seems. Houghton (1967) provides an excellent empirical study where staff were given extra time and effort and were motivated to 'try harder' to no effect.

Training duration and intensity often depends on the desired goal. Many counselling approaches can be put forward in a comparatively short period of time, but longer term therapeutic skills take both time and practice to acquire. Furthermore, training is ongoing and a skilled counsellor should be in a constant state of 'learning'.

(2) Burnout

Burnout, a term coined in 1974 by Freudenberger, reflects overexposure to a stressor, resulting in an inability to face the situation and provide output and care. The very nature of health care work in general and AIDS and HIV work in particular may increase the risk of experiencing burnout. Carroll (1979) examined the symptoms of burnout describing these as physical (exhaustion, sleep disturbances, eating disturbance); somatic (headaches, stomach aches, low resistance to illness); psychological (depression, anger, irritability, distrust, lowered self-esteem, withdrawing) and social (disrupting relationships, lowered morale, rapid staff turnover, job resignation, rigid work styles). The symptoms of burnout often follow extended exposure to stressful environments. Prevention is probably the most effective intervention. Many workers have catalogued ways in which burnout can be avoided (Corey 1982; Dowd 1981; Hershenson & Power 1987). These involve intervention at both the system and individual level ensuring a rewarding work environment, reduction of stress, provision of support, limitation of obstacles such as under-resourcing, overworking and understaffing, together with clear delineation of work and social environment and support systems.

(3) Cross-cultural problems
Hershenson and Power draw attention to obstacles of impediment by different social class, ethnic, or cultural factors. These could well be relevant in HIV work where some of the client groups may have particular behaviours or life styles which differ from those of the counsellors. Essentially, counsellors should be exposed to the groups they treat, should not form stereotypes, and should be open to modifying their approach to comply with cultural norms which may create access barriers for some sections of the population.

Overall, counselling is an approach which sees individuals as experts on their own lives and the role of the counsellor is to provide and facilitate an environment out of which positive change can develop. This model allows practitioners to involve patients actively. They can then participate in decision-making which affects their lives, and which confers action and control in place of passivity and compliance. It also means that patients take over some of the responsibility associated with key decision making. Counselling should not be confused with situations where direct advice is given.

Chapter 3

Epidemiology

It is difficult and perhaps impossible to estimate, with any degree of accuracy, the numbers of women and children infected with HIV world-wide. Mann (1989) summarizes World Health Organization (WHO) estimates of infection in the 1980s and concludes that of the estimated 600 000 people who have developed AIDS, more than 150 000 are women. The majority of women fall into in pattern II countries (mainly Africa) and a considerable group (30 000) come from pattern I and III countries. As childhood infection closely parallels female infection, WHO estimates that 200 000 infants may well have been infected via perinatal transmission in the past decade. The press have reported figures closer to ten million when estimating infection with HIV in children by the end of the century.

HIV infection in pregnant mothers can dramatically affect infant mortality. The numbers of pregnant women with HIV are increasing. In 1988, the USA reported 5600 HIV-positive women giving birth. By 1989, this figure had increased to 6400 (NIH 1990). By mid-1989, 82 cases of AIDS in women had been reported to the Centres for Disease Surveillance and Control in the UK (CDSC 1989) with a further 1087 laboratory reports of HIV in women.

The World Health Organization maintains an index of reported AIDS cases. These figures can give some indication of the spread of HIV but they reflect the severe end of the spectrum and essentially represent a vast under-estimate as figures are limited by under-recognition, re-luctance or impediments to prompt reporting, or confusion of deaths associated with other causes. By the mid-1990s, over 250 000 cases of AIDS had been reported to WHO (WHO 1990) from 150 countries. WHO estimates that by the end of the century that saw AIDS arrive, there will be over 5 million cases. As AIDS is the end point of disease, figures for HIV infection are much higher. WHO estimate that between 6 and 8 million people have already been infected (WHO 1990). Put in population terms this means that for every 400 adults in the world, 1 has HIV infection. By the end of the century this figure may well have tripled. The pattern of spread is not an even one and in areas of high infection (particularly sub-Saharan Africa), 1 in 50 adults is infected. Within countries there are clusters of infection, often around major cities. In the USA, for example, the CDC reports that 1 out of every 65 women giving birth in New York City is infected with HIV. At different hospitals within the city the rate varies with figures as high as 1 in 25 being reported. HIV is not confined to such cities and even cities which do not receive high media attention may have high rates of infection. Boston, for example, reports that 1 out of every 100 women who gives birth is HIV-positive.

As heterosexual spread increases, women and babies become more vulnerable. Current figures indicate that heterosexual spread accounts for roughly 60% of infections worldwide, and trends suggest that this percentage will rise by 15–20% in the next decade.

HIV and AIDS are not limited to region but is pandemic in nature. Some pattern III countries (such as Thailand and India) which showed low or non-existent infection only a few years ago are now exhibiting dramatic increases in spread. By March 1990, the USA reported 11746 cases of AIDS in women or young girls over the age of 13 years. Table 3.1 below sets out some examples of global patterns of spread.

Table 3.1   Global patterns of HIV.

Region	Study	Report
Africa	M'Pele*	0.5% to 18% general population affected. Between 2% and 30% of women in some urban areas are seropositive. Heterosexual transmission accounts for 80% cases approximately.
Latin America	De Menezes Succi*	Male: female ratio 9:1. Children account for 4% of all cases. Heterosexual transmission accounts for 68.5% of cases approximately.

Table 3.1 *(Con't)*

Region	Study	Report
Eastern Mediterranean	Trezi*	299 cases reported by Nov 89 – presumed an underestimation. Limited data available.
Europe	Brunet*	Much variation between countries. High infection rates among drug injectors. Heterosexual cases increase from 1% p.a. (85) to 10% p.a. (89). Male female ratio has moved from 10:1 (85) to 7:1 (89). 19 countries had declared total of 639 paediatric AIDS cases by Sept. 89 20% paediatric cases linked to blood transfusion.
South-East Asia	Ramachandram*	Relatively low infection rates. Of 2 318 822 tests, 12 107 positive with 67 AIDS cases (Nov. 89).
Western Pacific	Coden*	Variation. Australia and New Zealand higher rates (pattern I type) other regions lower.
USA	NIH	1989 Women account for 10% of AIDS Cases. 80% of paediatric infection is transplacental.

* Reports in 'The Implications of AIDS for Mothers and Children' WHO, Paris, November 1989.

Overall, a series of patterns and themes emerge:

(1)   HIV infection is worldwide. The most acute prevalence is seen in sub-Saharan Africa. WHO estimates (June 1990) that about 200 000 HIV-infected infants have been born in this region and in the next decade it is anticipated that there will be more than one million additional infected children.

Infection among women is proportionately lower in North America,

Europe, South America and Asia. Infection rates estimated by WHO (June 1990) are as follows (Table 3.2):

Table 3.2   WHO estimations of infection rates.

Region	Proportion
South America	1 in 500
North America	1 in 700
Western Europe	1 in 1400
Sub Saharan Africa	1 in 50
Eastern Europe/Asia/Pacific Region	1 in 20 000

(2)   WHO estimate that about 60% of global infection with HIV has been associated with heterosexual sexual intercourse.

(3)   The male to female ratio differs dramatically by region. Chiphangwi (1989) presents data as follows:

Table 3.3   Male to female ratio of spread according to pattern.

Pattern of spread	M:F ratio	HIV-positive women
I	10 : 1	250 000
II	1 : 1	1 250 000
III	1 : 1	25 000

Chin (1989) presents a global male to female ratio (based on 6 million infections) of 3:1.

(4)   Incidence of paediatric HIV infection and AIDS is more difficult to track. Chin (1989) points out the link between maternal and infant infection. Predictions are based on a vertical transmission rate of 25%, but Chin points out that the uninfected children of HIV positive mothers must also be taken into account as they may be potential AIDS orphans.

(5)   All estimations are limited and sudden identification of pockets of infection can affect these figures dramatically. Such examples as the infants in Romania and Elista (USSR) show, dramatically, how new infections may come to light revealing widespread nosocomial spread in these areas.

(6)   Risk groups vary according to region and in some regions they are

non-existent. With the passage of time, workers look more towards risk behaviours than risk groups. Risks of maternal or infant infection include:

- Present parental intravenous drug use;
- Previous parental intravenous drug use;
- Partner of the above;
- Blood transfusion;
- Prostitution;
- Partner of HIV-infected individual.

(7) Problems are not confined to the infected and their infants. A whirlpool effect is created whereby ramifications are dramatic. These include:

- Siblings affected by the trauma of an ill or dying sibling;
- HIV-negative children affected by ill or dying parent (s);
- Extended family carrying the burden of an ill child (children) and caring for orphaned (and perhaps ill) grandchildren or relatives;
- Well adult children dealing with premature loss of parents to AIDS or coming to terms with parental HIV;
- Children dealing with illness (such as haemophilia, thalassaemia, malaria) who have to take on the additional burden of AIDS/HIV;
- Parental guilt at exposing children to conditions which have, in turn, resulted in blood transfusion;
- Health care worker difficulties where they may have (unknowingly) provided blood transfusions of infected blood products;
- Multiple loss;
- Economic hardship or deprivation as a result of economic strains brought about by caring for infected infant/parent;
- Economic hardship or deprivation as a result of loss of breadwinner;
- Economic hardship as a result of reduced income shared among greater number of family members;
- All these are often made dramatically worse by the burden of secrecy and stigma associated with HIV infection and AIDS.

(8) Underdiagnosis may occur, especially in countries with poor diagnostic facilities or situations where women and children are not seen as potential HIV carriers. Chiphangwi (1989) notes that underdiagnosis in Africa may result from confusion with other common causes of death such as diarrhoeal illnesses, respiratory problems and malaria – all of which are common killers in Africa in their own right.

The increasing problem for women and children
It is sad to note that attention to women has somehow taken a back seat in the struggle against AIDS and HIV infection. Indeed, it seems that attention is now being focussed on women mainly because they are seen as vectors of infection to young children. This is despite the fact that the WHO estimates that of the 6 million presumed infections worldwide (up until 1990), 2 million have occurred in women.

In pattern II countries, women have always been implicated as the spread has been primarily heterosexual. The focus on women has been less acute in the West because of the predominance of male infection. Global figures are misleading in that they fail to identify the changing trends and the vulnerability of women (Pape & Johnson 1989).

Figures from South America (Brazil), for example, show the alarming changes. Spread, according to male : female ratio, is presented below:

1982:   0   female infections
1984:   120 males : 1 female
1989:   9   males : 1 female

Children with AIDS

Children with AIDS represent an increasing problem. In the USA, 2 192 children with AIDS have been recorded up to March 1990 (US DHHS 1990). The numbers of children with HIV are essentially unknown. Estimates suggest that for every child reported with AIDS, anywhere from two to 10 additional children are infected with HIV. In the USA, the majority of children are drawn from groups that are classified as minority or disadvantaged. In the UK and Europe, the majority of children to date are drawn from similar groupings. By the end of 1989, Davison *et al.* (1989) reported on 414 HIV-positive pregnancies in the UK. The European community has reported 558 cases of AIDS in children (WHO 1989).

The CDC reports that AIDS is the ninth leading cause of death for young children under four years of age in the U.S.A. Children are infected with HIV by a variety of routes. These include:

Transplacental spread. This is said to be implicated in over 75% of European cases and over 70% of North American cases. In these centres, injecting drug use has been implicated either directly or indirectly as a risk factor for a large proportion of the children. There have been no such risk factors identified in pattern II countries.

Infected blood products. This includes children with blood disorders that require transfusion such as haemophilia, thalassaemia and malaria who have been transfused in the absence of screening or heat treatment of products.

Nosocomal spread. This includes the use of unsterile medical equipment which has been implicated in the spread of HIV to hospitalized or institutionalized children (e.g. Elista, USSR where over 200 children have been infected by a web of contamination; or Romania where microtransfusions have been implicated).

Incest. Although cases via this route have rarely been identified the possibility exists and a 1990 study has identified two cases of infection via incest (Di John 1990).

Rates of vertical transmission

Differing rates of vertical transmission have been reported in the West and Africa. This may relate to many factors. Firstly, the efficiency and mechanisms of HIV transmission *in utero* are not well understood. It may well be that transmission is more likely if there is longer duration of HIV. The effects on the particular stage of pregnancy is not known.

In investigating gender differences, Des Jarlais and Friedman (1988) point out some consistent gender differences in USA groups. Essentially, they find that females have less severe outcomes than males. The data are preliminary and may reflect other social correlates rather than be the result of causative certainties. They also point out that the same effect is seen in children. However, they note that Rothenberg *et al.* (1987) find a shorter survival time for females. These studies supply few answers, but do raise the need to examine gender more closely.

Transmission rates for HIV 2 are not yet fully tracked. HIV 2 has been isolated mainly in West African countries. Blanch (WHO Conference 1989) reported on 18 mother/child pairs in West Africa who were followed up for 12 months where HIV 2 was detected. There were no infections and no positive cultures at birth. This may be due to structural differences or differences in replication patterns of HIV 2. However, it is early days yet and more studies are needed. There are no studies to date on women infected with both HIV 1 and HIV 2 and the corresponding epidemiology in their infants.

In conclusion, it can be seen that paediatric and maternal infection are widespread and will probably continue to increase. There are no data that suggest that this increase will not be of the exponential form seen in all other populations.

Chapter 4

HIV Testing in Pregnancy

At present there is an antibody test available which can detect exposure to HIV. Tests can be carried out prior to pregnancy, during pregnancy, on cord blood, the neonate and the young child.

HIV testing in pregnancy

HIV testing in pregnancy is like no other test. Screening should never be undertaken lightly nor should it be routine. Chapters 2, 5 and 6 set out many counselling issues related to screening. Essentially, the basic notions are:

- Limitations of the HIV test;
- Reasons for screening;
- Population to be screened.

The HIV test itself is limited. It can tell whether a person has been exposed to the virus and has made antibody. However, it does not tell how the person got infected, when the person got infected, the stage of illness, whether they will become ill, what kind of illnesses they will get or when and if they are likely to deteriorate. On the other hand, the test itself creates a high level of anxiety. People need to be sure they can cope with this. Much stigmatization and discrimination has resulted from positive tests. There is very little that the medical profession can offer someone who is HIV-positive by way of cure.

Counselling should be available, irrespective of sero-status. Drug treatments are not yet generally available and those that are currently in use have their limitations. They are not cures, and tend not to be used in pregnancy. AZT (Zidovudine) is the major drug used at present. It is effective in some individuals in delaying symptoms. It has been used, on a trial basis, with HIV-positive patients who are otherwise well. The data have not yet been fully reported. Any positive outcome must be viewed with caution as the long-term impact of AZT for well HIV-positives has not been documented. It is known that AZT can cross the placenta. A study of two pregnant women, HIV-positive and about to undergo termination of pregnancy (TOP), was used to verify this. The women took standard drug doses. After termination of pregnancy, fetal tissue examinations revealed the presence of AZT. The effect of AZT on the developing fetus is unknown. Thus, treatment options are limited for pregnant women and this has bearing on HIV testing.

Another problem with testing is that the timing is unclear. When should the test be carried out? As the antibody may take up to 12 weeks to be detected, early testing would not exclude infection if recent exposure has taken place. Continued testing may be unreasonable and impractical – but may be the only accurate way of monitoring antibody status over time. Pregnant women continue to have sex and thus exposure right through pregnancy is possible.

The reasons behind testing ought to be well thought out. The overriding reason why any procedure should be carried out is for the *benefit* of the patient. This obviously involves considerations such as informed choice and perhaps issues about management of HIV and related infections.

Some centres are eager to test to gather epidemiological data. This brings about many problems. Firstly, the need for this will vary according to background infection levels. The useless gathering of data should be avoided. The provision of data for service planning, funding and preparation is a much better justification. The aims and goals of seroprevalence studies need to be clearly set out prior to the introduction of any policy. Sometimes the cost of the study exceeds the available funding for subsequent service provision. Funding for screening must allow for counselling provision and follow up – and not simply cover the cost of the test. Staff training may also be a budgetary requirement.

In some areas the data yielded by these studies may limit the usefulness of the exercise and may call it into question. For a start, uptake needs to be high to yield meaningful results. Studies in New York have shown that it is the higher risk groups who tend to decline testing. Pregnant women may not be typical of the heterosexual population and thus extrapolation back may be impossible. The factors on which they vary include:

- They are more likely to be in a stable relationship;
- They have practised unsafe sex (evidenced by the pregnancy itself).

They are also vulnerable and this must be taken into account. No study has been reported where the partners of pregnant women have been screened – a fact that is not only astonishing but epidemiologically unsound.

Some staff would like to carry out testing as a result of their personal (misguided) fears of infection from positive patients. This is not helpful as it often also means that such staff would refuse to treat a patient found to be positive. The better way is not to dismiss staff anxiety but to allow for education so that these very real staff concerns can be addressed without the need to subject women to unnecessary procedures.

HIV testing in pregnancy has a varied uptake depending on factors such as midwife encouragement (Meadows 1990) and social acceptability in the woman (Moatti 1990). This often reflects the bias of the institution rather than the wishes of women attending it. Where informed counselling has preceded testing, allowing optimal, open choice, uptake is low. Workers should take care that they do not confuse counselling with informed consent. At antenatal clinics women may feel under great pressure to accept all tests and worry that refusal would jeopardize their care. A study by Ndugga *et al.* (1990) reported on high acceptability of HIV screening in a sample in Kenya. Acceptance after 'counselling' was high (95% of 783 subjects were tested). Yet 53% of the women screened did not return to the clinic for their results. It may be that these women did not clearly understand the nature of the test they were undergoing, or, alternatively, they 'refused' in their own way – by simply not returning.

Everyone who requests an HIV test should have HIV counselling available to them. If they still want a test this should be their right. For pregnant women, the standard procedures for the test should be adhered to. These include pre/post test counselling, confidentiality, no discrimination based on the outcome, and ongoing care. Full details on pre and post test counselling are outlined in the following two chapters. Santana *et al.* (1990) surveyed clinics treating in excess of 3000 pregnant women in the USA where HIV education had been recommended as part of policy. Their survey revealed that the education was well accepted. Stratton *et al.* (1990) documented the policies and practices at 49 obstetric centres in the USA. They found that all HIV-positive test results were given in person (though it is unclear how HIV-negative results were handled). Furthermore, they documented a high time commitment for post test counselling (average of over 30 minutes for

HIV-positive women and under 20 minutes for HIV-negative women). Thus all policies should incorporate the necessary funding and facilities to handle such time consuming (and perhaps costly) counselling into their testing protocols.

In some countries, HIV infection has been associated with higher risk behaviours such as IV drug use, haemophilia and bisexuality. Obviously, good history taking is important if such behaviours are to be addressed. In other countries, especially in Africa, so many women are potentially at risk that no such pointers exist.

Despite the fact that Griscelli (1990) has stated, 'the key to preventing the spread of infection in children does not lie in screening pregnant women but in preventing pregnancies in seropositive women', there is still widespread HIV testing. Table 4.1 below sets out a list of a number of studies reporting screening. Of particular note is the enormous number of women worldwide who have been screened for HIV.

Many studies report that 'counselling and testing' still have very low if not non-existent refusal rates. It is unclear to what extent subjects are objectively counselled, what form this takes, and whether refusal is a real option. For example, Johnston et al. (1989) report on 'all women presenting to an obstetric clinic'. Nesheim et al. (1989) report that 'since July 1 1987 all pregnant women at a large hospital in Atlanta have been offered counselling and testing. Over 95% of the women have consented to testing'. Medbo, in Norway, reports 'HIV screening has been offered to all pregnant women in Norway. More than 165 000 women (>98%) have so far been tested'. Lindsay (1989) reports on a study on routine antepartum screening in 3634 women where there was a 4% refusal rate.

Henry et al. (1988) reviewed 275 consecutive tests in a US hospital and found no record of consent or counselling for 44% of the sample. A study in Norway reported that every woman having an abortion is screened without consent (Brattebo 1988).

Denayer et al. (1990) looked at obstetric practice in Belgium. A sample of 815 gynaecologists in the whole country were questioned in a series of surveys. Of these, 91% offered HIV testing in pregnancy, 49% to all women and 42% to those falling into risk groups. Furthermore, these workers found that 49% of gynaecologists tested for HIV without informing the patient. The majority of clinicians (74%) screened for HIV at the first visit, while 15% screened twice: at the first and last antenatal clinics.

De Rossi has estimated that as ELISA (one of the HIV tests) has a 99% sensitivity and a 95% specificity, universal screening in Italy (700 000 deliveries per annum in that country) would allow an estima-

Table 4.1(a) Studies of HIV screening worldwide.

Study	Place	Number in Sample	HIV-positive Result: Number	%	Comment on Sample
Aguero	Lima, Peru	860	0	0%	
Araneta	New York	3425	21	1.4%	
Barbacci (1989)	Baltimore, USA	1406	49	5.3%	
Barreto (1983)	Maputo	1000	0	0%	high risk
Barton	Chicago	585	3	–	low risk
			0	0%	high risk
Berthaud	Brooklyn	301	–	5.8%	
Bird & Snow (1988)	Stockholm	8000	20	–	
Blanche (1989)	Kinshasa	8000	–	5.8%	
Boulos (1989)	Haiti	4336	–	8.9%	1986
			–	10.2%	1988
Boulos	Haiti	799	57	7.1%	
Braddick	Nairobi	2665	62	–	
Brattebo (1988)	Norway	24 825	3	0.012%	
Brossard (1987)	Paris	systematic all terminations	–	0.27%	terminations
	Paris		–	0.7%	
Bucceri A. et al. (1989)	Milan, Italy	214	138	–	
Bucherl (1987)	Munich	63	–	–	
(CDC (1987)	Carolina, USA	200	0	0%	
CDC	Wisconsin, USA	1000	0	0%	

Reference	N	Location	n	%	Notes
Chiphangwi (1985)	200	Malawi	4	2%	
(1987)	85	Malawi	7	8%	
Connor et al. (1989)	2619	Newark, USA	4	0.4%	
Ciraru Vigneron (1987)	–	–	–	1% & 3%	
Delaporte (1990)	108	Gabon	19	17.6%	
Delaporte	750	Paris	24	–	
De Rossi	310	Padua	2	–	high risk
	210	Padua	7	–	
	277	Padua	1	–	
Duerr (1990)	951	Rwanda	–	9.3%	high risk
Goedert (1989)	687		92	13.4%	
Halse (1990)	4599	Africa	443	9.7%	
Halsey (1987)	673	Baltimore 85	–	0.74%	
	1245	Baltimore 86	–	1.3%	
Harrison	532	San Diego	10	–	(anon)
Hauer (1987)	All	San Francisco	–	–	
Hira (1989)	1954	Zambia	227	–	
Hira (1990)	1954	Zambia	227	12%	high risk
Holman	126	Brooklyn	29	34%	
Holt (1990)	3754	Haiti	160	4%	
Hoff (1988)	30708	Mass., USA	–	0.25%	GU attenders
Howard et al.*	2800	Riverside, UK	–	–	GU an attenders
	982		2	–	

Table 4.1(a)   Studies of HIV screening worldwide.

Study	Number in Sample	Place	HIV-positive Result: Number	%	Comment on Sample
Ippolito (1989)	39 102	Rome, Italy	51	–	
Jenum	12 511	Oslo	–	1.008%	
Johnson (1987)	115	Baltimore	–	29%	high risk
Johnson J. et al. (1989)*	Baltimore	clinic attenders (no refusal)	–	1%	
Johnston F. (1989)*	436	Edinburgh, UK	–	18%	high risk
Kantanen (1988)	9202	Helsinki	1	–	
Kantanen	9738	Helsinki	1	–	
Kanti	92	Senegal	3	3%	
Kaptue (1987)	134	Cameroon	–	–	
Kozlov (1990)	2 229 000	Leningrad	50	–	
Lallemant	1833	Brazzaville	71	3.9%	
Lallemant	1531	Brazzaville	62	4%	
Landesman (1987)	602	Brooklyn	12	2%	
Landesman et al.	602	Brooklyn, USA	12	2%	
Larsson	7766	Stockholm	3	0.04%	
Larsson	7708	Sweden	3	0.089%	
Lindgren	39 500	Sweden	4	–	
Lindsay (1989)	3472	Atlanta, USA	10	0.28%	
Lindsay (1989)	513		–	5.6%	
Makawa	2000	Congo	203	10%	

Reference	n	Location	No. positive	%	
Malawi (1990)	3635	Malawi	–	20%	
Maynard (89)	all	Rhode Island	1	–	1985
			7	–	1986
			9	–	1987
			10	–	1988
Medbo (1989)	165 000	Norway	14	0.009%	(98% pop)
Mendez (1987)	366	Brooklyn, USA	–	42%	IVDU
			–	6%	Haitian
Miotti (1989)	461	Blantyre, Malawi	77	18.6%	
MMWR (1987)	2276	USA	–	–	Haemophiliacs
	973	Abidjan	102	–	
Neshaim (1989)	95% all women	Atlanta, USA	–	0.6%	(1987–89)
Ndugwa (1990)	3612	Uganda	1032	28.6%	
Novick (1989)	276 609	New York, USA	–	0.66%	
Nsa	8264	Kinshasa	479	–	1986
Ntabab	96	Malawi	4	4.2%	1987
	260	Malawi	19	6.5%	
Nzilambi	7000	Kinshasa	135	5.6%	
Pista (1990)	1519	Portugal	10	0.7%	
Pokrovsky (1990)	10 565 181	USSR	9	5.6%	
Pruzuck (1990)	2100	Burkina Faso	23	0.27%	
Rogers	8108	Baltimore	–	–	
Ryder et al. (1989)	21 655	Kinshasa, Zaire	466	4.23%	
Sangare (1989)	2602	Abidjan	–	38%	
Schoenbaum (1987)	276	Bronx	–		
Scott	2061	Florida	74	3.6%	

Table 4.1(a)   Studies of HIV screening worldwide.

Study	Number in Sample	Place	HIV-positive Result:		Comment on Sample
			Number	%	
Sperling et al. (1989)	224	New York	–	2.7%	
Temmerman (1989)	1507	Nairobi, Kenya	–	3.1%	
			–	8.6%	high risk
Tovo (1988)	89	Turin	–	32.6%	
Van Lith (1989)	224	Holland	6	2.7%	
Virnon	2300	France	–	0.2%	
Vranckx	1918	Badung	37	–	
Wenstrom (1989)*	349	Chicago, USA	–	0.6%	
	849	Chicago Labour	–	1.1%	
Wang	583	China	1	–	
Zohoun (1987)	83	Benin	–	0%	

tion of roughly 35 000 false positive tests. Confirmation by Western Blot, a different HIV test, on these samples would be expensive however – about $340 000 (£170 000). De Rossi has thus urged workers to examine the cost effectiveness of screening. The high costs invariably do not take into account the costs of counselling which ought to be added on to any estimate.

Barbour *et al.* (1989) studied uptake of AIDS counselling and testing at a Scottish family planning clinic over a three-month period. They found low demand but a steady request for advice and information from male and female patients. Advertising and awareness was promoted by use of written information (posters, information bookmarks, and information cards in all condom packs). Requests for HIV tests (17) were monitored over a three-month period. Out of these, 7 did not proceed to have a test. 14 of the 17 were counselled while the remaining 3 received information only. Wenstrom and Zuidema (1989) outlined a programme comparing anonymous and non-anonymous approaches to testing. They described a counselling process and reported that interviews took approximately 30 minutes. After such counselling there was a 34% uptake in screening.

Similar uptake rates were recorded by Holman *et al.* (1988). Of 322 patients who received HIV counselling and HIV test offers, 134 (40%) accepted testing. Furthermore, these workers found that only half of those who were HIV-positive acknowledged a risk factor, but after they were informed of their status all seropositive patients volunteered further information. Indeed all HIV-positive women had risk factors that were not identified during pre-test counselling.

Postpartum HIV counselling should also be considered. A study in the USA noted that a high proportion of women have little if any antenatal care. Many of these women also report behaviours which may carry risk for HIV and thus postpartum counselling should be considered. This is especially necessary given that many of these clients have limited access to medical care and may be missed at other venues.

A series of questions can be raised with regard to HIV testing in pregnancy:

Does testing result in a reduction of perinatal transmission?
There is no evidence to substantiate this. Sunderland *et al.* (1988) found that primary prevention of HIV was to be emphasized in the first instance. They found that many seropositive women continued their pregnancy and often presented with subsequent pregnancies. They found the need to examine a broad range of input covering contracep-

tion advice, involvement of women and their partners, and help in examining self fulfilment avenues for women who often find child-bearing to be their primary self fulfilment role. Thus any decisions against pregnancy had to incorporate viable alternative life experiences for these women.

Does HIV testing result in increased termination of pregnancy?

Current data suggest that women do not necessarily terminate if they are informed that they are HIV positive. Barbacci found only 3 out of a sample of 84 women proceeded to terminate and one of these had a subsequent pregnancy to term. Sunderland (1988) examined women who learned of their HIV-seropositive status while pregnant but in time for a legal abortion (the legal limit in New York, as in the UK, is 24 weeks gestation) and a second group who conceived a subsequent pregnancy after HIV-positive status had been established. Essentially, they found that 3 out of 18 women elected to terminate their pregnancy, with 15 continuing. Of the 11 who became pregnant after knowledge of HIV status, 9 chose to continue their pregnancy. Johnstone *et al.* (1989) noted that a high rate of drug-using women in his UK sample terminated pregnancy (irrespective of HIV status).

Of note was the fact that in this study one subject avoided hospital or medical staff until after 24 weeks gestation for fear of having to discuss the termination issue. The lesson from this study should be to ensure that women realize that termination is not the only option for seropositivity in pregnancy.

Stratton *et al.* (1990) surveyed 49 obstetric centres in the USA and reported that 85% of women found to be HIV-positive elected to continue their pregnancy. Griscelli (1989) reported that of 843 pregnancies in seropositive women in France, only 45% opted for a termination.

Irion *et al.* (1990) reported on surveys of 2364 pregnant women in Switzerland. Rates of HIV were low. They found that knowledge of sero-status did not have an important influence on pregnancy decisions.

Cowan *et al.* (1990) also documented that knowledge of sero-status had no effect on subsequent pregnancies. However, in this study, there was a greater effect on terminations in the index pregnancy.

Buckett *et al.* (1988) surveyed attenders (n = 299) with a 59% response rate. Of the responders, 59% felt they would request a termination of pregnancy if they were found to be HIV-positive.

What are the reasons women cite for termination or pregnancy continuation?

Johnstone *et al.* noted that the 38 women in their sample who continued their pregnancy despite knowledge of HIV did so for many reasons. They cited current good health, desire for a child, attitudes against abortion, or knowledge of other women with healthy children despite HIV as reasons for pregnancy continuation. Many of those who terminate cite HIV as a primary factor, but others have reasons that include social, support, and financial considerations which may precede HIV knowledge. Indeed, in many studies women who have terminated a pregnancy in the presence of HIV have gone on to term with subsequent pregnancies when social background factors have altered.

Does risk identification lead to more accurate targeting of HIV testing?
In general, studies have shown that women at higher risk are more reluctant to come forward for testing. It is unclear why this is so. It may be that they are generally more reluctant to come forward for anything. It may be that they fear that if they are identified as HIV positive they will suffer from discrimination. It may be that they do not want to contemplate termination and they are concerned that the staff may encourage this. It may be that they simply have taken an active decision not to have an HIV test as they feel uncertain about their ability to cope with the test result.

Barbacci (1990) reported on a study which examined whether selective HIV screening based on risk factors would identify all (or a significant proportion) of HIV-positive women in the Baltimore area (USA). They introduced two systems of screening. One comprised routine screening for pregnant women and the other was selective screening based on risk factors. Overall, they found that routine screening identified 87%. They subsequently examined blood from women who did not volunteer for testing and found that only 53% of HIV-infected women had acknowledged risk factors. Based on these findings, Barbacci *et al.* advocate routine screening for HIV in antenatal clinics. However there are some problems with these data. Their rationale for the benefits of knowing HIV status may be open to question. They claim it allows for identification before 20 weeks gestation which would allow for termination. However, other studies have shown a low uptake of termination (indeed Barbacci's own study shows that of the 81 women identified as HIV-positive, only three terminated – one of which proceeded to a subsequent pregnancy to term). Another benefit claimed is 'preventing subsequent pregnancies'. However, there are scant data to support this. Indeed, Holman's study showed a steady group of HIV-positive women with multiple pregnancies. Another benefit claimed by this study is the ability to 'prevent breast feeding'. This is currently an issue under debate and there does not seem to be sufficient supporting data to back this up. Indeed, the European Cohort Study is examining the advantages of breast feeding for its immune conferring abilities on immune compromised babies. The counselling cost and implications of routine screening may be enormous or simply unattainable.

Wenstrom and Zuidema (1989) reported on a thorough protocol whereby all women in a Chicago clinic were given a standardized (scripted) counselling session. HIV screening uptake after such counselling was 34% and counselling sessions took approximately 30 minutes. A further group were queried but received no counselling and were subsequently tested anonymously. Risk factor reporting was significantly higher in the group receiving counselling. Systematic counselling was much more effective in eliciting risk factors than was questioning. In the latter group, 9 women tested HIV-positive yet only 4 of these had reported risk factors.

Lindsay *et al.* (1989) screened 3472 women in Atlanta and identified 10 HIV-positive pregnancies. 30% of the seropositives compared to 10% of the seronegatives identified risk factors.

Can HIV screening discourage women from attending antenatal clinics?
This question raises a problem which must be urgently addressed. A consistent group of HIV-positive women have been identified as late attenders at antenatal care or as women who receive no antenatal care at all. It is difficult to know whether fear of screening is a deterrent to attendance or whether these are women whose lifestyles tend to expose them to HIV risks as well as to discourage their attendance at clinics. However, Lindsay *et al.* (1989) found significantly more seronegative women registered for care in the first trimester compared to HIV-positive women. In addition, there was higher reporting of past sexually transmitted diseases.

What are the attitudes of pregnant women generally to HIV testing in pregnancy?
It is difficult to address this question with great clarity as, globally, pregnant women differ greatly. A series of attitude surveys has been reported, often with different results. It may well be that there is an enormous difference between attitudes towards testing and the reality of testing. It may also be that questionnaire design may affect the detailed nature of the response. Generally, Stevens *et al.* found that although over 80% of women thought that HIV testing should be available generally, when probed about it themselves, one in two would not take up testing if it was offered. Furthermore, over a third of

subjects would mind if their blood was taken anonymously for seroprevalence surveys. Buckett *et al.* (1988) reported that 11% of responders thought clinic attenders should not be screened; 35% did not know, 34% said they themselves would not wish to be screened, and 29% did not respond. If screening was introduced, a high proportion of responders in this survey (85%) wanted to be informed and 87% wanted their results. These workers also pointed out pockets of information gaps in ethnic minorities.

In 1987, Scrimgeour *et al.* surveyed 153 pregnant women and reported that 81% wished to be tested at the booking clinic (i.e. the antenatal clinic first attended); 86% would want to know if screening was being carried out, and 90% wanted results.

Stevens *et al.* (1989) also reported high rates of anxiety associated with HIV testing and that the reassurance generated by HIV test results (if negative) was not as effective as that for other antenatal tests.

HIV testing for neonates and children

Cord blood can be sampled to test for HIV. However, this test will not differentiate between passive maternal antibody transferred to the infant and infant antibody, i.e. that produced by the infant itself in response to viral infection. Early studies which have reported on neonatal infection based on cord blood sampling are limited and indeed may be inaccurate. They can accurately reflect maternal infection. Similar markers have been taken and utilized in epidemiological studies. Those most often quoted are taken on blood samples used in the Guthrie test – routinely carried out – involving a small blood sample taken from a newborn which is checked for phenylketonuria (PKU), a disease which can have dramatic cognitive implications which can be avoided by dietary adjustments. After this test, the blood spots, which are gathered on a small card, can be used for HIV testing. As Guthrie tests are often carried out on extensive proportions of the population, they may be useful alternative tools for prevalence screening. Indeed, such studies have been used (Peckham 1989).

Regular screening of children may be needed for the following reasons:

(a) To check for vertical transmission. Different centres have different protocols. Essentially, they involve regular screening to detect change in sero-status. A child who reverts from HIV-positive to HIV-negative may have shed maternal antibody and not be infected. Such studies give personal feedback to anxious parents. They may have many dif-

Table 4.1(b)   Studies of HIV screening in infants (cord blood) and children.

Study	Sample	Source	Centre	HIV-positive N	HIV-positive %
Araneta MR (1987)	3425		USA	–	1.4%
	1934	terminations		–	1.44%
Armson	366	cord blood	Pennsylvania	0	0%
Donegan	500	cord blood	Boston	1	–
Gayle H. (1989)	1009	children	Abidjan	67	6.6%
Ippolito	23 492	children	Italy	28	0.119%
Ippolito *et al.* (1989)	39 102	Guthrie	Italy	–	0.0013%
Peckham C. (1989)	115 000	PKU	London:	29	
			inner		0.049%
			outer		0.004%
Schuerman (1989)	1050	children	Dabou C/Ivory	85	8%
Wang	95	cord blood	Chongqing China	2	–

Note: some workers publish in different sources and thus the data may include some samples twice.

ficulties as it may take up to 24 months for a child to shed maternal antibody. Some variation has been monitored with recent African studies showing a shorter time for sero-reverting (9 months). Such studies are also useful in longer term data as knowledge of vertical transmission rates may be useful for a pregnant woman who is considering a pregnancy in the presence of HIV.

(b) There has been discussion about the use of screening for children prior to adoption or fostering. The limitations of such screening must be linked with the inability of the test to differentiate between maternal and child antibody. Thus a positive test result would only provide information on the baby's mother and not necessarily on the baby. Some centres provide risk factor information rather than HIV test results.

Clearly the major reason for infant screening must be the clarification of infant status and monitoring of vertical transmission rates. The latter is of no (or limited) benefit to the child directly but may be helpful for future generations. Children's rights must be jealously protected while they are too young to stand up for themselves.

Rouzioux (1989) summarizes the current notions surrounding early HIV diagnosis in infants, as follows:

- 'Early diagnosis requires a combination of tests;
- Antibody testing must acknowledge passively transferred maternal antibody;
- Virus culture can be used for early diagnosis;
- Complete Western Blots at nine months may be predictive of later symptoms;
- Polymerase chain reaction (PCR) tests are valuable as a research tool at present but has some limitations in terms of diagnostic value'.

Table 4.2 below sets out a series of studies which have monitored vertical transmission rates.

Table 4.2   Studies reporting vertical transmission rates.

Study	Sample	n	% transmission
Blanche *et al.* (1989)	France	117	27%
Bohlin *et al.* (1990)	Sweden		33%
Boulos (1990)	Africa	199	23%
Datla (1990)	Nairobi	–	46%
Delaporte *et al.* (1990)	Gabon		17.6%
European Collaborative Study (1991)	10 European centres	372	12.9%
Fortuny Guasch *et al.* (1989)	Barcelona	90	19.04%
Giaquinto C. *et al.* (1989)	Italy	120	20%
Grosch Worner *et al.* (1989)	FR Germany	59	30%
Halsey *et al.* (1990)	Haiti		25%
Halsey (1989)	Haiti	154	20–40%
Halse (1990)		443	25%
Hira (1990)	Zambia	227	39%
Holt (1990)	Haiti	160	15.4%

Table 4.2　(Cont'd)

Study	Sample	n	% transmission
Ippolito	Italy	660	30%
Lallemant *et al.* (1990)	Congo		42%
Lepage *et al.* (1990)	Rwanda		33%
Maynard (1989)	Rhode Island (13–15 m follow-up)	–	31%
MMWR (1987)	USA (Haem)	13	69%
Mok *et al.* (1989)	Edinburgh	49	7.1%
Medbo (1989)	Norway	23	21.7%
Mworozi *et al.* (1989)	Kampala, Uganda	87	20–30%
Ndugwa *et al.* (1990)	Uganda		31%
Oleske *et al.* (1990)	Newark, USA		19%
Pruzuck (1990)	Burkina Faso	23	36–45%
Rickard *et al.* (1990)	Buenos Aires		40%
Ryder *et al.* (1989)	Zaire	475	39%
Schoeller *et al.* (1989)	Milan	85	35.2%
Tovo (1988)	Italy	89	32.6%
Tovo (1989)	Italy	231	30%
Tovo *et al.* (1990)	Italy		19.2%
Van de Pere	Rwanda	218	33%
Van de Pere *et al.* (1990)	Rwanda		34%
Zucotti *et al.* (1990)	Milan		22%

The above table should be read in the light of the fact that there may be duplicate reporting, especially for ongoing cumulative population studies.

Pre-test counselling is impossible to provide for a young baby; the rights and needs of such a child must, however, be taken into account. Under the general principle of law, the rights of minors or those incapable of making their own decisions are protected. Such laws should be examined in cases of HIV testing of minors. Those who act *in loco parentis* need to be given the same information and decision-making time as those who are directly contemplating HIV testing. Clearly, if a child is tested, the results of those tests must be respected as confidential and a clear protocol must exist for informing that child when he or she is old enough to understand.

Chapter 5

Pre-test Counselling

HIV antibody testing is now widely available in the West. In third world countries, such tests may be less readily available through financial, prioritizing, or expertise constraints. However, the presence of many research studies in such centres may mean the tests are more freely available. The giving of an HIV test has many ramifications and should always be accompanied by pre- and post-test counselling.

Aims of pre-test counselling

Any person considering taking the HIV test should be given counselling. Pre-test counselling presumes that the test is optional, that the recipient has the right to refuse, and that there are no negative outcomes reliant on the test results. Thus people living in areas where testing is compulsory, or those who have to be screened prior to employment, would not be able to receive counselling in the true sense of the word. In such cases, accurate information is a must, and testers should be honest with those who are to be tested.

For those who are contemplating the test, either because of their own desire, or a recommendation from their carer, counselling should attempt to:

(1) Give the person time, opportunity and information to understand the implications of the test. They should be certain about the reasons why they are having the test, and the effects that the test and possible test outcome will have.

(2) Explore the underlying reasons for the test, whether this is based on accurate factual knowledge and whether the decision to have the test follows on logically from the reasons why the individual thought

this was necessary. Check the decision making procedure. One woman in the UK, for example, presented to an antenatal clinic with arm tattoos. She was given a referral letter and sent to her nearest sexually transmitted disease (STD) clinic with a request for HIV testing. Counselling revealed a stable relationship, a steady partner, no drug use (intravenous or oral) and a history of tattoos (dating back six years) which were carried out in what appeared to be sterile conditions. The woman initially thought that the antenatal staff knew something she did not and was anxious about HIV and thus willing to have the test. After counselling, it emerged that she felt she had no risk factors, would find it difficult to cope with waiting for a test result, and was reluctant to be tested.

(3) Explore coping and support resources for an individual who may be HIV positive. When someone is told of a positive result, their coping abilities may be strained and whilst in shock they may be less likely to make sensible, useful moves to deal with the trauma of a positive result. Thus it is preferable to set these wheels into motion during the pre-testing phase.

(4) Promote health education. Irrespective of whether the client goes on to have the test or not, one of the major aims of pre-test counselling is to address behavioural factors which may have put the client at risk of HIV acquisition in the past and may do so in the future. Clear guidance on safe sex, needle hygiene, and condom use, may constitute an important preventive tool. If the individual does not go on to have the test, they may address aspects of their behaviour in the future to limit their risk. If they do have a test and it turns out to be positive, the same behavioural risks need addressing. The advice for exposure prevention and HIV transmission to a third party is the same.

(5) Create a good supportive and trusting relationship between the counsellor and the client prior to test results. This often proves invaluable when a positive test result has to be fed back. The counsellor will have a pre-existing knowledge of the client, hopefully have a good rapport, and provide continuity of care.

(6) Respond to the personal and individual needs and requirements of the client. No pre-test counselling session will be the same for all clients. Although it may have common ingredients, each individual will have different needs and circumstances and place a different emphasis on background factors. One of the major skills of the counsellor will be to provide a holistic counselling intervention together with a response to the individual needs of the client.

The process of pre-test counselling

Prior to pre-test counselling certain background issues must be re-solved. These include:

(1) Location

All counselling should be carried out in a private location. Ideally, this should be a room where a door can be closed, where there are no interruptions, and where the woman can feel secure about confiden-tiality.

(2) Confidentiality

Prior to testing, all units should work out very clearly who is to have access to test results, how they will be filed, discussed, and passed on. In the UK, STD clinics have confidentiality guaranteed under the law. This is not true in other clinics and in other countries. The guiding rule should be that only those who are essential to the medical care should be told – and always with the consent of the woman herself. Consent is usually withheld when there is no trust. The task for the professional is to create the trust rather than to insist on breaches of confidentiality. Where social stigma and adverse reactions exist, this is of paramount importance. When social climate changes, HIV testing and HIV itself may generate less fear and stigma. In some countries, there is a high uptake of testing (e.g. France, Sweden), and social reactions may differ (Moatti 1990).

(3) Should the counselling be part of routine testing or separate?

An early decision needs to be made as to whether HIV testing of pregnant women should be part of the routine testing encounter or whether it should be separate.

These decisions will be based on routine policy, background infection in the local area, and client population factors. If testing is part of other routine antenatal tests, then it is important to gather clear information. Sometimes it is very difficult to raise the topic of AIDS and HIV and staff fail either to inform people adequately or to elicit relevant in-formation. The best way of overcoming these problems is to practise various kinds of opening questions to lead in to the subject and to allow time for the patient to talk. It is quite easy in such a format to include generalized relevant information as well as specific HIV risk factor or relevant information. For example:

COUNSELLOR: During pregnancy we need to monitor all aspects of your health.
PATIENT: Yes, I know that.

With this opening, it is easy to ask the patient questions to examine their individual risk situation. Such questions can be:

Are you taking any medicines at the moment?

Followed by:

What about other sorts of drugs?

(4) Designated counsellor
It should always be clear who is carrying out the role of counsellor. Where there are specially trained counsellors, clear referral channels must exist. Where this is not so, a designated individual should be appointed or should undertake the counselling. It may be easy for everyone in the chain of care to think that someone else has done the counselling and in the end it is overlooked.

The common elements of pre-test counselling should include:

(1) Establish the following factual information:

- Is the client currently pregnant?
- Is her partner HIV positive?
- Are they contemplating pregnancy?
- How far has the pregnancy progressed?
- Do they have other children?
- What is their support like?
- Do they want to talk to a counsellor?
- Do they know who the counsellor is?

(2) Establishment of risk and exposure factors
In different countries levels of risk may differ dramatically according to background infection data. For example, in the European Collaborative

Study, intravenous drug use has been identified as a major risk factor. However, in Africa this has not been seen as a problem. In some countries there are no discernible risk behaviours beyond sexual contact. Risk assessment is a shaky tool, an inexact probe for an inexact science. It runs the risk of overinclusion of individuals who seem to have risk factors, or exclusion of those who may be infected, but who do not obviously fit into a given group. In order to carry out an adequate risk assessment, the background risk factors for the given culture must be known and taken into account. Some factors are universal and these include:

(a)   Sexual activity of the individual including not only their past sexual history but the behaviour of their partners.

(b)   Sexual orientation of their partners. This is obviously very difficult to ascertain. Many homosexual men report heterosexual contacts. Furthermore, female partners of bi-sexual men are often not aware of their partners' sexuality. Such sensitive questioning and disclosure can only take place within a trusting, non-judgemental and truly confidential environment.

(c)   History of personal and family illness. There are some conditions which must be noted as they may have particular relevance to HIV. These cover all blood related conditions which involve transfusions such as haemophilia or thalassaemia. Illnesses in previous babies should be noted as many women with HIV go on to have subsequent pregnancies. Also there is some evidence to suggest that if a previous child dies of AIDS or HIV the risk of vertical transmission is greater in the subsequent pregnancy.

(d)   History of personal and partner behaviour. This is difficult to elicit but ought to focus on sexual and skin piercing behaviour. Thus the presence of intravenous drug use in the client or partner should be noted.

(e)   HIV status of the partner. This seems somewhat obvious, but must not be overlooked. Often people imagine that hospitals are homogeneous entities with perfect communication between departments. In the case of a pregnancy where the death of a spouse has not been identified as HIV related, it is worth noting the cause as certain illnesses – tuberculosis, for example – may be HIV-linked.

(f)   Blood or blood product transfusion.

(g)   Skin piercing in the absence of sterilization of instruments.

Risk assessment can be difficult to carry out. If it is carried out by means of a series of closed questions, clients may find it difficult to discuss vague worries and possible risk exposure.

For example:

COUNSELLOR: Do you use drugs?
PATIENT: No.
COUNSELLOR: Does your partner?
PATIENT: I do not think so.
COUNSELLOR: Do you have any other partners besides your husband?
PATIENT: No.
COUNSELLOR: Have you had a blood transfusion recently?
PATIENT: Not recently.
COUNSELLOR: Are there any illnesses in you or your family that we should know about?
PATIENT: Well my partner is colour blind and we are quite worried. . .
COUNSELLOR: No, that is not really a problem with HIV.

Here the counsellor uses a barrage of closed questions which prompt the patient into short, monosyllabic responses. It also presumes that the patient has a knowledge base which may not in fact exist. An alternative way of handling this situation would be:

COUNSELLOR: There are some risk factors which may be linked to HIV and may help point out if a test is helpful. Do you know what these are?
PATIENT: Yes, and I think I am okay.
COUNSELLOR: Good, should we go through them?
PATIENT: Yes, well my husband is my only partner and we have been married for some years now.
COUNSELLOR: Any others?
PATIENT: We don't use drugs or anything like that.
COUNSELLOR: What about illnesses?
PATIENT: None that I can think of, other than colour blindness.

COUNSELLOR: That does not involve the passage of body fluids so although it is something you may want to talk about it does not affect any decisions about HIV testing.
PATIENT: Does blood from a blood transfusion count?
COUNSELLOR: Tell me about the blood transfusion.
PATIENT: I have had a blood transfusion after an accident. . . .

In the second example, the counsellor allows the patient to explore possibilities and is able to check out that the patient truly does know which factors to consider and which ones to reject.

The counsellor may want to preface the session by giving the patient the information, for example:

COUNSELLOR: In the studies there are some things which are associated with transmission more than others. Although it does not mean that all people who have these are positive, it may point out where testing can be focussed. What I shall do is tell you about all of these pointers, and we can examine whether any may apply to you.

The important points are:

- Do not take client knowledge for granted;
- Do not worry a client – emphasize that risks do not equal infection;
- Do not make judgements based on anything but information – all sorts of people can be infected with HIV;
- Do not make light of any risk that the patient brings up as it may be relevant;
- Do allow the patient to talk openly and freely.

(3) Clarification of the test

As a diagnostic tool, the HIV test has certain limitations. The patient should have these clarified.

The test can tell one thing:

- Whether the individual has antibodies present in their blood.

The test cannot tell:

- Where the individual became infected;
- How the individual became infected (sexually, by blood transfusion, by contaminated needle);
- If the person has AIDS;
- Whether the person will get AIDS and when;
- The clinical state of the person;
- The length of time the person has been infected;
- Whether the virus will be transmitted to the baby.

The limitations of the tests are that, on occasion, they may throw up a positive result when one does not exist, or a negative result when the person is truly positive. The accuracy of the HIV test is high, but not perfect. One way around this is the use of confirmatory tests. All positive results can be subjected to another test which uses a different method and is targeted at a different aspect of the virus and the presence of two positive results may thus be taken with greater certainty. This does not help false negatives.

As an antibody test, the test is limited in time. Some antibodies are produced very quickly by the body. However, with HIV, it can take up to three months for the body to express sufficient antibodies for these to be picked up on HIV testing. Thus, a negative test result only refers to a period three months previously. Risky behaviour in the interim would not be reflected and infection could occur during this 'window' period.

The test cannot identify whose antibody is present. Thus, in a newborn baby, passive maternal antibody will be present and will not necessarily mean that the baby is infected with virus. New tests (polymerase chain reaction tests) are being researched which may give a clearer idea of virus presence. Although the results of these are promising, at the moment they are still in the research phase; the tests are also expensive, require trained personnel and are not widely available.

Finally, the test cannot tell whether HIV has been or can be transmitted across the placenta to the fetus.

(4) Preparation for test results

Most people undergo testing in the hope that the result will be negative. This is particularly true of other antenatal tests which are essentially tests to confirm the well-being of the baby. The negative results are often seen as a reassurance which can counterbalance any anxiety created by the test. Systematic research on other tests have shown that this is not always the case (Farrant 1981, Stevens *et al.* 1989). The desire for a negative result may expose an underlying concern by the individual as to why they feel they may be at risk for a positive result. A major goal of pre-test counselling should be to discuss these risks as well as the test. They may be more fruitful in terms of pathways of help and may be key sites for health education.

While the person is still in a position of 'not knowing', and while the option to undertake an HIV test is still open, it is often helpful to think through the full implications of a positive test. This may sound strange. This may be as a result of the fact that many people often invoke denial as a protective strategy. Few people proceed in their everyday lives thinking about all the possible problems they may encounter. However, in the absence of such thought, coping, planning and adjustment cannot be explored or rehearsed. Thus it is at this time that the interviewer can give permission to the client to explore the possible meaning of a positive test, a range of possible emotional and practical consequences, and, of greatest importance, the avenues of support and methods of coping that would work for them. This process serves two purposes. On the one hand if the client goes ahead with the test and this turns out to be positive, in those early moments, when the news strikes and they feel overwhelmed or shocked, they will have some plans already formulated to fall back upon. On the other hand, some clients may see, with some clarity, that the enormity of the test outcome may be something they are not ready for or able to cope with. In such circumstances they may want to rethink the decision to have the test in the first place. In the absence of a cure for HIV this may well be an option they choose to take up.

(5) Exploring the possible implications and ramifications of a test on an individual's life

These may be wide ranging and numerous. They may vary dramatically according to circumstances, cultural background and personal factors. They include:

Relationships. A positive test result has been known to result in breakdown of relationships, straining of relationships and shunning of the infected individual. On the other hand, there are many examples of strong relationships which withstand this news. A pregnant woman and her partner may want to examine this.

Economic considerations. There are many economic implications of an HIV test. Sometimes these apply whether or not the test is positive. For example, some insurance agencies may turn down insurance on the grounds of a client 'having been tested for HIV'. Some employers may terminate employment or fail to employ someone in the first instance if they have been tested positive to HIV. More and more countries are excluding HIV-positive individuals from entry. These are practical considerations but they can have far reaching effects on the emotional well-being of an individual. As such, they should not be underestimated.

Planning. Future planning may be affected by HIV. However, some people would prefer to have bad news than to live with uncertainty.

Decision-making

At this time some people do go ahead with the test, while others wait to think about it, or decide not to go ahead. It is important to bear the following in mind:

(a)   A person can change their mind and although they choose not to have a test at one particular point, they may want one in the future.

(b)   Sometimes counselling sessions and clinics can be overwhelming and patients cannot think clearly. They may want to have time to think or to talk about the test with their partner. They should not be hurried into the test and they should be allowed, wherever possible, to go away and spend some time in contemplation before coming back. Some centres never test on the same day as a counselling session, whereas others are willing to do so.

(c)   Women should not feel that counselling is directed for or against testing. They may want a test and feel they are being put off. On the other hand, they may not want a test and may feel pressured into accepting it.

(d)   If a woman is determined to have a test and the counsellor thinks she should think about it in greater depth, there is a difficult problem. Such women may go to other venues. At all times, after attitudes and desires have been explored, the decision needs to be one for the client to make and not the counsellor.

(e)   It is of utmost importance that the pregnant woman attends for antenatal care. Testing should not be a barrier which may turn them away from the clinic.

Proceeding to test

Pre-test counselling does not cease at the moment a woman decides to have an HIV test. Rather, where facilities and resources are available, this signifies the start of an ongoing process of help. The stress of the procedure can be reduced if the counsellor bears the following in mind:

- The test is an anxiety-provoking one;
- Psychological difficulties are often at their greatest at times of uncertainty;
- The intervening period between blood sample and test result provides such a time;
- Information reduces anxiety;
- Pacing reduces anxiety;
- Confidentiality is an overriding issue;
- Always have a procedure for test results;
- Information recall is often limited at times of anxiety – use alternatives such as written information, or telephone help lines, to supplement personal input.

Once someone has decided to have an HIV test there are many procedural items of information that can help them minimize anxiety. They need to pace themselves according to the timetables of test results. A clear programme for this should exist and should be outlined, with clarity, to the patient.

The time taken for tests should be kept to a minimum. A clear programme should be set out for the provision of test results. The client should have it made clear that this will be done in person. It is important to keep a consistent policy. Thus, do not give negative test results over the telephone and request others (i.e. those whose test is positive) to come in. Clients will soon learn that if they are not given their result over the telephone it must indicate that it is HIV positive. Results should not be given at times when all services close down. Mid-week is usually the preferable time. However, the weekend often signals the availability of family and days off from work and may have advantages if support can be set up from services over the weekend.

The client should have some written information to take away with them to allow recourse to informative and helpful reading material during the wait before their next visit.

It is well documented that anxiety is increased during periods of uncertainty. The client should be forewarned of this and coping strategies together with support avenues should be set up for this period.

It has often been found in antenatal care that negative test results are not conveyed to clients. This is a bad practice in general, and specifically so for HIV. Clients sometimes generate a time scale (often arbitrary) by which time they feel they should be informed. They can experience extreme anxiety until this point. It is preferable for patients to be given negative results as well as positive results. This should be done as soon as the results are to hand.

Some case examples:

Case 1

Jane has presented late in her pregnancy for antenatal care. Her baby is due very soon, but she is uncertain about her dates. Jane reports a history of intravenous drug use. She lives in a squat and is not supported by her partner. She has stopped sharing needles. She wants to have this baby and sees her future as rosy now that she has a baby to care for. The midwife has suggested an HIV test.

Problems presented by this case:
(a)   Jane is unsupported and may need a lot of input.
(b)   Jane is well advanced in her pregnancy. She may have avoided antenatal care as she was unaware of the pregnancy, was not motivated to attend, was worried that she would be coerced into a termination, or she simply did not see the need to attend.
(c)   Jane is pinning a lot of her hopes and her future aspirations on the baby.

Aims of counselling:
(a)   the counsellor needs to clarify if the HIV test is what Jane wants.
(b)   The counsellor ought to reassure Jane that her medical care is not reliant on her HIV test and that she is free to choose.
(c)   The counsellor ought to use the session to provide basic health education on risk avoidance and harm reduction.
(d)   The counsellor ought to check the support channels that Jane has available irrespective of HIV status.
(e)   The counsellor needs to prepare Jane for possible outcomes of the test if she decides to go ahead. She needs to have clear information on the effects of the test, the implications for her and her baby, and some of the longer term issues.

Case 2

Mindy is attending the antenatal clinic. This is her first baby. The clinic is busy and there is not much time to take a full history. Mindy seems slow and does not have much insight. She is married and does not work. She is having a whole series of antenatal tests and it has been suggested that an HIV test be done as well.

Problems presented by this case:
(a)   Mindy has not consented to the test. It may be all too easy to include the HIV test within the battery of tests, but this may raise particular problems for Mindy.
(b)   It does not seem that anyone has spent much time talking to Mindy. Her risk levels are unknown.

Aims of counselling:
(a)   Pre-test counselling should focus on Mindy's needs rather than clinic protocols and policies. The counsellor should inquire from the referer who suggested the HIV test and why.

(b)   The counsellor should use the session positively for health education.

(c)   The counsellor should ensure that there truly is informed consent before Mindy has a blood sample taken.

Case 3

Hanna is a patient in a busy clinic where HIV testing is done routinely. She has been seen by the doctor who has checked her pregnancy and she is now about to have the HIV test. She has murmured some reservation and has thus been sent to you.

Problems presented by this case:
One of the problems of routine screening is that it gives individuals little right or the power to question. In Hanna's case, her carers may find it very difficult to handle if her test is positive.

Conclusion

Pre-test counselling should not be overlooked with this client group. It may be tempting to simply include HIV tests into the total package of antenatal tests but workers should resist this.

Pre-test counselling is a costly facility and all testing packages should include budgetary allowances for this resource. Although specially trained counsellors are available at some resources, this is a luxury and one which cannot be afforded at others. In such cases, the front-line workers need to be trained in the basic counselling skills. If this is not possible or practical, then special workers can be trained.

Chapter 6

Post-test Counselling

Post-test counselling comprises an initial session during which the individual is given feedback of test results. Follow-up counselling and support can often ensue in the long term. The initial session, during which test results are given, is a key intervention. In some centres where resources are limited or where women do not return, this may be the only form of counselling they receive after their test result. This contact will be discussed in detail and then some of the key points for long term support will also be outlined.

Giving test results

It is never easy to break bad news (it is always much easier to tell women that their test is negative). In the event of a negative test the patient should be told the result as soon as possible. It should also be noted that, according to the literature, negative test results have sometimes been found to confer 'permission' on patients to continue indulging in risky behaviour. The key focus of the interview is to emphasize the importance of behaviour modification and, if the circumstances warrant it, to suggest re-testing within three months to rule out the window of infectivity. This window covers the period where a person may be infected but due to the time take for antibodies to be produced in sufficient quantities to be detected on the test a time of up to 12 weeks may need to elapse. Over this 12-week period a person may test negative despite the fact that they have been infected with HIV.

Many workers forget that pregnant women continue to have sex and this is, invariably, unprotected.

If the test is positive the news is difficult both to deliver and to receive. Sometimes patients expect a positive result, and the interview simply confirms something that they already know. At other times the patient will be completely surprised.

There are no rules about giving bad news. Good counsellors will be prepared, will understand what they are doing, how they are picking up signals from their client, what reactions to anticipate, and how to deal with these. If a session goes badly, the good counsellor will try to reflect on problems and try to rehearse ways in which to handle things differently in future. The inexperienced counsellor will 'blame' the client, ignore or forget the incident, push it away, and perhaps be much more wary (and distant and unhelpful) on subsequent occasions.

Sometimes the interview simply could not have been handled any differently. Counselling skills are then concerned with helping the client on an ongoing basis, despite the difficult news breaking session. If counsellors do not look at the process and simply try to detach themselves, they will slowly build up a barrier (mostly one of self-defence) and may become cold and indifferent to clients' emotional needs. Some common elements to post-test counselling sessions include the following:

Before the meeting

In anticipation of the meeting counsellors should:

- Ensure they have a private place where they will not be interrupted with a client;
- Ensure that they have the correct test results for the correct person;
- Ensure that confirmatory tests have been carried out;
- Ensure that they have follow-up information such as support group telephone numbers, referral agents, and so on;
- Ensure that they have time available to spend with the client;
- Ensure that they are able to provide follow-up sessions if the woman or the couple need it and if not, be able to suggest someone else to whom they can turn.

Giving the news

Counsellors vary in how they initiate a session and they divide roughly into the following groups:

Those who give the news immediately –
COUNSELLOR: Good morning, Jennifer, I am afraid I have some bad news for you.

Those who set the scene of emotional care prior to the news –
COUNSELLOR: Good Morning, Jennifer, come on in and let me take your coat. Would you like to sit down?

Those who set the scene and ensure support is available –
COUNSELLOR: Hello Jennifer, is there anyone with you who would like to join us? This may be difficult for you.

Those who give the news very quickly –
COUNSELLOR: Jennifer (placing arm around her shoulder), the test was positive.

Those who make the client verbalize their worst fears –
COUNSELLOR: Well, Jennifer, what sort of result are you expecting?

It is clear that there are no right or wrong ways of breaking such news. What is important is that counsellors, who after all have different styles, use one that is comfortable for them. A counsellor who feels comfortable will probably be more helpful to a patient in need than one who is following a menu or prescribed formula which is difficult and does not fit the client. The key instruction is for counsellors to understand the style they use and understand why they use it. Often it is designed to meet their own needs and not those of the patient (although they may try and persuade themselves that it is the best method for the patient). Counsellors must not be rigid. They should constantly be aware of the feedback and reactions of the client and adjust their behaviour to their perception of the client's need. Some items to bear in mind include the following:

(a)   Be comfortable with the words. Before the interview, repeat them aloud if necessary in front of a mirror. It is often surprising how difficult it is to say sensitive words aloud.

(b)   The essence of the bad news may not come as a surprise to the patient. There may be a part of her that is expecting it. It is rather the fact of the news, or its confirmation, that is difficult to bear. For such people, the counsellor's willingness to help, sympathy and expressions of care may make this very difficult time somewhat easier to bear. On the other hand, this news may be a bolt out of the blue for the recipient. This is especially true in circumstances when incomplete consent was obtained. This makes the task of breaking the news very difficult indeed.

(c)   When such an interview becomes difficult, the counsellor should stick with the client, not wind up the session with some quick cursory comments and leave. Opening statements such as 'what is your most immediate worry?'; 'does this come as a shock?' indicate to the client that the counsellor is willing to talk.

Reactions to the news

For a good proportion of women the results will be negative. This is an altogether different session, filled with relief and the challenges in such a meeting are to:

(a)   Ensure clients are aware of the window period and, if there is some real concern of risk or exposure, that they will return in three months.

(b)   Ensure that they are aware of risk avoidance and can reconfirm discussions about limiting their exposure to risk in the future and the behaviour changes they will need to adopt to carry this out.

(c)   Ensure that they do not see this as permission to go out and continue a risky life style in the presence of this 'reprieve'.

More attention, however, will need to be focussed on the group who test positive. No two patients react in the same way. Some theory has likened the reactions to a grief or bereavement reaction. Although it may provide a helpful framework, counsellors must remember that in bereavement there is no set pattern and there are no set reactions here. However, forewarning of possible reactions is helpful. These include:

Shock
'My God, you are joking'.
'Not me, surely not'.
Silence.

Denial
'It cannot be right, it just cannot'.
'Are you sure those are my test results'?
'You are wrong, you are wrong'.

Anger
'I hate the world – this cannot happen to me'.
'I don't want to die, I just don't want to die'.

Anxiety
'I am going to die!'
'AIDS, I have AIDS!'

Information seeking
'Does this mean I have AIDS?'
'Does this mean I will die soon?'
'Is there a cure?'

Emotional reactions
Crying.   It is common to cry – the counsellor should reassure clients that it is okay and they need not feel embarrassed.

Silence.   This may be a difficult reaction for a counsellor to respond to. Silence can often promote questioning. It may signify that the client is taking it in at her own pace, that she is dumbstruck and cannot find anything to say, or that she is overwhelmed and lost. In all instances, the counsellor should allow the silence. If the woman breaks the silence, pay particular attention to her response or questioning – it may be of crucial importance to her. If she does not break the silence after a period initiate some short undemanding questions to allow her to slowly unfold. This may be a good time for the use of closed questions which are pacing and easy to answer.

Verbal Crying.   Sometimes patients repeat questions or phrases over and over again. This is known as verbal crying. It can often be done in the form of a question such as 'So I have AIDS? I have AIDS, do I? So I have AIDS?' It is important to recognize that this is a form of crying and not a request for didactic conversation. By launching into a long stream of explanations at this point the counsellor runs the risk of talking completely above the client, who is neither concentrating nor requesting dialogue. At some later point, when patients do ask questions the counsellor may think they have been given all the information and not repeat it.

Loss of control.   Clients may have severe emotional reactions: they may start to shake, to lose body posture, to crumple over and to have a period where they seem out of control. The task of the counsellor is to hold them – either physically if this is appropriate – or emotionally. Do not dismiss their intense emotional reaction or hurry them up with reconstitution. There are many theories which point to the cathartic nature of such deep emotional expression. A counsellor should give the patient some time and then slowly help her gather herself together. Reassure her that such reactions are in order, perfectly acceptable, and may precede efforts of adjustment and coping.

Nightmares.   Some patients report having disturbing and incessant nightmares. Essentially, these occur after the news-breaking session and they can be prolonged and exceedingly disturbing. In general, sleeping tablets are not a long-term solution to these. An exhausted patient who has had a series of disturbed nights can well benefit from induced sleep in the short term, but she also needs to talk through her worries. Nightmares often occur when there has been no planning and coping skills are low. Help with planning, discussion, coping, and support, is often the remedy for nightmares. These seem to recede and disappear with time.

Implosive thoughts.   For some clients, life after the news seems like it will never be the same. A constant implosion of HIV-related thoughts intrudes upon their everyday lives and they are unable to put aside the test results which seem to enter their minds and scream at them wherever they are. This reaction may recede, but indeed for some people it may never go away completely. Time and positive action can alleviate this.

Physical panic reactions.   Many clients report some of the classic physical signs of anxiety and panic. These include heart palpitations, sweating, churning of the stomach, skin burning sensations (especially facially), weak knees, diarrhoea, dry throat, loss of appetite, early waking. This is very disturbing and may set up a cycle of worry as some of these physical symptoms are those associated with symptomatic HIV disease. Relaxation and anxiety intervention can help reduce or even eradicate these symptoms.

How should the counsellor react?

The first rule is to listen to the client. Hear what she is saying, how she is talking, what she is asking. The counsellor should not enter the room determined to recite a prepared speech, but take the client's pace and respond to her. The full meaning of a positive result may differ for each person. Furthermore what it means to the counsellor may not be the same as what it means to the client.

Follow the client's reaction closely. There are multiple reactions and although every session may differ, it is helpful if the counsellor maintains a thread of continuity in his/her head to provide structure and pacing. The most difficult time to react is directly after the client has been told the news. It is at this moment that the counsellor is locked into the client's emotion. If the intensity of the emotion is hard to bear, the inexperienced counsellor will attempt to distract, cover up or gloss over the reaction. It is more helpful to go at the client's pace. Allow her to verbalize thoughts, to be quiet, or to cry. Be practical – have some tissues handy, get her a drink.

For pregnant women, a positive HIV test result is often made all the more difficult because of the pregnancy. The woman may be torn between the news of HIV and her thoughts of her baby. She may oscillate between concerns for herself and her baby. Unlike any other test result HIV not only tells her of potential harm to her unborn child, but simultaneously gives her dramatic news about her own health.

The task of the counsellor at this point is to:

- Help clients through an emotional crisis;
- Provide longer term assistance with support and coping strategies;
- Allow them an opportunity to reflect, question and plan in a safe, non-confronting and therapeutic atmosphere;
- Allow clients a time and place to address their concerns, plan through their decisions, and try out options;
- Act as a resource centre;
- Provide sound basic information;
- Provide a lifeline when clients leave. They may panic or a delayed reaction may hit them later on. A telephone helpline, a follow-up appointment, or a self help group would all be good ideas.

The provision of information

Generally, the information covered at this interview may be limited by the fact that the client may have difficulty taking too much in. The follow-up of clients and the flow of information may stretch over a series of sessions where information is given piece by piece. It is important that they simultaneously incorporate the information into their reality so that it makes sense and has meaning for their personal situation. The points covered will probably be:

(a)   HIV is infection with the virus. It does not imply that the person has AIDS. The distinction may be blurred and difficult for a client to take on board. The test will not provide information on how long the person has been infected, how she became infected, and if or when she will proceed to develop the disease.

(b)   In a pregnant woman, HIV can cross the placenta and infect the fetus. The chance of vertical transmission varies. In the West the good studies show a rate of approximately 25%. In Africa the rate seems to be higher, closer to 33%. The reason for this difference is unclear. It may be that the samples include women who have been infected for longer periods of time; it may reflect background health factors such as previous illness, nutrition and so on. The long-term outcome is not known as research is still in its infancy.

(c)   There are large gaps in our information about progression of disease. The passage of time does not diminish the likelihood of AIDS progressing.

(d)   A number of co-factors for infection and disease progression have been shown in some studies. Although the studies are not perfect, one could allow for benefit of the doubt and take the findings into account as safety measures if possible. The major finding of note is that other sexually transmitted diseases may be co-factors in either the onset of infection in the first place or disease progression. Thus safer sex can protect against these and so protect against AIDS.

Facts to bear in mind are:

- Infection with HIV is lifelong and the virus can be transmitted to others;
- Treatment for opportunistic infections has progressed dramatically and continues to do so;
- The epidemic is in its infancy and there are many unanswered questions. There are individuals who have survived with AIDS for the duration of our knowledge so far (now over ten years);
- Hope and optimism should never be dashed;
- Individual predictions and figures should be avoided (statements such as 'you have two years to live', for example).

Infection control
This is often a primary concern. Make sure the client knows the facts about how the virus is and is not transmitted. This can be backed up

with written guidelines which the client can take away. Rehearse incidents that occur in daily life and how she should to react. These could include blood spillage, dish washing, laundry, kissing, touching, and so on. Be specific. The list of do's and don'ts includes:

DO:
- Continue to share toilets, baths, linen and cutlery;
- Look after your health;

DON'T:
- Share needles and syringes;
- Share any personal item which may pierce skin such as toothbrushes and razors.

Safe sex
HIV is essentially sexually transmitted; the client should have full and clear information about safe sex. This may be very difficult for the client and she may want extended sessions to discuss this. Her partner should be able to attend if he/she desires. Written guidelines that the client can take away are also helpful.

Initiation of coping

A positive HIV test has the ability to make people feel totally out of control, strangers to themselves, and devoid of coping strategies. One of the first challenges to the counsellor is to initiate coping. This does not mean that the counsellor should tell the client what to do and how best to do it. Rather this means that the counsellor should help draw out the coping tools that the client has and help to start utilizing them in ways that work for each individual. This may well differ from client to client.

With a pregnant woman, the decisions about the future of the pregnancy may loom large and be the first and foremost issue to be addressed.

James (1988) described a series of psychosocial problems encountered in 15 females referred for psychiatric evaluation during pregnancy on receipt of a positive HIV test result. He documented high rates of co-morbidity in this small sample (including drug use, mood and adjustment disorders, and personality disorders). He points out the need to address the dynamics and impact of a pregnancy in addition to HIV. Of note in this study was the fact that many of the psychiatric problems preceded both the pregnancy and the HIV infection. Furthermore, he recorded 26.6% in this sample had made previous suicide attempts.

Counselling schema

This seven-point counselling plan can be presented in summary form which can be a useful guide for counsellors.

Counselling plan (Sherr & Hedge 1989)
(1) Fact Finding
   This includes facts such as whether the client is currently pregnant or not, a drug user, in a relationship or not, sexuality issues, clinical state (whether they are symptomatic or asymptomatic), support network, communication access and back-up, current drugs (for example are they on AZT?)

(2) Explore options and possible consequences
   This enables clients to think through all possible avenues and outcomes be they positive or negative, rational or irrational, practical or impractical, hopeful or feared. Examples include:

 • To conceive or not;
 • To terminate or not;
 • To utilize alternatives (donor semen if male is HIV-positive, adoption, fostering).

(3) Explore own and partner's reactions
   In a couple, reactions, needs, feelings and expression can differ. This may be a source of conflict. Some couples feel similar things at different times. Some relationships are put under considerable strain and help may be needed to allow for expression and negotiation.

(4) Decision making
   Decision making is both a process and an event. In the short term, help is given in making specific decisions. A longer term counselling goal is to help a client build up a process for decision making. Future decisions can be tackled with greater efficiency and less trauma. The short-term goal is to solve problems whereas the long-term goal is to create strategies.

(5) Living with the Consequences
   Once a decision is made, the options that a client has thought through become reality. In reality some options may have unanticipated components. They may need to be re-examined. Decisions are rarely perfect solutions. Compromises are often made and the client may need to address these.

(6) Practical assistance

This element of counselling should never be underestimated. It is a useful tool throughout the process. Although it does not necessarily comprise the whole of counselling, it can often be used when a client does not feel ready or able to explore other issues. The provision of practical help will be invaluable and will also serve as a vehicle on which trust can be built up so that when future needs arise the client can turn to the counsellor. The kind of practical avenues are:

- Social services;
- Help with housing, finance and medical care;
- Helplines;
- Support groups;
- Respite care;
- Information;
- Provision of condoms.

(7) Continuing support

This process marks the entry point of counselling and is not an end in itself. HIV brings with it long-term problems and ongoing counselling may be needed. The problems include:

- Living with uncertainty;
- Feelings of responsibility;
- Guilt;
- Low self-esteem;
- Feelings of failure;
- Purposeless future;
- Incomplete family;
- Death and its implications;
- Loss of relationships;
- Loss of sex;
- Secrets;
- Hurdles of practical difficulties;
- Separations.

Psychological factors after positive test result

There are a number of psychological factors which have been identified. These are briefly outlined below together with some practical interventions.

Anxiety.   Anxiety has been mentioned before. Its symptoms are distressing and it is unnecessary for a client to suffer these unduly. It is also important to tease out anxiety reactions from early HIV disease symptoms and thus it is always advantageous to provide input for anxiety. Intervention can be focussed on relaxation and anxiety management. Distraction can be useful, especially in someone who may have much free time to dwell on their problems. Exploring alternatives such as work, hobbies, relaxation, and enjoyment aspects of life, can alleviate some anxiety symptoms. Symptom control techniques such as thought stopping can be used.

Panic attacks.   These are often seen in conjunction with anxiety. Here, individuals are suddenly overcome with overwhelming panic. They experience physical symptoms and the fear associated with this experience can lead them to attempt to avoid subsequent exposure to a situation. Again, the techniques used to intervene with anxiety ought to be useful in relieving panic attacks. Clients often find it helps to have the link between the physical and psychological explained.

Depression.   A variety of mood fluctuations can occur. A depressed individual often has slowed reactions and may stop eating properly, lose sleep and be lethargic. Theories such as those of Beck (1976) and Ellis (1979), have provided some useful input for general patients and they can be put to good use here. Generally, these aim to alter cognitions and attributions and to mobilize a client. Other insight therapies may also be of use.

Obsessive compulsive behaviour.   Obsessive symptoms have also been noted in clients. These have been seen in the worried well as well as those with HIV. They often take the form of body checking for lesions, or tracking other physical symptoms. Accurate information together with some symptom control can be helpful.

Neurological symptoms.   The fears of AIDS dementia are often more common than the syndrome itself. Although there is brain pathology found on autopsy, AIDS dementia itself is not very common. Furthermore, these symptoms seem to appear much more at the end stage of disease if at all. Most often, neurological disturbance is related to mood and relationships. It can also be affected by stress, opportunistic infections which themselves can directly affect the brain (but can be reversible), or medication. Losses tend to occur in both memory and motor areas.

Psychosexual disturbance. Whether or not a client was infected with HIV sexually, they can transmit the virus sexually. This often puts severe and profound strain on existing sexual relationships or causes difficulty for clients in future relationships.

Suicide. Although few people complete suicide there is a growing literature on the effect of HIV on suicide rates, and an increase in suicide attempts (para suicides). Often the attempts are associated with relationship strain. Furthermore the lack of counselling may be linked to suicide. Although it is often not possible to stop people killing themselves if they are determined, there is much that can be under-stood which may prevent suicide. This includes:

(1)   Often it is not the desire for death which prompts a suicide but an inability to cope with life. Help with life is important.

(2)   People who have clearly thought through suicide plans are at greater risk of carrying them out than those who have had a transient thought about the worthlessness of life. The latter thought is common, and indeed, counsellors can reassure people that death thoughts are not 'abnormal'. A good counsellor ought to ask clients about their thoughts and explore the extent of planning. It is a myth that discussing suicide can prompt action.

(3)   People who kill themselves often let others know of their inten-tion. Thus all suicide comments should be taken seriously.

(4)   If clients want to talk about suicide do not push them away. Listen to what they have to say and slowly pace them. The key is to give them a link into the future – either a lifeline or a plan which will give them something to cling on to (such as a meeting the next day). If someone talks about suicide over the telephone, the counsellor should avoid the temptation to get a name, address and whereabouts imme-diately, or to begin dissuasion instantly. The client may need to talk about problems and the necessary information can be gathered at a later point when some trust is built up.

(5)   Sadly, there are some people who do go on to kill themselves. Their family and friends may need much support.

Longer term issues of post-test counselling

Post-test counselling can extend well beyond the initial contact where test results are given. The major aim of such counselling should be constructive and client-centred. It should provide an opportunity for the client to examine some or all the problems brought about by HIV and to explore solutions that are acceptable. The kinds of problems include:

- Telling others;
- Keeping well and avoiding illness;
- Reducing the risk of transmission;
- Sexual relationships – past, current and future;
- Maximizing factors which may be protective (such as social support, good health, sensible diet, reduced drugs).

Vogler (1989) studied the impact of an HIV diagnosis in sexual partners in a study of 31 couples. Although they found some considerable changes, with many individuals reporting abstinence, reduced anal intercourse, and increased uptake of condoms, they also noted inconsistent condom use in 40% of their sample. Thus, in the long term, risks from sexual exposure may be considerable.

More data are needed on the rate of transmission for heterosexual partners. In a study of haemophiliac partners over 5 years, Forsberg noted that the transmission rate was low. The exact nature and extent of behaviour change needs to be monitored, together with obstacles and problems that couples experience and interventions they find useful.

HIV positive test results and children

The situation for children is no less difficult and it is made more awkward by the fact that the child may not have full understanding – especially in the case of an infant or young toddler. This means that the child's parent/s, guardian or carer needs to be involved.

For transplacental spread one cannot tell with any certainty what the meaning of a positive test result is for quite some time (up to two years in the European cohort study, shorter periods have been reported in Buenos Aires and Africa where there were no new conversions after 12 months). Thus a parent may have to live with positive test results over an extended period of time. During this time, they will constantly hope that this will turn out to be maternal antibody rather than a sign of HIV infection in the baby and that it will revert with time. The final decision that the child is indeed HIV positive may be difficult for them to take in. They may struggle with the problems surrounding uncertainty.

The number of children who are infected via blood products will decline in centres where blood products are screened. In centres where they are not screened there may be recrimination and anger. The situation may be more difficult given the medical condition that the children were admitted for in the first instance (such as haemophilia, malaria and so on.)

Few writers have addressed the problems of telling children of their status. The difficulties concentrate on who to tell, who not to tell, who should do the telling and when the telling should be done and how.

In a study by Mok (1990), HIV was found to be a closely guarded secret. People do not talk to others and in many instances children are not told. The reasons behind this are many. Parents are reluctant to tell children. They fear the child will tell others; will not understand. Or they cannot face telling the child; they do not know how to tell the child or they fear that the child may get more ill if she/he knows.

In practice, the counsellor should work closely with the parents or carers of the child. They should develop a trusting relationship and should raise the issue of telling. When the parents put this off, the counsellor ought to establish why they are doing so and when they will change their mind. For example:

COUNSELLOR: Have you told Jamie that he is HIV positive?
PATIENT: We could never do that.
COUNSELLOR: Can you see a time when Jamie will need to know?
PATIENT: I suppose in many years, when he is grown up and wants to start a life of his own.
COUNSELLOR: Yes, can you think of other circumstances?
PATIENT: No, not really. Well perhaps if he gets sick. But he is so well at the moment. . . .
COUNSELLOR: If he got sick would that be a good time to tell him?
PATIENT: Well, perhaps we could have raised the topic a little before hand.
COUNSELLOR: When you decide to tell Jamie, who will do the telling?
PATIENT: I think we both would – it will be terribly difficult, I mean how do you tell a child? Perhaps you could be with us, no, maybe we should do it at home, I am not sure about that really.

In this dialogue, the counsellor has moved from the general, far distant future, to the particular. The parents are now beginning to think about possible outcomes and plans. Although they do not need to make any firm decisions, by raising the issue, the counsellor may allow them to think it through.

There is also the situation of well (uninfected) children whose parent/ parents or sibling has HIV. The advice must be that those entrusted with the care of such children should make sensible decisions appropriate for each individual child. The ingredients in the balance should be the emotional readiness of the child, the insight of the child, and the pace at which the child should move. People often think that the obstacles to telling children are overwhelming. In reality, children are able to take much on board. Indeed, children seem to respond much better to truth (even if this is painful) than to lies, deceit, uncertainty and confusion. Often children have a clear sense of strain or stress and cannot understand what is going on. If they are given the truth this is much easier for them to deal with. Children can often determine their own level of need. Essentially the child can be the guide as to the depth and extent of information given. The counsellor should either work with the child and the parents, or work with the parents to help the child indirectly. Tell the child as much as they can take in and then raise the subject subsequently. The child may need time to take the message in. With changing circumstances the child's questions and level of need may alter. A step-wise progression based on truth and multiple opportunities for discussion is often the most productive.

Children need simple and straightforward explanations. Jargon should be avoided. Children need the same reassurances, support, comfort and practical help that adolescents and adults need.

Some clinical examples of post-test counselling cases

Case 1: Post-test counselling in a woman who is 22 weeks pregnant

Maria attended for routine antenatal care at a large urban hospital. Maria works in a good job at a large industrial company. She has been recently married and is excited about her forthcoming baby. Her husband (Alan) is local, but she comes from Spain. Her routine antenatal care reveals that she has been a former drug user. She reports that she is now on a drug maintenance programme (methadone) and does not use any other drugs. Her husband is also a former user. He reports that he has given up altogether. They have shared needles together in the past. Maria is seen as part of the clinic and is 'advised' that an HIV test should be done. Her counselling was done by a doctor responsible for her medical care. He feels he outlined the situation to her completely. He has spoken to both her and her husband. The couple have both been tested. They are due to return to the antenatal clinic. Alan has tested HIV negative. Maria has tested HIV positive. Both are well. The doctor telephones the counsellor to ask advice on how to break the news and what to do.

Problems posed by this case
(a) Maria is well advanced in her pregnancy.
(b) It is unclear to what extent pre-test counselling was carried out. Clearly there has been some input but the extent of this is uncertain.
(c) The doctor's role is uncertain. Clearly he will have an ongoing input into the case and needs to be involved.
(d) The fact that one partner tests negative and the other tests positive may create some problems.
(e) Maria has used drugs in the past as a coping mechanism – to what extent is she drug free and will this news lead to increased drug taking?
(f) What support is available to the couple and to Maria (whose family are abroad).

Ideal solution
There is never an ideal solution. Clearly the couple need to take the news in and to address the following:

(a) What are their decisions with regard to the pregnancy?
(b) What are their desires with regard to future childbearing?
(c) What are their immediate concerns about infection control, safer sex and medical follow-up?
(d) Timing is a key factor here as termination becomes difficult the further the pregnancy has progressed.
(e) Longer term follow-up should be available.

Reality
The tasks the counsellor faces are:

(a) To make decisions regarding the involvement of the doctor. Although the counsellor may be proficient at counselling, the doctor may benefit from involvement. He may see, by example, how a counselling approach works. He may utilize the session to build up skill by role modelling for future cases. He may have a good relationship with Maria and Alan and his involvement may be helpful to them. The counsellor may find it difficult to work in the presence of the doctor, but such concerns should be secondary to the needs of the clients and the future usefulness to the front line doctor.

(b)   To discuss alternatives available to the client.

(c)   To discuss decisions, their implications, and how to help the couple come to an agreement.

(d)   To ensure that the couple are not rushed by the doctor who sees an overriding medical need to make early decisions if a termination is to be carried out.

(e)   To examine the future for this couple.

(f)   To examine the individual needs of the couple.

(g)   To anticipate possible differences in opinion between Alan and Maria and to help them accept that they may hold different views, may react differently, and may have to discuss this.

(h)   To provide other input channels (for example, telephone help lines; discussions with other women who are HIV-positive and pregnant).

(i)   To reassure them that they will be supported in their decision both emotionally and practically (if this is possible).

(j)   Not to make promises that cannot be kept.

(k)   Not to deny, reduce or minimize the circumstances.

Case 2: Post-test counselling where there was no pre-test counselling

Counsellors may have to break bad news to a client they have never met. They will not have the luxury of creating a relationship, rehearsing reactions, setting up support strategies. Consider the following example:

> Mercy is a 28-year-old woman. She is attending the paediatric clinic for a follow-up visit with her sick child. Her child is one year old and was brought to the clinic with symptoms of severe diarrhoea and lethargy. An HIV test was carried out on the baby. This turned out to be positive. The clinic has asked you to attend to counsel Mercy who also had blood taken at the time and this has turned out to be HIV positive as well.
>
> Mercy is married and has another child. She lives in a semi-rural area and has to travel into the city to visit the hospital. Mercy's husband works away from home during the week but returns at weekends. Mercy has many close family around her who help with the children and provide support.

This is not an atypical case history. Many women may present with an ill baby and it is the first time that HIV infection in the mother has been considered. However, it makes a very challenging counselling scenario.

Problems posed by this case
There are a series of levels of problems with the case which the counsellor needs to understand prior to counselling. These include:

(a) No-pre test counselling.
(b) Little or no expectation and preparation for a positive result.
(c) No personal contact or relationship which pre-exists the bad news.
(d) Double bad news (mother and child are infected).

Ideal solution
In an ideal world Mercy will:

(a) React appropriately.
(b) Return for follow-up visits.
(c) Initiate the use of condoms in her relationship.
(d) Discuss the problems with her husband.
(e) Examine risky behaviour such as other sexual partners or exposure to piercing or blood products.
(f) Form a close and supportive relationship with the counsellor.

Reality
In reality the situation is very different. Mercy may well:

(a) Find it impossible to take the news in, either not believe it or feel it is lies.
(b) Mercy will probably be reluctant to return to a clinic who has given her such awful news (or who 'lies' or who 'upsets people').
(c) Mercy may never tell her husband.
(d) The use of condoms may be unthinkable, unaffordable and may result in the break up of her marriage (the worst possible outcome for Mercy).
(e) Mercy may have much distrust.
(f) Mercy may never want to talk to the counsellor again.

Aims

In the ideal world the aims would be straightforward. In reality, they may be so difficult to achieve that the counsellor ought to set more realistic (and achievable) goals. These should address:

(a)   What are the limitations of Mercy's intake for this session?
(b)   What are the priorities?
(c)   Will Mercy return? If yes, rank order priorities differently. If no, ensure that she has all the basic information she needs. The latter situation may be highly likely although it is obviously the least desirable.

Counselling decisions

A series of practical decisions should be made to ensure optimum outcome rather than to attempt 'total' (and perhaps unachievable) success. These should be:

(a)   Creation of trust.
(b)   Helping her with the news.
(c)   Discussing practical and immediate problems with her (such as who to tell, how to tell).
(d)   Do not tell Mercy what to do. Encourage her to come up with suggestions and endorse and encourage these. Follow them through.

Lessons to learn

(a)   Post-test counselling without the provision of pre-test counselling is difficult and may be less useful or successful as a result. This means that wherever possible counsellors should attempt to be involved with women prior to testing or even while they are waiting for results. This allows for a more productive relationship and may allow the woman to use the counsellor to greater effect.
(b)   Counselling is not magic. It is hard work and it is a two-way process. It involves an enabling counsellor and a willing client. A client who does not want to hear the message or do any of the work will not benefit from counselling.
(c)   Counselling which comes across as a series of commands (do not have sex; do not have sex without a condom; tell your husband; come back to the clinic) may result in a client taking power or control in the only way left open to her. She has the decision as to whether to return or not. Demands may alienate her and chase her away.

Case 3: Post-test counselling after the birth of a baby to a HIV-positive woman

Sylvia is HIV positive and well. She has recently given birth to a baby girl (38 weeks gestation). The baby appears well. Sylvia's partner is not really available to her. They seem to have a relationship with ups and downs. They live separately. He sometimes comes to visit and acknowledges the baby as his. Sylvia is hopeful that the relationship will continue. Sylvia worked as a cleaner before the birth of the baby and took in any casual work. With the arrival of the baby she has stopped working and is dependent on state welfare provision and family and friends.

The baby is now 7 weeks old. Cord blood was positive for HIV and the first blood test has also come back positive.

Problems posed by this case
(a)   Sylvia herself is HIV positive. She needs to have counselling both for herself, her baby, and the family unit.
(b)   It is not yet possible to differentiate between passive maternal antibody and infant antibody. Sylvia will have to wait for many months before she knows the true status of her baby.
(c)   Irrespective of status, Sylvia may have many problems concerning the future of the baby, both short and long term.
(d)   The apparent good health of the baby may prompt both Sylvia and the counsellor to think that all is well. The counsellor should not provide glib statements which may prove to be wrong.

Aims
Aims of the counselling should be:

(a)   Set up a good long-term relationship with Sylvia and her baby.
(b)   Reconfirm the uncertainty and examine how she is coping with this.
(c)   Explore some reactions and practical problems in all eventualities.
(d)   Look at the practical problems Sylvia may be facing.

Conclusion

Post-test counselling includes the provision of bad news and ongoing support. Remember that there are some people who will need a lot of support. On the other hand, there are others who may need relatively little support. This may change over time, so that the counsellor should tailor availability to need and make sure that the client knows how to make contact.

Chapter 7

Termination Counselling

HIV in pregnancy does not necessarily mean that the outcome will be termination. Indeed, the literature worldwide shows the contrary. For many people, in any case, this option is unthinkable. In many countries this option is not even available. Studies have shown that when termination is available HIV-positive pregnant women often do not take this up (Johnston *et al.* 1989; Sunderland 1988). The only predictor found for termination of pregnancy in one study was previous termination. This does not mean that termination counselling should not be part of the range of health care worker skills nor that termination should be ruled out as an option.

The key theme for workers as far as termination is concerned must be to acknowledge that decisions are always those of the mother or parents and counselling is the process which may help them come to that decision, live with the consequences of that decision, and plan a future in the presence of the decision. Counsellors should never assume that life with HIV is worse than no life.

There are many places where people can turn to for advice. Such sources include mothers, fathers, grandparents, doctors, siblings, teachers, and friends. It seems that people are surrounded by others telling them what to do. This marks the very difference between advice givers and psychologists. Counselling is the one place which is not concerned with telling people what to do. People need counselling when the other mechanisms no longer work. Counselling involves helping people make their own decisions. Once these are made, it involves supporting people through these decisions and maximizing their ability to cope.

Literature on termination of pregnancy and HIV

The literature on pregnancy decision-making in the presence of HIV is mixed. Johnston *et al.* (1989) looked at the extent to which knowledge of HIV antibody status affected decisions about continuing or terminating pregnancy. They studied 163 pregnancies in drug-using women (spontaneous abortions, data gathered before 1986, and woman not knowing their HIV status before 22 weeks of gestation were excluded). They found that termination was common in both groups of women, with and without HIV, for this client sample. They identified that more women had terminations with HIV than without but this finding did not reach statistical significance. They found that 44 women knew that they were positive to HIV when they became pregnant and 21 of them went on to have a termination. Thus knowledge of HIV is not an effective contraception. It must be remembered that for a proportion of these women (9) HIV was quoted as the main reason for having a termination. 4 of these 9 had AIDS or AIDS-related illness. Such factors are known to increase transmission risks to the baby and this may have interacted with their decision. A group of 25 women were identified as HIV positive and well during their pregnancy. Ten of these proceeded to have a termination (nine of the ten, however, had previously requested termination on other grounds).

The data from this study also give an insight into the reason why women want to continue pregnancies. This is important for counselling in order to understand the reasons for all decisions. Thirty-eight women in the sample continued their pregnancy in the presence of HIV. The factors identified by these workers were:

- Current good health;
- Desire to have a child;
- Feelings against termination;
- Normative judgements based on knowledge of women who had babies in the presence of HIV who are currently well and seemed uninfected.

These workers concluded that decisions were rarely altered from original intentions especially when the pregnancy was wanted. The desire to have a baby was strong for these women. They caution that when normative data alters, subjective decisions may vary.

Counselling sessions have been evaluated by a series of workers. Sunderland (1990) found no difference between groups of women with regard to a termination decision based on HIV status. This was confirmed by Selwyn (1989) who also found no difference in termination or pregnancy rate for those counselled. Cirara (1990) found that under half (23 out of 60) of the subjects in her study terminated a pregnancy in the presence of HIV. Barbacci (1989) found that 20% of her sample terminated pregnancy. She also found that 16% of her sample became pregnant after being informed of a positive HIV result. Wiznea (1989) found that in her sample 27% terminated their pregnancy and a proportion of those went on to a subsequent pregnancy.

Termination

Termination of pregnancy is one option for women who are pregnant and infected with HIV. It should be emphasized that this is but one option and termination counselling is part of a much wider support service. All good termination counselling should commence with decision making about the termination itself. The following section will examine the role of the counsellor, the general and specific counselling skills needed for termination counselling, and the ongoing psychological problems and support requirements associated with termination.

There is widespread belief that termination of pregnancy is associated with considerable emotional reaction. However, there are few prospective studies which have systematically evaluated this. There are no such studies for women with HIV. The literature tends to be more general and in recent studies which have followed women over time, short-term psychological reactions to termination were common but severe long-term difficulties were unusual. The extent to which these data can be extrapolated to women with HIV is unclear. HIV and AIDS may pose an extra factor. Few long-term problems have been identified in various studies (Greer *et al.* 1976; Illsley & Hall 1976; Donnaie *et al.* 1981). Furthermore, few workers take into account that there may be psychological benefits from termination. For example Shusterman (1979) found that some women expressed relief after termination. Thus it seems that for many women there are short-term crises and, for a few, longer term problems. This proportion seems to be in the region of 1 in 10. No studies of long-term follow-up of HIV related terminations have yet been done.

If one is to learn from the current data, the most important lessons are to acknowledge the benefits as well as the traumas of termination and to try and identify and predict factors which may be associated with longer term problems. Workers such as Dunlop (1978) Shusterman

(1979) have recounted risk factors (but not on samples where HIV is a factor). The findings may well apply to HIV, and they list risk factors as follows:

(1)   Pressure or coercion in the termination decision-making process. Such pressure could emanate from many sources, including medical, family, spouse or peers.
(2)   Previous psychiatric history may be a predictor of subsequent coping problems. Thus a comprehensive medical and psychiatric history should be taken when women present for medical check-ups.
(3)   Dunlop (1978) noted that terminations which are associated with medical reasons may create subsequent difficulties. It is unclear whether this is caused by the stress of facing up to the medical problem or whether the medical problem recurs and over the long term these contribute to psychological difficulties.
(4)   The emotional reaction on discovering the existence of the pregnancy has been found to be a useful predictor of subsequent distress. Essentially, those who feel immense anger may need special input.
(5)   Poor relationships and lack of intimacy with a partner has been associated with poor prognosis. It is unclear whether this is a direct problem: that it is the unfulfilling relationship which contributes to long-term difficulties rather than a termination in the presence of such a relationship. However, it does indicate that good counselling in the first place should involve a comprehensive discussion on the nature and level of the relationship.
(6)   Shusterman (1979) found that dissatisfaction with termination decision was a predictor of poor outcome. This finding points out the necessity to check the decision with the woman and to allow, at all times, for decisions to be re-examined and altered.

From these data it seems that social support, plus the supportive decisions of others, are desirable ingredients for protection against future emotional disruption. When women think through their decision more clearly and feel in control, the prognosis is better. Counselling sessions which can provide or address these factors may help to equip women and protect them against short- and long-term distress.

Counselling should be a key element in termination decisions providing both an occasion and an opportunity for full discussion and thought.

Marcus (1979) found that counselling prior to termination was beneficial although in this study subsequent contraception and termination problems were still apparent. This study has clear implications for HIV where some of the key themes in counselling could be adapted, for example, to look at:

- Current pregnancy;
- Future safe sex;
- Future conception.

Holman (1989) found that many women who were HIV-positive and pregnant returned to their clinic with subsequent pregnancies. This lends support to the idea that it is necessary to provide comprehensive future family planning at the time of termination. It also highlights the fact that one termination does not rule out a subsequent pregnancy.

Approach to counselling

A good counsellor is faced with a difficult task, and has to understand that there are no right or wrong decisions. A decision which is right for one person at one time may be wrong for another person at another time. The basic ingredients needed to help somebody with decisions are as follows:

Accurate factual information

Factual information is often overlooked as a commodity. It is also sometimes undervalued. For example, many people who are in possession of much information, feel that counselling is the mere imparting of this. They are wrong. It is only one portion. On the other hand, people with factual information sometimes feel they have no counselling skills and are intimidated by the counselling demands of their patients and may feel reluctant to embark on anything vaguely resembling counselling. Once again, this is sad as they have a major tool in their hands and if used wisely could benefit many clients.

The advice to anyone starting counselling is 'get informed'. With AIDS and HIV this has become a challenging prerequisite. As the database expands nearly to explosion point, it is often quite a feat for somebody to become knowledgeable and to stay updated. It is important to find the time to do the best job possible. It is also important to understand and acknowledge one's own limitations. In some instances, the client may be in a position of more knowledge and possess more facts than the counsellor – the counsellor, however, can still offer help.

The objective – do not judge

One can have strong opinions on behalf of patients, friends and relatives. In counselling there is little room for strong opinions: the job is
to listen to the needs and thoughts of clients, help them to come to the
best decision for them, and ensure that they have thought through all
possible options. It can be difficult to abandon personal opinions and
strong views. Take, for example, the following case outline:

A young unmarried woman presents for advice. She is pregnant for
the second time. She terminated her previous pregnancy. The father of
the child has no commitment to either the relationship or the pregnancy. He is a heavy drinker, to the extent of possibly being labelled
alcoholic. He is often found in an alcoholic state and has a history of
beating up his girlfriend. The woman is ambivalent. Housing is inadequate and finances are poor. This is a true case history: try and analyse
your first reactions. Also analyse the extent to which you hold a view
on the 'pros and cons' of termination in this case.

In reality, this woman went on to have the baby, a boy. He was born
in Germany. These are the circumstances surrounding the birth of
Ludwig van Beethoven.

The above example may help highlight the necessity for a counsellor
to withold judgement and not to think that termination is always a
clear and obvious option.

The process of counselling

Real life cases are rarely simple and the following example will highlight some of the many issues which can be involved in counselling
and some of the strategies to be adopted.

Case 4:

> Martine was a 28-year-old woman. She had been an injecting drug
> user some 4–5 years ago. She had been involved with a regular
> partner for the past 5 years. He too had been an injecting drug user.
> They had shared syringes with each other. With this history, the
> antenatal clinic suggested an HIV test. The test came back positive.
> Prior to the consultation the midwife requested counselling input
> and advice.

Faced with such a case, the counsellor needs to go through a process.
The first stage involves pre-counselling planning. The second stage

, concentrates on the counselling session or sessions and the final stage is one of longer-term planning.

Stage 1: Pre-counselling planning

Who should do the counselling?
The midwife concerned may well also be involved in the counselling process. Decisions therefore need to be taken as to whether the midwife and the counsellor should jointly counsel the woman. The advantages of this may be many. The midwife may benefit from learning by example so that in a subsequent case she will be better able to provide a counselling model. On the other hand the midwife already has a pre-existing relationship with the woman and may be ideally placed to provide ongoing help and trust. The disadvantage may be the time limitations. The midwife may have a different model of care and may be reluctant to allow the woman to explore decisions and options for herself. Although a learning procedure could help the midwife with this alternative model, this may be at some cost to the woman concerned. The counsellor needs to work out the level of this cost and whether it is acceptable.

Who should be counselled?
A counsellor needs to work out whether the mother should be seen alone or with her partner. Once these basic decisions have been made the process of counselling should ensue.

Setting the scene
Good counselling relies on many basic elements which ought to be considered as a matter of course prior to the beginning of counselling. Special attention should be focussed on the following:

Place. The counselling venue is important. It needs to be a comfortable place in which to conduct a confidential conversation without fear of interruption or breach of privacy. Facilities such as coffee or tea, easy chairs, access to a telephone, writing materials and tissues may be necessary.

Timing. The timing of the counselling needs careful planning. Miller *et al.* (1986) cautioned, 'never on a Friday at 5'. The message there is that one should anticipate emotional trauma after counselling and the availability of support services should play a role in determining timing.

Preparation.   The first step in counselling comes from the counsellor. Prior to any interaction, the aims and goals of counselling must be clearly worked out. This does not mean to say that variations will not occur according to individual needs. What it does mean is that the counsellors need to be very clear about both their role and their remit. The underlying goal of all counselling is to provide a non-judgemental environment where a woman can explore, in an open and unpressured way, the decision that she would like to make.

Long-term commitment to help.   Counselling must involve as much help as an individual woman needs to come to the decision, support through that decision, support if she changes her mind about the decision, and long-term support after she has made such a decision. Such decisions are far reaching and will remain with the woman and the woman and her partner as a couple forever. They may have important bearings for some of the future life of the woman and the counselling process should ensure that the woman has the best opportunity to come to a decision which is right for her.

Stage 2: Counselling intervention

Beginning the interview
Some counsellors work alone, others in pairs. A woman faced by too many counsellors may feel intimidated. Most counselling is usually done in a one-to-one situation. Women should always be given the opportunity to choose whether they would like their partner or another special person present with them. There is a fine balance between somebody wanting to be seen alone and somebody being pressured to be seen in a couple. The counsellor should give the woman the opportunity to make this decision. This is often best done alone with the woman who can then bring her partner if she so chooses. It also allows the possibility for the woman to have some time on her own and the partner to be brought in at some later point.

   Counsellors should always introduce themselves fully to the patient and ensure that they have the correct name (and pronunciation of that name) of their patient. The counsellor should be seen as helpful and friendly. The way an interview begins may often determine the extent to which this goal can be achieved. Go out and fetch the patient rather than have a receptionist call her name, letting her find her own way to the room. Do not abandon normal social interactions such as greetings, introduction, seating arrangements and the ensuring of comfort. This may require the provision of a place to hang a coat, the provision of items which break social distance such as a cup of coffee or tea. Such an atmosphere is important with all counselling but of particular importance with HIV. Shaking hands, sharing tea cups, and general warmth, convey an acceptance for someone with HIV which may be an important pre-requisite to any ongoing trust.

Setting the scene for counselling

In an ideal situation, pre-test counselling should precede any sessions which may deal with termination and HIV. If this is so, subsequent input may be easier and commencement is less difficult as there is a pre-existing relationship and some ground may have been covered. Furthermore, such ground will have been covered at a time when anxiety levels may have been lower and thus chances of recall and understanding are heightened. However, there is much literature which points out that people screen out items which they see as highly fearful or irrelevant. It may be that at pre-test counselling the individual (who perhaps may not have anticipated a positive result) may have been selective in attention, absorption and recall of information.

If pre-test counselling was not carried out, the task is somewhat more difficult. At the point when termination is to be discussed, the counsellor also needs to gain basic trust of the patient and to form a good rapport.

However this is done, it is important to set out in the first instance what counselling means and what the session will entail. The patient, and her partner if present, need to understand that the counsellor will spend time exploring the options, discussing the information that exists, and helping her (or them) to come to a decision. The woman needs to know that she is not being rushed into making a decision and that she will be given as much time as she needs. There should be no pressure to come to decisions by the end of the meeting. It may well take more than one session and the woman may want to go home and think about it before deciding.

The woman also needs to have a clear indication that the counsellor has no particular learnings either way. It is crucial that she does not pick up an impression from the counsellor one way or the other. This may colour her decision; it may also make it difficult, or even impossible, for her to explore her own feelings.

Basic background
At this stage the counsellor ought to establish basic background facts. These form the foundation for any subsequent information giving. It is very important in the area of HIV to know the basic facts as this may affect many of the decisions and have bearing on current knowledge.

The kind of information that should be gathered includes the following:

How far the pregnancy has progressed.   The legal limitations on termination vary from country to country. In any event, there are widespread accepted medical criteria which would dictate safety limits for termination. Generally speaking, terminations should be aimed for a time prior to 16 weeks gestation. After that time, the risks to the mother increase. The method of termination will also vary according to the gestation time of the fetus. In the UK the legal limit for terminations has recently been brought forward from 28 weeks to 24 weeks gestation.

HIV status.   It is important to know whether the woman is symptomatic or asymptomatic at the time. This has specific implications for pregnancy outcome. Data suggest that vertical transmission in an HIV-positive mother who is well is somewhere in the region of 21%–29%. This changes dramatically for a mother who is symptomatic. The risks of vertical transmission increase and are closer to 50% or 60%. If the mother was unaware of these facts she may well want to undergo medical tests to examine T4 (CD4) cell counts or other markers which may help her come to a decision. She ought to know that these tests are available. This is a key stage in counselling and one where the psychological and medical disciplines need to interact; good channels of dialogue are therefore crucial.

Parity.   The counsellor should establish whether the mother has other children. Studies have highlighted an increased risk to a mother of transmitting HIV to her baby if she has had a previous birth where the baby has acquired AIDS. The health and well being of other children ought to be established.

Social factors
The social background of the pregnant woman may have many implications for her decision and subsequent support for that decision. In the West, drug use has been associated with HIV transmission. It is important to establish whether the patient is a drug user or not. At times of crisis somebody who has used drugs in the past may feel the

need to use them again in the future. A termination decision may well represent a crisis point for such an individual.

Support factors

No counsellor can be available all of the time. One of the goals of counselling must be to establish other support networks that the patient can turn to. This will include both personal and community support: partner, parents and friends on the one hand, and professionals and agencies such as Women's Groups, HIV support groups, or termination counselling agencies on the other.

It is also important to differentiate between different forms of support such as social support, professional support, and financial support (Kincey & Saltmore 1988).

The timing of support is also a key factor. If the correct ingredients of support are theoretically 'available', but not readily available when they are needed, their efficacy may be reduced or even negated.

Pacing the procedure

Many of the procedures involved with termination require pacing and timing. These need to be made clear to the woman at an early stage. Information includes knowledge about availability, forms and procedures, practical details such as hospitals, convenient dates, and so on.

Discussing termination

The issue of the termination should not be raised directly as a confirmation for the woman of a wish to terminate. Rather it should be raised with regard to the pregnancy generally. This will allow for a new and fresh beginning so that the woman can go through the decision-making process from start to finish without preconceived conclusions. It is necessary to explore the pregnancy with the patient and to understand what it means to her. She may want to discuss how she came to conceive, what she think about childbearing, what her plans for the future are, and to explore possible strategy outcomes. There are many ways of dealing with an unwanted pregnancy. It is erroneous to assume that a pregnancy in the presence of HIV will be an unwanted one. At all times women's views must be respected. They need to know basic facts and information to help them come to a decision which is correct for them. Furthermore, often there are no ideal solutions. The solution at the end of the day, invariably, will be a compromise. What is important is that a woman feels happy about the decision she has come to, and about the process that has resulted in this decision and that she is well practised in the effects the decision will have on her in the future.

It is at this point that a woman ought to be given the full facts as far as they are known. These are simple and straightforward. Women need to appreciate the difference between the large body of data and their own individual circumstances. They also need to be given, without ambiguity, the fact that knowledge is limited. To many of their questions there are simply no answers. Furthermore, given that information is still in its infancy, what we know today may be proved to be wrong in a few years time. Great care must therefore be taken when interpreting this data for clients. This is perhaps one of the most challenging aspects of counselling. For professions used to having answers, this is a situation where there are no answers. Although clients may initially be angry, upset or disappointed, in the long term they will know that the counsellor was the one source who did not pretend to know it all, who was honest about the limitations. The counsellor needs to practise saying 'we do not know'.

Essentially, the facts a woman wants to know will include:

(1) The estimates of vertical transmission. These have changed over time. The current estimates in the West are chances of between 20% and 29% (even as low as 12.9% in the most recent European Cohort Study Report 1991) for a mother who is HIV positive and well. They appear to be closer to 30% in African studies.

(2) The prognosis does look gloomier for a mother who is symptomatic or who has had a previous baby with AIDS. In such cases, recorded vertical transmission rates have been as high as 65%.

(3) Clinical state can be examined by a series of tests, including T4 (CD4) cell counts. Cost and technological expertise may limit the availability of these.
    A discussion on termination should include the following:

- The future and prognosis;
- The effects on subsequent pregnancy;
- Personal effects, such as discomfort, pain;
- Practical information such as length of waiting time, method of termination;

- Time limits – how long does the patient have to make a decision; can it be reversed?;
- Medical care available;
- The effect of continuing pregnancy on the patient's own health.

In the early days, it was thought that the mere fact of a pregnancy could exacerbate illness in the mother. This has now been found not to be the case. Further studies are needed to confirm this situation. On current information, women can be reassured that no detriment in their condition has been recorded because of pregnancy. Even if this were the case, it is unclear whether a termination would reverse the situation.

Other options
Termination is only one possible outcome of a pregnancy. The reasons why a mother is contemplating termination ought to be explored. Continued reassurance and an undertaking of support are very important. If the mother is concerned about the future care of her baby in the event of her death, for example, then issues of fostering and adoption can be discussed.

Decision making
At the end of the day, women must be able to make their own decisions. They need to know that they have time to make these decisions. No woman should be hurried into making a decision because a session is nearing its end. It is a good idea to allow a woman to go home and ponder her decision before calling it final.

Once a woman has come to a decision to terminate, the counsellor should then discuss with her all the possible outcomes of this decision. The counsellor can explore how she would react in a variety of circumstances, encouraging her to try and think through the consequences of the decision and plan some of her responses and the avenues to which she would turn for support in such a time.

Longer term problems
Part of the counselling procedure should be devoted to longer term problems. This involves a discussion of future conception and contraception. Questions of infection control and safe sex may well be raised at this point. The counsellor should be in full possession of the

facts and know how to give the woman clear and accurate advice as well as providing her with supplementary literature.

Concerns and anxieties

Appropriate details about termination need to be discussed with any woman about to undergo this procedure. This should be done by a qualified member of staff. If the counsellor does not know the facts, it is good idea to involve one of the medical practitioners. Anxieties are most common and most acute in the face of the unknown. People are often much less anxious when they have accurate facts. The presentation of the facts also allows for good cognitive rehearsal of stressful events and may often prepare the woman for the forthcoming procedure.

The method of termination may depend on the gestation of the fetus. Good history-taking skills form an important part of the counselling procedure in this instance. When dates are unclear, the client's doctor may want to be involved in terms of prescribing an ultrasound scan.

Planning

The counsellor needs to help the woman plan through both the practicalities of the termination and her emotional responses to it. She may want to discuss her anxieties, worries and concerns. She may want to express sadness or relief. The counsellor should ask clear and unambiguous questions. It is often helpful to invite the woman to contemplate all the possible ramifications and to explore how she thinks she would cope. These include adjusting to the loss of the pregnancy, problems of self-esteem, relationship difficulties, long-term guilt and mourning, and possible effects on subsequent pregnancies. Very often people simply shut out stressful or worrying thoughts. This leaves them unprepared when reality hits. By simply opening the door to such discussions, the counsellor may allow the patient to think of worrying thoughts within a safe environment.

Subsequent pregnancies

One of the important issues in termination counselling centres around subsequent pregnancies. Some workers have found raised anxieties and concerns during pregnancy for women who have had previous terminations. This is an issue which ought to be dealt with since with

HIV, the situation is unique. If a woman cannot face a pregnancy in the presence of HIV she may be dealing not only with current termination prospects but also with the issue of procreation and childlessness for herself and her partner in the future. The reassurance that 'some-day' there may be a baby may not be something that a woman with HIV can hold on to. In addition when a wanted pregnancy is terminated because of such 'illness' factors there may well be sadness and feelings of guilt and blame. It is no less so with HIV. The situation may be worsened by the fact that HIV is a condition affecting the mother as well as her baby. The termination may symbolize not only the end of her pregnancy but a turning point in her own life. This may be the first opportunity she has had to discuss the effects of HIV on both herself and her partner as well as her future relationships. Much of the post-test counselling and ongoing support sessions could be evolved or initiated at this point.

An opportunity to reflect
Towards the end of this interview the counsellor should summarize and reflect back to the woman some of the process that she has gone through. This serves to confirm that the counsellor has fully under-stood the woman's thoughts and feelings and has found a way of putting them into a digestible form. It also allows an opportunity for asking questions.

Preparation for termination
Termination of pregnancy is a surgical procedure with an increased emotional component. There is a common association of anxiety and concern with surgery in anticipation of the event, during the procedure, and often for extended periods afterwards (Johnston 1980; Janis 1971). Furthermore, there is a considerable amount of psychological literature which shows an association between pre-operative emotional state (including anxiety, cognitive preparation and satisfaction) with post-operative outcome (Johnston & Carpenter 1980; Janis 1970).

A series of studies has been carried out on the provision of varying forms of information with beneficial effects (Ley 1988). One of the difficulties in the research is the failure to use systematic measures, the utilization of vastly differing operative procedures, and the measure-ment of post-operative outcome by a variety of indices. The net result is that it is difficult to generalize from one study to the next. However, the overwhelming finding is that there does seem to be a positive impact (Matthews & Ridgeway 1981). A range of medical situations have been examined: gynaecological surgery (Johnston & Carpenter 1980), laparoscopy (Wallace 1983), ultrasound scanning (Reading 1982) and labour (Enkin 1982). Input has varied from instruction booklets, written information, verbal information, improved communications, brief psychotherapy, counselling, instructions, role-play, sensitization, procedural information, and so on. Outcome measures have included pain ratings, satisfaction, analgesia uptake, length of hospital stay, psychological well being, anxiety, medication, and psycho-social adjustment.

Generally, the literature indicates that the provision of information has an overall beneficial effect. The addition of information about sensory experience enhances the effect of any procedural information (Johnson & Leventhal 1974). In conclusion, psychologists have pointed out the need to address the particular needs and fears associated with the given medical procedure. More recent work has developed these ideas to incorporate a tailoring of input to individual coping styles (O'Sullivan & Steptoe 1986).

Post-termination
After termination, there may be an ongoing demand for counselling. Among the many issues the client may need to address are:

(1)   Immediate feedback.
(2)   Pain experience, reassurance, and immediate feelings of difference, sadness, mood fluctuation, worry and fear.
(3)   Pain management.
(4)   Pacing and queries which include general information, basic facts, things to anticipate, simple advice, and clear signs of what to look for. Supplement with written information as there are limits to the amounts of information patients can absorb.
(5)   Anticipation of psychological reaction: support access, set up follow-up meetings and use the time to discuss contraception, infection control, handling of blood, future safe sex, and future planning.
(6)   Discussion of contraception and safe sex.
(7)   Mood changes: after termination it is helpful for the woman to be prepared for mood changes and to have patience and understanding if she experiences these. She may react intensely to the sudden change from being pregnant to non-pregnant. She may feel a mixture of feelings ranging from sadness and emptiness to relief and detachment. She may feel touchy and sensitive. She may view the world very

differently and fail to find relevance, importance or meaning to any events in the outside world. This can frighten and worry her. She may be left wondering whether she will ever be the same again.

(8) The partner. It is all too easy to forget the partner when termination is directed at the woman. Remember that every baby has a father and he may be a key figure in the support of the woman; he may have a whole range of emotional reactions himself as it is his baby, too, that has been lost. Problems with partners sometimes arise when they are forgotten, pushed aside, ignored or relied upon without adequate appreciation of their feelings. It is common for couples to have similar emotional reactions but at different times. Often a partner is so busy providing support that he puts aside his own feelings. It may be at a later date that these emerge. A relationship may be based on mutual understanding and support. Yet at a time of crisis people have different opinions, different demands, and different reactions. This can be a source of immense strain. Indeed there are some relationships that never recover from crisis while others are strengthened.

(9) It is important to allow a woman to have open discussion and dialogue after a termination. She may need to go over some of her feelings, examine her decisions, or simply discuss the termination. She may need to examine telling her partner if she had not done so before.

After discharge

Follow-up is vital. Counsellors should anticipate change in psychological reactions after termination and should prepare both the mother and father for this. Immediately after a termination someone may express one emotion and some days later may oscillate to a very different emotion. Prepare them for the possibility of this and explore how they may cope.

Self-help groups, such as 'Positively Women' in London, may be very helpful. Here, women can gather support and perhaps discuss their experiences with other women who have undergone a termination or faced such decisions.

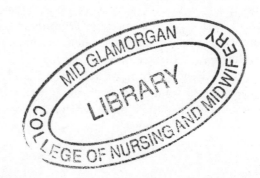

Chapter 8

HIV and AIDS in Pregnancy

The quality of experience during pregnancy is a major focus of obstetric care. There is no reason to assume that an experience is any different or less meaningful for a mother when HIV infection is present. The differences may be associated with the trauma, psychological burden, and crisis decision-making that she and her partner will be faced with. As such, the goals of management should include the medical and psychological well being of mother, baby, and the wider family. The literature on HIV in pregnancy has focussed on immunological markers, medical outcome, and decision to terminate. There is little investigation on the psychological experience for HIV-affected women – the pain, tears, happiness and joy.

This chapter will review the literature from general obstetrics to highlight the counselling implications which may apply to HIV and AIDS and to circumstances where HIV issues may extend to the uninfected.

Consultations

For all women, consultations during pregnancy may be stressful. General communication between doctors and patients is often unsatisfactory (Ley 1982). This has also been documented in obstetric consultations (Reid 1981; Sherr 1989). Many of the barriers to communication are raised by the over-use of jargon, complex explanations, inadequate information, and speed of interview. From the woman's point of view, communication barriers may be related to anxiety, forgetting, incomplete factual bases (which render some information confusing), timidity in asking questions, discomfort, alienation and unfamiliarity. Such communication problems have been demonstrated in a wide range of medical settings, but may be most difficult in obstetrics.

All obstetric patients are women and in many countries the majority of obstetricians are men. Areskog-Wijma (1987) surveyed women awaiting gynaecological consultations and found that 4% preferred a male doctor and 42% preferred a female doctor. This gender difference plus the non-availability of female doctors may pose problems. The discreet nature of sexuality may create embarrassment and hinder open dialogue. The physician may be very familiar with many cases, but for the individual woman this may be the first exposure to such a doctor. Obstetric consultations are often accompanied by vaginal examinations. Oakley (1979) reported that one third of her sample were given their first vaginal examination at their first antenatal visit which frightened them, caused them embarrassment and was painful. There is a considerable literature which encourages such examination on medical grounds, and further literature for HIV which underlines the importance of such routine screening (Minkoff 1989). However, from the point of view of the woman, this can be awkward and difficult. It may well be worth postponing a vaginal examination to the second visit. Writers have documented degradation, anxiety and emotional upset when exposed to vaginal examination (Magee 1975; Osokosky 1967; Areskog-Wijma 1987). Reading (1982) has also noted that vaginal examinations may result in failure of a woman to return for medical care.

Two studies have demonstrated that interventions can be used to good effect to reduce any anxiety surrounding vaginal examinations (Fuller *et al*. 1978; Reading 1982).

Psychosexual problems may emerge during gynaecological examinations and this may be an ideal time for intervention and help. This requires both a skilled and sensitive practitioner who will pick up cues and problems from the client and allow for help either by intervention or referral. Some such problems may precede HIV infection or, more commonly, may be directly linked to HIV.

In other settings, the provision of full information in written form has been shown to reduce anxiety and pain and enhance speed of recovery for patients undergoing gynaecological surgery (Wallace 1984). Such information could well be integrated into the care packages of HIV-positive women during pregnancy.

Psychological factors during pregnancy

Anecdotal evidence has usually marked pregnancy as a time of anxiety. More rigorous studies have provided a complex picture. Anxiety did not vary dramatically in studies by Murai and Murai (1975) and Elliott (1984), but did increase over the course of pregnancy in other studies (Grimm 1961). In a comprehensive review of pregnancy anxiety, Elliott concludes that specific labour related concerns may emerge at the latter stages of pregnancy, but generally pregnancy was not necessarily a time of anxiety and, indeed, there were many positive mood states associated with pregnancy which are often overlooked. Some of this anxiety, if it exists, may well be iatrogenic. Garcia (1983) notes poor levels of communication, lack of continuity of care, abhorrence of a mass 'depersonalized' approach to routine treatment, and criticism at the difficulty in obtaining feedback and test results. Problems in routine antenatal systems may be of particular relevance to a woman concerned about HIV. Numerous intervention studies have shown ways of ameliorating these and may be helpful. Although it would be useful to ensure that HIV affected mothers benefit from such changes, staff should be aware that not all HIV-positive mothers will acknowledge their status and thus universal examination of procedures and protocols will raise the level of psychological care of all women in obstetrics.

Women in many countries go to considerable lengths to attend antenatal clinics. In some countries, attendance is often late in the day. In others, women only attend at the onset of labour and thus antenatal care needs to reach out to them. There is some evidence (Hira *et al.*, 1989) that in Africa HIV-positive pregnancies are associated with significantly earlier onset of labour, and a correspondingly lower birthweight baby. It is unclear whether this is causative, but antenatal intervention which may promote full term delivery may enhance the health status of the baby.

Given the varying pattern of attendance, it is worth considering how women are treated once they do arrive for care. In the UK, Garcia (1982) reported an average hospital wait of 156 minutes. This clearly seems to be a result of the system rather than due to the women themselves: a Royal Commission Report stated that over half of their patient sample (n = 1652) managed to arrive within five minutes of their appointment time, with two out of five arriving early. Furthermore, late arrivals, although rare, were often associated with hospital transport failures. The commission reported that only 1% of those making their own way to the hospital were late.

In general obstetrics, O'Brien and Smith (1979) found that only four out of 200 UK women had no antenatal care. Studies in the USA have found that women with HIV are more likely to appear later for antenatal care. This may reflect the factors associated with HIV positivity in this group (namely drug users) or may be enhanced by fears that HIV-positive pregnant woman have about undue pressure to terminate. It is worth remembering that dissatisfied women make poor attenders.

In the West, there is high attendance at antenatal clinics generally – despite the fact that MacIntyre (1979) reports that only 17% learned anything during their visit and 69% reported that they did not enjoy their visit. Continuity of care was seen as desirable and feedback was always endorsed when it was received even when this was negative feedback (MacIntyre 1979). Sherr (1980) controlled for personalized feedback in conjunction with explanatory information and found that this took up very little physician time, but resulted in lower post-consultation anxiety and higher satisfaction. Sherr (1981) also noted that women wanted full explanations and preferred medical sources for these. Desire for information was high and common to primiparous and multiparous women of all social classes. Success in obtaining such information, however, varied according to parity and class, and was determined not by the desire for information but by the willingness of the carer to engage in dialogue. Lower social class and higher parity were factors militating against explanations by doctors (Sherr 1989).

Antenatal screening generally has been a source of much investigation. Some workers are critical of the extent to which routine screening can identify problems and subsequently ameliorate these (Hall & Chng 1982). However, as the medical debate surrounding the pros and cons of screening in pregnancy continues, it is important to note that there is some psychological cost to screening (Marteau 1989; Sherr 1989; Reading 1982; Campbell 1982; Farrant 1979). Psychological interventions which have provided explanation, anticipatory information, visual feedback of ultrasounds and relaxation training for stressful procedures, have all shown beneficial effects on the appraisal of the event, the understanding of the outcome and the satisfaction of the consumer, as well as on more indirect behaviours such as attitudes to pregnancy and the heeding of advice about cessation of alcohol and tobacco use (Reading 1982).

Psychological problems such as anxiety and depression have been recorded in some pregnancies. However, such problems are often correlated with previous obstetric abnormalities (Davids 1961; McDonald 1963; Crandon 1979) and with previous miscarriage (Kumar & Robson 1978). As HIV may present such stressors, such psychological difficulties may well arise. Health carers need to be sensitive to this. Antenatal anxiety has been shown to be unrelated to labour complications (Beck 1980; Astbury 1980). Crandon (1979) did show correlations between antenatal anxiety and birth outcome. However, this was a poorly controlled study and it seems possible that the anxiety was related to medical conditions which were responsible for the poor outcome rather than the anxiety in isolation. It is poor comfort for an anxious mother to be told that her anxiety itself can harm her baby.

Elliott (1984) charts some of the positive mental health aspects associated with pregnancy. These are often overlooked. To many women, pregnancy is an enjoyable experience and may have particular personal, societal and cultural meanings.

HIV and the uninfected during pregnancy

Despite the fact that the numbers of HIV-positive pregnant women are relatively low in some centres, pregnancy must constitute an ideal occasion for health education and safe sex counselling. At this stage, the passage of simple information, within a broader informational package, may be well placed. It will allow women to examine their possible risk exposure, to contemplate whether safe sex is an issue for them, and to address their subsequent sexual behaviour. It will also allow for possible prevention of HIV infection in pregnancy. The sheer volume of women at antenatal clinics will often mean that such counselling is rarely carried out by a professional counsellor. Under these circumstances it is important for midwives and obstetricians to:

- Have a basic knowledge of AIDS and HIV;
- Have sound knowledge of risk factors, modes of transmission and ways of preventing transmission;
- Ideally have some training and practice on basic counselling skills;
- Be able to identify those women who, during counselling, appear in need of further counselling. If this goes beyond the expertise of the carer, they need to know when, how and who to refer patients on to.

In addition, prior to HIV infection being identified in a clinic, it is helpful for staff to have training and for policy to be clearly worked out. Counselling obstacles may include:

- An unwillingness to talk about sex;
- An acknowledgement that all women should have clear accurate messages and selecting out those who do 'not appear' to be at risk is short sighted and potentially dangerous;
- Lack of time.

Counselling takes time. If such time is not available the task can be delegated to specially trained personnel who have more time available. Other possibilities include group discussion (which may cause individual embarrassment but may be helpful for many), written material, or visual/audio-visual messages.

HIV-negative partners of HIV-positive men

For these women, there are many issues which they may want to discuss. These include:

- Childlessness;
- Children;
- Desire for a child from the dying spouse.

Patients may want to consider alternatives such as artificial insemination by donor. Such procedures may in themselves be anxiety ridden. In the UK, all donor sperm is stored and an HIV test is carried out on a blood sample of the donor. After three months, a second HIV test is carried out. If this remains negative the stored semen can be used. Women may want to confirm the procedures current in their own countries prior to artificial insemination. There have been documented cases of HIV infection after insemination from infected donor sperm.

Counselling and drug users

Women whose pregnancies are affected by drug use in the presence of HIV form a major group of clients. The pregnant woman is either a drug user herself or is the partner of a drug user. Drug users in the child-bearing age groups are high in number. On the whole their use of contraception is low (Mulleady & Sherr 1989) and, contrary to some myths, they maintain sexual contacts and their behaviour accounts for a large number of pregnancies.

There is a growing knowledge about drug use, drug users, and the variations in surrounding cultural aspects which may play a decisive role in behavioural expression (Des Jarlais & Friedman, 1989). Some years ago, the major thrust of intervention in drug use was to promote abstention. Although this may be a fine aim, the presence of HIV must necessitate an alternative focus where risk reduction (rather than elimination) may take precedence. Some workers may find this difficult.

Counselling, however must aim simply to minimize risk when drug abstention is not possible.

Drug use may play a role in HIV transmission – from the sharing of contaminated needles and from unprotected sex with an infected individual. Drug users form a heterogeneous group. Counselling a woman who is pregnant and may have a drug use risk factor should commence with the formation of clear baseline data. In order to establish this, the counsellor must find out:

(a)   Which drugs are used, mode of use (injection, inhalation, smoking) and frequency.

(b)   Sharing behaviour should be examined in detail. This includes tracking sharing behaviours and who they share with. Some women think they are not at risk because they only share with their sexual partner. However, if their partner, in turn, either has sex with someone who has HIV or shares with someone who has HIV, there is still a risk.

(c)   Sterilization of equipment. Do they use bleach, boil their syringes, or clean them in other ways before use? Do they have any other physical problems (such as ulcers or infections) as a result of injecting?

(d)   Risk in general. A good discussion on risk factors should start with the client recounting their understanding of risk, and exploring a range of possible risk avenues to which they may have been exposed. This includes other contacts that their partners may have (sexual or needle sharing), and other partners they may have (sexual or needle sharing). They may then address how they can examine such risks, whether they feel able to reduce the risks, and what the obstacles to such behaviour change may be.

A pregnant woman will need to discuss drug management. If she is a non-drug using partner this will not be paramount. Sexual behaviour may need to be discussed. This can be difficult for staff who see themselves as drug workers. Drug users may, on occasion, solicit for sex in order to fund their habit. Condom use, even in the presence of pregnancy, should be discussed. Women need to know that sexually transmitted diseases may be a risk factor. Often carers forget that pregnant women still have sex and can still expose themselves and their babies to risks.

In the West, drug users may be a group who have low access to care agencies. Indeed, many present late in their pregnancy and receive reduced antenatal care as a result. In some centres, they are put off attendance as they fear that their baby will be put into care or separated from them. They may have a distrust in professionals. Therefore it is important that the professionals reach out to them and do not alienate them.

Addictive drugs themselves can cross the placenta and babies can suffer from withdrawal at birth. Not only is this a problem which may require medical management, but such babies are often fractious and difficult, which may make mothering difficult. Preparation for this can be constructive.

Practical help can often precede or supplement emotional support. Even if a woman has decided to alter her drug habits, she should still be provided with practical help in case this is not as easy as it sounds. The provision of clean needles is paramount. Mulleady (1989) also stresses the importance of prevention programmes to prevent initiation into drug use in the first instance.

Counselling and haemophiliacs

The majority of infections for this group occur via contaminated blood products. Thus the members of this group are caught in a cycle whereby the treatment of one major life threatening condition comprises the source of infection for another. This may be compounded by the fact that the very staff who were perceived as 'life saving' may now be the source of anger and recriminations as they were the ones who could be held responsible for introducing, albeit innocently, the infection via the blood product. Although incidence of new infections in this group is not expected since the start of heat treatment of factor XIII, there is still a web of infection surrounding this group. Notably, sexual partners have been infected and now, in turn, some of the children will become HIV-positive (Evatt 1989).

Counselling for couples in this group should include:

(1)   Discussing their desire for a pregnancy.
(2)   Thinking through alternatives and checking that the couples agree.
(3)   Some couples still want to proceed with a pregnancy whatever the risk.
(4)   Practical advice could be helpful (for example, one case has been reported where a couple were advised to self-artificially inseminate at the time of ovulation. This still allowed for exposure of the female to the male semen, although this exposure was of a limited nature. It also meant that the single exposure had a maximum chance of succeeding to a pregnancy).

(5)   Examining short- and long-term issues including the practicalities of the pregnancy, financial costs, physical costs, longer term problems, and solutions.

Effects of HIV on pregnancy

The effect of HIV on the course of pregnancy and maternal health is unclear at present. In the early days, it was felt that pregnancy exacerbated immune deficiency and could result in the deterioration of maternal health. This would, obviously, have severe implications for counselling. However, to date there has been no empirical evidence to back this up. It may be that pregnancy involves a time factor of 9 months which overlaps with the time-related progression of AIDS. This may confound outcome measures. At present there is no evidence that pregnancy, of itself, is harmful to the mother's medical condition (Schoenbaum *et al.* 1988). There is no study which looks at changes or reversal of postulated harmful effects if a termination of pregnancy occurs. This is clearly an area where more research is needed. Minkoff (1989) claims that the natural history of HIV disease is only marginally affected by pregnancy. Slight increases in rates of T4 (CD4) level depletion have been noted.

Pregnancy was not associated with progression of HIV infection in studies by Berrebi (1990) in France, and Bledsoe *et al.* (1990) in the USA. Lasley-Bibbs (1990) found that HIV-positive women had a significantly higher pregnancy rate than HIV-negative controls among USA army women. However, it is unclear from this study what the direct role of HIV is in the rate of conception. It may well be that frequency of intercourse was a predictor of exposure to HIV and to pregnancy.

HIV and pregnancy decision making

The effects of HIV on the decision to become pregnant are unclear. Kaplan *et al.* (1989) studied 151 women who were HIV-positive and of childbearing age. They found that, over time, and in the presence of counselling both in relation to safe sex and pregnancy, that a number of women (11/134) conceived. Although these authors conclude that this is as a result of poor safe sex counselling, perhaps workers need to be more open minded and note that women may well proceed with a pregnancy, whatever their status.

Wiznea *et al.* (1989) tried to identify factors which would influence pregnancy decision making in a cohort of 33 HIV-infected women. They noted that 6 of the 22 women who were eligible for termination (27%) took up this option. A comparison failed to reveal factors which would affect decisions. Factors examined included the presence of an HIV-infected older child and HIV-associated symptoms.

A similar study (Barbacci *et al.* 1989) of 89 HIV-positive women found no association between knowledge of HIV status and termination or pregnancy avoidance in the future.

Sunderland *et al.* (1989) found that HIV infection had no clear impact on decisions surrounding reproduction. Indeed, psychosocial and economic variables had greater influence.

Cowan *et al.* (1990) examined current and subsequent pregnancies. Knowledge of HIV had some effect on termination decisions in the index pregnancy but no effect on subsequent pregnancies.

Jakobs *et al.* (1990) described the psychological needs of HIV-positive women and outlined the trauma faced by women on learning about pregnancy and HIV at the same time. They examined stress caused by misinformation, decision making about the future of the pregnancy, and the stress resulting from hospitalization whether this was for delivery or termination.

Prognosis

HIV can cross the placenta and infect a fetus. In the early days, the rate of vertical transmission was recorded as high – close on 65%. However, these early studies were based on small samples and comprised women already identified as symptomatic with AIDS. As time progresses, larger data bases have accrued and the position seems less negative than originally thought. Current data (see Chapter 3) quotes figures of 20–29% (or perhaps even less) for mothers in the West who are HIV-positive and well. The transmission rate is higher in African studies (25–35%). This may be due to virus strain, background medical health, medical care, nutrition, or greater progression of disease in the population at large. The prognosis is poorer for women who have AIDS or for those who have had a previous baby with AIDS.

HIV infection in infants is more severe than in adults. Mean survival time from diagnosis to death is also shorter in infants than in adults. The first year of life evidences the highest pathology. Opportunistic infections differ in some respects. The type of infections differ. It may be that the impact of HIV on an immature immune system is more dramatic.

Much of the Western data are confounded by the fact that many pregnant women are also intravenous drug users. Drug-related problems such as drug withdrawal may affect these infants. Many indirect factors associated with drug use may also have an impact on the pregnancy and the baby. These include poor housing, poor nutrition and poor background health.

The prognosis may well be linked to timing of infections and disease progression in the mother. No data exists to tell us if there are critical infection periods – such as there is with Rubella, for example.

It is worth noting that the presence of other sexually transmitted diseases have been seen as co-factors for infection and disease progression. Thus good antenatal care should include education about avoiding sexually transmitted diseases and treatment of such diseases if they are identified.

Delivery

Infection could theoretically occur during delivery; many workers have tried to examine whether Caesarian Section (CS) would be preferable to vaginal delivery. Studies from Edinburgh, the European Collaborative Study (7 centres), CDC, and reports from the Milan Cohort have failed to note any advantages of Caesarian Section over vaginal delivery in adjusting vertical transmission rates.

In the absence of any evidence to the contrary, current knowledge would not therefore point to a Caesarian Section unless this was required for other obstetric reasons.

During vaginal delivery, care should be taken to minimize risk of exposure to HIV. As the virus is present in maternal blood, vaginal secretions and amniotic fluid, specific precautions should be taken for the baby's safe passage down the birth canal. Any monitoring which requires puncture of the fetal scalp should be avoided (scalp electrodes, for example). Such open wounds would provide a point of virus entry to the baby.

To minimize body fluid exposure, any procedure which involves blood spillage or skin piercing should only be undertaken if absolutely necessary. Maternal pubic hair shaving and episiotomy should be avoided where possible.

Drug treatment and decision making

At present AZT is not given routinely to women who are pregnant. Trials of newer drugs (e.g. deoxyisonine, or DDI) do not include pregnant women. It is unclear what the effects of such drugs on a developing fetus are. There are a few studies which have examined whether the drugs permeate to the fetus. Gillet *et al.* (1989) studied seven HIV-positive women who were pregnant and had all opted for a termination of pregnancy. All women, with consent, were administered with AZT and subsequently tissue from the aborted fetus was examined to ascertain whether the drug had crossed the placenta. They found that the glucorinide of the drug was detectable in the fetal tissue. They examined blood concentrations and found that these were comparable to maternal concentrations in six of the seven cases.

A case report study by Crombleholme (1990) reported that continuation of AZT during pregnancy in a woman who had commenced therapy prior to conception did not prevent vertical transmission. However, it may well be that the woman concerned was in an advanced stage of illness (and thus in receipt of AZT in the first place) and so this data cannot be extrapolated to women who are HIV-positive and well.

Pregnancy outcome

The questions that pregnant women and their carers want answers to are still the subject of research. It is difficult to deal in uncertainty and not to raise undue anxiety in women while research investigations are examining the possibility of certain outcomes.

The kinds of questions are:

- What effects will pregnancy have on my HIV status?
- What effects will HIV have on the course of my pregnancy?
- Will my baby be premature?
- Will my baby weigh less?
- Will my labour be normal?
- Am I more likely to miscarry?
- Will HIV affect onset of labour?

Counselling can only allow for the provision of research data as they are known. Women need to have the facts, however incomplete, and to understand the possible implications for their behaviour and well being and to be able to cope with some of the uncertainties surrounding their pregnancy. It is important to draw out the comparison with other factors in normal pregnancy which are unknown, uncertain, unpredictable and cause consternation.

Johnstone et al. (1988) studied 50 seropositive women and 64 sero-negative women with histories of drug use, and their seropositive partners. They noted that in terms of general obstetric risk, these women could not be compared to normative data as they were, on the whole, young, heavy smokers, unmarried, and suffered from socio-economic deprivation and unemployment. Such factors would, any-way, possibly contribute to different obstetric outcomes without the complications of HIV. Yet the comparison between the two groups revealed a possible effect of HIV itself.

Johnstone found an increase in spontaneous abortion in the HIV-positive women. Overall, complications such as prematurity, intra-uterine growth retardation and low birth weight were present in greater quantity than in the population as a whole. Yet these did not differ between the two groups under study. These workers conclude that despite many indices of poor obstetric outcome, their small study did not reveal factors directly associated with HIV that could account for this. They emphasize that all their HIV-positive subjects were asymp-tomatic and well. Thus this study highlights some poor pregnancy outcomes for the group as a whole.

Lopita et al. (1990) found no association between the presence of HIV infection and spontaneous first trimester abortion.

As early as 1987, Morbidity and Mortality Weekly Report (MMWR) reported on a consistent number of pregnancies in haemophiliac cou-ples affected by HIV. They found that 12% of their nationwide sample reported pregnancy during January 1985 to March 1987. Of this group, 61% had been tested for HIV; 13% (n = 22) were HIV-positive prior to pregnancy. They recorded 22 babies born to this sample (with 2 multi-ple pregnancies). Despite the presence of antibody in 69%, the data were gathered too early to comment on transmission rates after passive maternal antibody could be shed. Of note was the fact that none of the children had been diagnosed as having AIDS.

Ndugwa et al. (1990) studied a group of 3612 pregnant women in Uganda. 1032 were found to be HIV-positive (28%). They were younger than the HIV-negative subjects but did not differ on other variables such as previous history of tuberculosis or blood transfusions. A high proportion of the HIV-positive group were symptomatic (44.8%). 60.8% were reported as having a pregnancy complication. There were no tests carried out in this study to differentiate the symptomatic and asymp-tomatic subjects in terms of pregnancy complications, something that would have been of considerable interest. The HIV-positive group did not differ from the HIV-negative on delivery factors. Caesarian Section had no effect in this study. Gestation was significantly lower (38.3 weeks compared to 39 weeks) with correspondingly lower birthweights. The vertical transmission rate in this study was 31%.

The European Cohort Study reported on perinatal outcome for 271 children born to 264 HIV-positive mothers. Drug-related problems were evident in 25% of the babies. Mean gestation was 38 weeks. Perinatal findings were 'unremarkable'.

Selwyn *et al.* (1989) studied 39 HIV-positive women and compared pregnancy outcome in this group with 58 HIV-negative controls all of whom were recruited from a Methodone programme in the USA. Their measures revealed no difference in the rate of termination, spontaneous abortion, premature delivery, stillbirth, or low birthweight babies. Furthermore, there were no differences in medical complications for mother or neonate.

Feeding

Transmission of HIV from mother to baby via breast feeding is thought to have occurred in eight cases to date. These are the only documented cases and need to be fully understood if policy decisions are to be made based on their findings.

HIV has been isolated in breast milk (Thiry *et al.* 1985). Infection by breast milk, however, has been isolated to single case reports (Weinbreck *et al.* 1988; Ziegler *et al.* 1985; Ziegler *et al.* 1984; Lepage *et al.* 1987; Nanda & Minkoff 1989). The majority of the case reports (n = 7) describe women who were HIV-negative during pregnancy and were exposed to HIV through blood transfusions from subsequently identified donors or through needle sharing after delivery. The remaining case was of a baby born to an HIV-negative woman who was wet-nursed by a woman with AIDS. In all these cases, there is a common theme. All the women were viraemic at the time. They were either in the phase immediately after exposure to virus or progressing to illness. Thus there are no data to hand on the breast feeding impact for HIV-positive and well mothers. Nor are there data to hand on the effects of breast feeding for a mother who is not newly infected.

Breast feeding is under scrutiny in many of the prospective studies. Peckham *et al.* (1989) noted a possible beneficial effect of breast feeding. Obviously there cannot be any random allocation of infants to feeding mode and the issue may be one that can never be clearly described. However, it does seem necessary to ensure that advice is based on clear understanding of facts. To date, the number of infections via breast milk are low and do not come from typical cases. In areas where bottle feeding is impractical, workers must weigh up the costs of other diseases through malnutrition or infection as well as the benefits of breast feeding for the emotional well being of the baby and mother prior to giving advice at all.

Manzila *et al.* (1989) studied a group of 108 infants in Kinshasa to examine perinatally acquired HIV-infection by examining those receiving mothers milk compared to those receiving formula. They found no significant association between infection and infant milk source and concluded that there was no additional risk factor from breast feeding for a child already exposed during pregnancy and delivery. They also underline the potential benefits of breast feeding in an African setting.

Ziegler *et al.* (1989) reviewed current cases of infant infection and breast feeding and concluded that the risk of breast feeding for infants of women infected during lactation was comparable to the overall risk of perinatal transmission with a reported rate in the region of 30%. In cases where the mother was already infected at delivery, no evidence of additional risk was found. Ziegler notes the need for more accurate testing and a need to understand co-factors.

Thus, although virus has been identified in breast milk and it is theoretically possible that it can be transmitted in this way there is no evidence beyond these studies that singles out breast feeding as an added risk factor. Indeed, there are studies which show the contrary.

Chapter 9

Labour and Delivery

Labour is a human ritual which is often, if not always, surrounded by societal customs and norms. These may determine place of delivery (hospital, home, birthing hut, or under a particular tree), and also birth attenders (doctors, midwives, birthing women). There are often social taboos surrounding labour and delivery. They concern the do's and don'ts and vary from culture to culture. They may determine who is present with the woman (some are alone, some are with doctors, midwives, students, mother-in-law) and who is forbidden (sometimes all men, siblings, lay persons, and so on).

Help should not come in the form of judgemental appraisal. A good model to learn from emanates from the area of recreational drug use where a policy of harm reduction has been seen as helpful. This entails workers accepting that some behaviours ought to be stopped, but while they still occur the client should be given help with all levels of harm reduction to minimize exposure to risk and HIV. This model may well have a place in childbirth. Though some workers may frown at the practice of packing cow dung on the vagina, others may find episiotomy equally abhorrent. — *what is normal for one, way not be normal for another.*

Infection control

Labour brings with it many concerns. Staff may have possible exposure to blood, amniotic fluid and vaginal secretions. Staff anxiety about delivery of an HIV-positive mother has been documented (Sherr 1987). Such anxiety can be significantly reduced with full information and education (Sherr 1988). Routine infection control measures should be adopted for all deliveries. A two-tier system of infection control which advises specific precautions for known HIV infection, and lax attitudes in unknown cases, may expose staff to unnecessary hazards. Even in the presence of routine screening, women who test HIV-negative may indeed be infected. The test may have been carried out at the start of pregnancy and they may have become infected in the intervening period or the test may have been negative but taken in the window period thus hiding true infection. Infection control guidelines are clear and should be implemented routinely. The rule of thumb should be to always exercise caution when handling all bodily fluids.

In some settings, this cannot happen due to physical constraints, limitations on medical expenditure, sheer volume of patients, or other obstacles.

Safety procedures should include the following:

(1)   Gowns and gloves should be used – wherever possible – during deliveries. Some staff prefer long gloves as opposed to shorter gloves. If this is easy to accommodate and if it raises assurance it is worthwhile. Gloves should be used while handling the baby if it is still covered with any maternal secretions. If gloves are not available, workers should ensure that any lesions on their hands are covered with waterproof plasters.

(2)   Frequent handwashing should always be adopted.

(3)   Eye protection should be considered. Extreme protection by use of goggles may reassure the midwife and limit exposure to fluids but may also interfere with the relationship between the health care worker and the parturent woman. Some centres report the use of clear glass spectacles which afford good protection but also do not interfere with a developing relationship. Some centres require spectacles to have a side protection. However, some workers find these uncomfortable. Eye splashes should be washed out immediately. This means that eye wash should be handy.

(4)   The use of mucous extraction devices needs to be re-thought. If the carer uses their own mouth to draw out the secretions, there is a possible risk of neo-natal secretions coming into contact with the health care provider's mouth. No cases of HIV transmission by this mode have been recorded to date. However, in the light of theoretical risk, it is possible to use alternatives to manual suction devices.

(5)   All sharp instruments should be properly disposed of, particularly needles. Needles should not be resheathed. Good disposal facilities must be available.

(6)   Restriction of blood spillage should be kept in mind at all times. This means that routine disposal of placenta should be carried out and blood spillage should be maintained within as confined a space as possible. The use of disposable bags and routine incineration can mini-

mize this risk. The use of placental material for other purposes must be reconsidered in the light of AIDS and HIV.

(7) Blood spillages should be cleaned with hypochlorite solution as per usual hospital routine.

An excellent review for Western centres can be found in the study by Minkoff (1989).

Remember that at all times a woman who is delivering a baby with known HIV infection will have continued concern about the well being of her new baby.

Mode of delivery

In the early days it was postulated that Caesarian Section might reduce exposure of the baby to HIV virus. However, a series of studies have now been carried out looking directly at Caesarian Section and the idea that Caesarian Section may reduce transmission has not been upheld. The studies which have examined this include work carried out in Edinburgh, data from the European Cohort Study, data from the CDC, and reports from the Milan Cohort. Although it is theoretically possible that infection can occur at the time of birth, data to date suggest that rather than opt for elective Caesarian Section, other procedures should be monitored and perhaps adjusted in order to take into account this possible risk. Fetal scalp monitoring and the use of scalp electrodes should be avoided in known HIV-positive mothers and minimized in unclear cases. Such skin puncture would provide a vector for transmission from maternal secretions to the baby's blood. If transplacental infection has been avoided this would be a tragic iatrogenic route of infection; thus, wherever possible, external monitoring should be the option of first choice.

In line with this problem, the baby should be washed as soon as possible to eliminate surface secretions. These may possibly be contaminated with the virus and this procedure can protect the baby. The baby's hair also should be washed clear of maternal blood. Great care should be taken that babies do not lose body heat and are kept warm at all times.

Psychological care during delivery

Labour and the birth of a baby is a momentous time for all mothers, irrespective of HIV status. Emotional needs are usually paramount, perhaps heightened by HIV. Trust and confidence are always important. For a woman with HIV, it may relieve many aspects of uncertainty if she knows who she can turn to during labour. This will also allow for planning and prior decision-making which can be discussed with care givers. Discussions before the labour provide an opportunity for the midwife or obstetrician to outline any infection control procedures that they intend to utilize. It is helpful if women realize that this is routine and not specifically for them.

An HIV-positive mother needs to have good support during labour. Confidentiality, fears of rejection, and overwhelming concern for her baby may dominate the labour. Support needs to be continuous as far as this is possible. The privacy of the labouring woman should be respected. Midwifery and obstetric guidelines which have been worked out for HIV deliveries are seldom very different from those for all deliveries. They usually involve common sense (Brierly 1989). From the counselling point of view, the carer needs to examine:

- Rapport and trust;
- Use of medication;
- Place of delivery;
- Medicalization of child birth;
- Involving partners;
- Ongoing dialogue.

Preparation for labour

Preparatory information and the acquisition of coping skills have often been used to cope with pain. Pain may be unpredictable and individual reactions vary dramatically. Labour may involve pain experience and there is a known time during pregnancy in which to prepare for this. Janis (1971) has proposed that cognitive rehearsal is an important tool. There are many studies which examine the efficacy of antenatal (prenatal) classes. These may well suffer from methodological bias given that self selection on attendance may be more predictive of outcome than class content. Furthermore, where classes are available, it is unethical to deny them to a particular sector. Indeed, those who are denied access may well turn to alternatives and thus there may never be a true 'control' group, but rather comparison groups. Enkin (1982) has reviewed a number of studies and found a consistent impact of classes in reducing analgesia uptake. Whether these women feel less pain is unclear. This consistent finding may reflect the fact that women who do not desire medication seek out classes as an alternative, or that classes have an anti-medication bias and persuade attenders to adhere to their approach.

It must be remembered that formally taught classes are a luxury which the majority of childbearing mothers in the world have no exposure to. Indeed, even in Western societies such as the UK, Reid (1980) noted that 42% of primiparous women did not intend to go to classes. In some countries there is no financial provision for such input and in others women do not attend. This does not mean that this large group of women do not have informational needs. What is important for psychologists is to understand the nature of their needs and how they can meet these. Often this may be through informal channels where they learn from the experience of their contemporaries (sisters, mothers, friends). Such channels may have overwhelming salience but may provide biased and sometimes uninformed accounts.

Without prior information, women are reliant on others. This essentially brings with it passivity and feelings of helplessness.

Pain management

Pain management in labour is universal. Different cultures have different ways of managing labour. In the West, there is high uptake of analgesia. The British Births' Survey found that 97% of women had some form of analgesia during labour. The place of birth varies and may affect the kind of pain management available. In the West, hospitalized birth is ever-increasing (in the UK, 97% of births occur in hospitals). In some countries (for example, The Netherlands), home deliveries are still available and are encouraged. In developing countries, there are systematic differences according to availability, urban or rural settings and financial constraints.

Obstetric complications are often accompanied by increased use of analgesia. For example, Cartwright found that women with still births were more likely to receive analgesia. It may be that practitioners want to protect the woman from pain and suffering because her baby has died. It may also be that the complication itself necessitates medical attention which in itself increases the likelihood of medication being offered. These data should be remembered with HIV deliveries. They may well attract medical attention – especially in centres where such deliveries are rare. Women should be allowed to choose their own pain management as far as possible. Workers need to remember that 'choice' is an uncertain concept, and often the provision of options, the way information is framed, and the social pressure on a woman who feels out of control, can all determine her response.

There are no studies which examine the efficacy of current pharmacological pain management routines on HIV-positive mothers or chart any implications for their babies. In the absence of such knowledge, existing data should be taken into account when decisions are made on the following:

Use of pethidine.   This is a commonly used analgesic during labour. Its limitations may be associated with the fact that drug using mothers may need high doses for it to be effective. Timing of pethidine administration is important as it can cross the placenta and affect respiration in the newborn. This may not be desirable in the presence of HIV.

Epidural analgesia.   Various accounts of epidurals have been given. Consumer satisfaction has been reported. Morgan *et al.* (1984) studied 1000 women in London, just over half of whom received epidural analgesia during labour. Their reported pain relief was greater than for women receiving pethidine, but their labours were significantly longer and assisted delivery was markedly increased (51% versus 6%). Thus, for women with HIV, the advantages of reduced pain must be weighed against the disadvantages of assisted delivery. The added need for specialist skills for insertion of the epidural and monitoring must be taken into consideration.

Relaxation techniques.   Although the literature on such techniques are limited, it is common for some form of breathing technique to be used in pain control. These often prove effective if there has been prior training.

Post partum

There is no special need to treat HIV-positive women any differently to other women. They may, however, have some special extra needs which ought to be taken into account.

The practical needs:

(a) Disposal of sanitary towels and care during post partum bleeding may require good hygiene standards and instruction.

(b)   There is no need for a woman with HIV to be isolated or treated in a separate room.

(c)   A mother may be particularly anxious about her baby. The HIV status cannot be established for anything up to 24 months. If HIV testing on cord blood has been carried out the mother will need to understand about passive transfer of antibody. Reassurance when there is uncertainty cannot be given. Rather the mother needs to be given help to deal with the uncertainty and pacing for the future.

(d)   The health of the mother needs continuous monitoring.

(e)   Staff should limit their own exposure to all blood and blood products by adopting sensible health care routines. For example, they should encourage mothers, under instruction, to carry out cord care and clean their own babies' cord. This serves the dual purpose of teaching the mother, giving control to the mother, and limiting the health care worker's exposure to blood. Any examination of the perineum should be carried out with the use of protective gloves.

There are no published studies on post partum psychological state in HIV-positive women. In the general literature, it is known that a small group of women suffer from childbirth-related psychological problems. Sometimes these become severe and necessitate psychiatric help (Dalton 1982; Martin 1988; Braverman & Roux 1978).

Kumar and Robson (1978) found that post partum disturbance correlated with marital tension during pregnancy and doubts about going through with the pregnancy. They identified these factors retrospectively and have not carried out prospective studies which follow all patients with marital tension and all those with doubts to see if they all progress to psychological disturbance. Thus workers need to be aware that these factors do not necessarily predict post partum problems, but are potential problem areas worthy of input. HIV in itself may create marital tension and relationship problems in couples have certainly been recorded (Ussher 1990; Sherr & Hedge 1989). Furthermore, some mothers with HIV may have doubts about the pregnancy. The best preventive intervention is to tackle marital discord and doubts when they arise and encourage problem solving and decision making which may help women handle these crises at the time and may minimize their future impact.

Whalen *et al*. (1990) have documented that many pregnant women, especially those with risk behaviours for HIV, do not receive health care during pregnancy. Thus the post partum period is an ideal time to provide services and counselling.

Caspe *et al*. (1990) examined post partum HIV counselling and testing in New York City. They found that 45% of 80 consecutive subjects had received late or no antenatal care. Drugs had been used during their pregnancy in 74% of cases and, based on these findings, the authors emphasized the need to target services to this group – one which may have few contacts with care agencies.

The wider family

Staff should extend their support and inclusion to all members of the wider family who will not only provide care for the child and mother, but who may have their own particular needs. This should include the spouse, other children, and the wider family.

Chapter 10

HIV/AIDS and Children

AIDS in children is more severe than in adults. In one study, mean survival from time of diagnosis to death was estimated at four months. However, the paucity of data together with the increased expertise in treating opportunistic infections may alter these figures over time.

Most children are infected perinatally. Over 600 children with AIDS have been reported to WHO from European countries. Over 70% of these children acquire HIV perinatally. The extent and nature of paediatric HIV in Africa are unknown, but estimates are high. In the USA, perinatal transmission accounts for over 75% of AIDS in children. The remainder of the children are exposed to HIV from exposure to blood or blood products which have been infected with the virus. There is also the possibility of infection from sexual encounters in young teenagers, and from child abuse in younger children. In New York City alone 583 child AIDS cases had been reported to the end of March 1990, and as with the adult figures, roughly half these children have already died.

In Europe and the USA, most perinatal transmissions are associated with a drug-using parent. Thus, data worldwide are difficult to co-ordinate and difficult to make use of for extrapolation. The effects of drugs on the child with HIV is unknown. The indirect effects of drug use must also be charted. These include the standard of parental care and parenting skills, the availability and socio-economic status of parents, and corresponding nutrition, housing, and medical attention.

Thus, although a body of data is emerging for children, these data must be interpreted with care. Collaborative studies are the most hopeful in terms of revealing systematically useful prospective data. (European Collaborative Study 1988, 1991).

If one speculates about the future, the problem takes on alarming proportions. Unfortunately, many child care agencies find the prospect of high HIV and AIDS prevalence in children very difficult to contemplate and plan for, and services may be stretched and arrive late in the day. There is considerable evidence of the significant extent to which AIDS in children comprises both a medical and societal problem. For example, in New York City in 1988, the Department of Health indicated that one in 53 babies born was HIV-positive. Longer term follow-up (providing seroconversion rates after two years) would provide more accurate data. Forward planning is still urgent given the high numbers of projected cases and the demands that are essential to meet the needs of these children.

The use of AZT (zidovudine) for children has lagged behind its use in adults. Wilfert (1989) reports on some of the issues and findings. Essentially, tolerance, safety and efficacy of AZT in children needs to be clearly established. Wilfert reports on data from 88 treated children over 10 months. Although there were some benefits noted, the challenges for this group are still to monitor toxicity, to target treatment appropriately – given the difficulty of identifing infected children in the presence of passive maternal antibody – and to monitor the long-term effects of drugs on developing children.

Neonates

To date there is no test which can easily tell whether a neonate has been infected or is virus free. Changing technology may allow for identification of infant infection but at present the antibody test may show a positive result yet reflect maternal (passively transmitted) antibody. The care of the infant should always be seen in terms of the family. Numerous studies have been used to examine outcomes for neonates. These are summarized below.

A study by Goedert *et al.* (1989) followed up a sample of fifty-five infants. They found sixteen (29%) to be infected with HIV: nine of the sixteen had AIDS, six had less severe clinical problems, and one appeared symptom free but remained HIV-positive beyond fifteen months. They also found that babies born at or before thirty-seven weeks gestation had an increased risk of HIV compared to those born at thirty-eight weeks or above (60% compared to 20%). These workers conclude that prematurity may be related to HIV transmission. It is unclear how the relation exists. It may be that early HIV infection *in utero* results in prematurity, or that prematurity itself heightens the risk of becoming infected – perhaps during labour, delivery, or after birth. They found that prematurity was generally a common problem for drug-using women, in those who were seropositive as well as seronegative. Ryder (1988) found that for non-drug using African women, premature delivery was more common for seropositive than seronegative women (13% versus 3%). However, this study included women with AIDS rather than those simply with HIV infection and well. These workers feel that effort to maximize the chances of full-term delivery are important short-term goals in this group.

Hira *et al.* (1989) in Zambia, examined 109 babies born to seropositive mothers. They found eighteen had died before eight months of age. Fourteen had been diagnosed with AIDS while 23 of the remaining 91 babies were HIV-positive at 8 months of age. This figure stayed constant by 24 months. However, by this time, a further five infected babies had died; four were terminally ill; 17 had AIDS and two were symptom free. Based on these data, they find a vertical transmission rate of 39%. The major symptoms found in this group was pneumonia, recurrent coughs, failure to thrive, diarrhoea, fever, candidiasis and lymphadenopathy. A 34% vertical transmission rate is generally higher than studies reported in the West. This may be due to route of transmission, background medical factors, or sampling. Within this sample, although no mothers had AIDS, 16% had AIDS-related complex (ARC) and 38% had generalized lymphadenopathy. When comparing positive and negative women (n = 227 and 1727 respectively) there were no significant differences in stillbirth or prematurity rate. However, this sample showed a significant effect of low birth rate for HIV-positive women. It is also interesting to note that four deaths occurred in this study. Generally, transmission, disease expression and mortality of infected babies was higher for the African study than in the European data. They also found that two-thirds of the children born to HIV-positive mothers were not infected despite breast feeding for up to eighteen months. These workers also point out a high mortality figure (44%) and comment on the high level of morbidities. Indeed, all but two of the children experienced recurrent episodes of illness and had frequent hospital admission.

Lallemant (1989) followed up 64 babies born to HIV-positive mothers and compared them with 130 control babies born to HIV-negative mothers for 12 to 22 months. There were no differences in still-birth rate, gestational age, sex ratio, or infant weight. They found that mortality was high. Deaths occurred more frequently and earlier than in European studies. Only 1 in 10 HIV-positive women in the study had AIDS at time of delivery. These workers found a greater incidence of twin births in HIV-positive mothers. It is unclear whether this is related to HIV or is a chance factor.

Krener, in an interesting study, revealed difficulties in relation to the hospital care of a newly diagnosed baby with AIDS. She found individual variation in the interaction (especially when this was physical by way of touch) with the baby and she comments on the impact that this could have for the potential stimulation development and psychological well being of infants.

Boulos (1990) found that infants lost maternal antibody faster than the rates reported in the European studies. This African study showed that by 7.5 months 50% had lost antibody (compared to the timing of 9–10 months as reported in the European studies). No infant lost antibody in this study after one year.

In the European Collaborative Study (Peckham 1990), criteria for HIV infection have been set. This study renders a comprehensive data set for eight participating European centres where children are followed prospectively to examine pregnancy outcome and paediatric progress.

This study presents a working criteria for HIV-positive categorization as follows:

- Clinical presence of AIDS/ARC;
- Virus or antigen identified;
- Antibody persisting for more than 18 months of age.

From this study, continuous recruitment allows for a more comprehensive prospective insight. It is important that counselling advice is based on findings from populations that are relevant to both the individual and the circumstance. Thus in London, Edinburgh, Milan or Padua, findings from the Cohort Study may be highly useful to an HIV-positive pregnant woman. In Burkino Fasso or Nairobi, such findings may be limited. Local studies may be better indicators of outcome ranges, prognosis and infant mortality.

An early comprehensive report from the European Collaborative Study (November 1988) reported on follow-up for 271 children. In all, 123 children had been followed for one year, of which 10 had developed AIDS or ARC. All children who had developed AIDS or ARC had been ill by the age of nine months. Although the median age for antibody loss was 10.3 months there were still a group of children losing antibody at 15- and 18-month check ups. No child in this report had lost antibody and then become antibody positive. However, loss of antibody did not necessarily prove absence of infection. No AIDS dysmorphic syndrome was confirmed in this study.

Overall, the studies show that where HIV antibody is shown to persist, children, in the main, tend to suffer from ill health. Some workers have described a bi-modal distribution of illness with age.

What seems to emerge from the data is a group of children who become ill before the age of one year. A second group seem to survive longer and have more chronic type of illness. The paucity of data, the limited time span, and the fact that comprehensive studies are only now under way, means that the long-term outlook for HIV infected neonates is simply not known. It is difficult to generalize from adult studies as HIV may have a different impact on a developing organism. It seems that earlier onset of symptoms is associated with a poorer prognosis.

The majority of perinatal diseases occur in the first and second years. Studies seem to show that the earlier a clinical diagnosis is made (independent of mode of transmission) the higher the mortality.

Scott (1989) sets out prognostic factors as follows:

- Age – less than one year is linked to a poor prognosis;
- Type of disease;
- Development of opportunist infections;
- Development of AIDS.

Counselling issues with neonates

Groups of neonates.   Within the group of neonates who need care and attention, there may be systematic differences. They include:

- Babies born to mothers known to have HIV/AIDS;
- Babies with AIDS;
- Babies who are HIV-positive;
- Babies who are HIV-negative.

Limitations of HIV testing.   HIV tests offer crude help at present. They cannot differentiate between passive maternal antibody and infant anti-body. The tests are unable to shed light on how the baby was infected, when the baby was infected, if the baby is indeed infected, or whether the baby will go on to get AIDS (and if so when). Thus the tests often fail to clarify anything for parents and are a constant reminder of uncertainty which can result in swings from hope to despair.

Promising work on polymerase chain reaction (PCR) tests which detect virus genome may be helpful in the future. However, at present, they are expensive, accuracy and specificity are still under research, and they are not yet commercially available. (Brandt *et al*. 1990; Henrion *et al*. 1990; Vendrel *et al*. 1990). Ferris *et al*. (1990), utilizing polymerase chain reaction, studied 35 babies born to seropositive mothers. They cautioned that a higher frequency of maternal transmission of HIV may exist compared to previously inferred findings from serological and clinical detection.

Evaluating vertical transmission. This is difficult. Children can shed maternal antibody for anything up to 24 months. Some children who test negative die of AIDS. AIDS itself is a clinical diagnosis which may possibly be missed or overlooked. Essentially, a child is deemed as not infected if antibody is lost, there are no clinical indications of infection, and no virus and antigen has been detected on tests. Long-term data for such children are not available. Despite the fact that parents can feel reassured if children appear uninfected, they may still be subjected to uncertainty while the long-term outlook for these children is established.

Some workers are trying to examine prognostic markers which could be helpful in the early identification of HIV infection. Van de Perre (1990) and Henrion *et al.* (1990) identified higher incidence of transmission to infants where mothers had T4 (CD4) counts $<150/\text{mm}^3$ positive antigenaemia p24 and displayed a high replication rate of HIV in cultures. Ndugwa *et al.* (1990) noted that a reverse T4/T8 ratio at 6 months may be an early marker of infection.

Based on the above, it seems helpful that regular medical work-ups on children are carried out to enhance predictability of infection and to give feedback to parents.

Neonatal HIV infection. This issue is surrounded by high levels of long-term uncertainty. This hampers decision making, coping and adjustment. For example a recent report on the European Collaborative Study (Peckham 1989) reported on a sample of 350 children of which '47 were infected, 166 presumed not infected and 137 with an unclear diagnosis'. From this study then 303 children had futures which were enfolded in uncertainty and described in the study by phrases such as 'presumed' or 'unclear'.

Particular challenges. There are particular challenges for counselling clients in the presence of uncertainty. They need:

- On-going support;
- Regular medical check-ups;
- Help with planning;
- Discussion of coping;

- Pacing;
- Realistic expectations and advice;
- A balanced focus on the present and the future.

Obstacles to counselling. There are many obstacles to counselling for such neonates and their families. Confusion can emerge as a result of:

- Unknown interaction with drug use and drug user effects;
- Respite care options;
- Implications of fostering and adoption;
- Infection control;
- Confidentiality.

Illness in one or both parents. The situation is further compounded by additional uncertainty linked to parental illness. With transplacental transmission, one or perhaps both parents will also be affected by HIV. This means they are also coping with their own personal life crises and uncertainty. Planning may be particularly difficult, hindered by such obstacles as:

- Guilt;
- Fear;
- Anxiety;
- Lack of confidence;
- Bereavement;
- Lethargy;
- Panic attacks;
- Limited energy to meet the demands of a young baby;
- Desire to be constantly available and helpful;
- Becoming pregnant again (Sunderland has documented that many women continue to a subsequent pregnancy);
- Lack of support;
- Secrecy. Mok (1990) reported that all subjects in her group in Edinburgh kept AIDS as a closely guarded secret. Secrecy places a burden not only on those who keep the secret but also on the small group of professionals who need to meet all their needs.

Pacing. Pacing should allow families to differentiate between short- and long-term issues and their point of overlap. Some of these issues demand a lot of attention and can be difficult and painful. They include:

- Care for themselves and their child;
- The future of the child – especially if it is a future without them as parents;
- Who to tell. This involves many decisions. Not only do they need to work out who to tell, but when and how. Most families to date have a veil of secrecy surrounding an HIV diagnosis;
- Prognosis is both a long- and short-term problem. Parents may weigh up the issues of treatment and face side effects;
- Subsequent children are also an issue. Many parents who have a baby in the presence of HIV go on to have subsequent babies.

Uncertainty.   Professionals may find great difficulty dealing with this level of uncertainty. They are used to having advice and answers at the ready (indeed this is the very definition of a professional!). In terms of facts it is important to tell patients the nature of the findings to date, help them interpret them, and point out the limitations. It is never helpful to tell people what to do when there is a paucity of facts and an overwhelming amount of uncertainty.

Professionals should be aware of the common reactions that people have in the face of uncertainty and watch out for these in their patients and themselves. People often do the following:

- Make irrational decisions;
- Draw on the most readily available information and ignore the background;
- Simply deny the uncertainty;
- Defend and put up barriers to protect themselves;
- Look to the extremes (most pessimistic or most optimistic) and forget that there is much middle ground;
- Abandon logical reasoning;
- Use 'railway track' thinking (that implies that they get caught on one train of thought and abandon alternatives). Sometimes help can take the form of constantly reminding them of alternatives;
- Often do nothing – becoming frozen or anaesthetized into inaction! Help can take the form of mobilization.

Help in the presence of uncertainty can take many forms. The goals are:

- Attribute cognitions to realistic causes;
- Replace paralysis with action;

- Help pace people;
- Help with problem-solving.

Counselling can help people by enabling them first to list the multitude of problems they face. They can then group these into sub-groups. This may allow people to act on those which can be dealt with and bide their time for other problems rather than grind to a halt on everything. Practical steps that can be taken include:

(1) Planning assistance may help people brainstorm solutions, examine ways that they coped in the past, and think through how they can adapt previously successful methodologies to new situations and challenges.

(2) Support may be a new concept for some people. They may be unused to turning to others for support – let alone a professional. There may often be a stigma associated with 'psychological help'. Yet the secrecy that surrounds AIDS often means that this small group of specialized health care workers is the only group available (Mok 1990). People may need permission to acknowledge their own needs and accept support. Support may take many different forms. There are often no single solutions and people may gather different elements of support from different sources. They may be given help in seeking these out and maximizing input to meet their needs.

(3) Practical help is often of paramount importance. Many hurdles and practical obstacles can be overcome with help. For individuals who are unwilling to engage in counselling and emotional support, care can help alleviate some of their practical problems. This may free up some of their own resources to deal with their emotional needs or may provide a trusting and mutually helpful relationship which can then progress to a supportive one.

(4) Some people benefit from mutual support groups. These are groups (led or unled) of people facing similar crises. This should be used in addition to rather than instead of input. Some people find it difficult to reach out to such groups and some who do reach out do not find them helpful.

(5) Alternative approaches are often sought out. Do not be judgemental. Help clients have a health critique and if something is doing no harm it may well do good.

(6) Care and attention will help minimize the extent to which the child will be treated as a 'medical novelty' with multiple (often unnecessary) hospital visits and constant rounds to clinics, research centres and doctors.

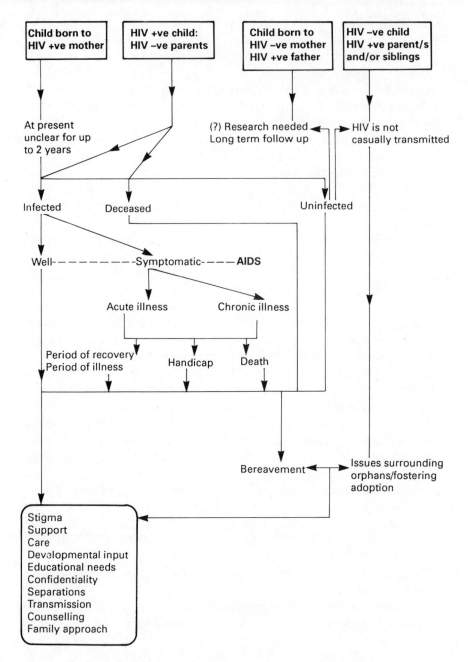

Figure 10.1   Diagrammatic representation of the effect of HIV and AIDS in children.

Neurological problems in children

The results from studies examining neurological problems are incon-clusive. The most comprehensive data emerges from the USA, but data from Europe and Africa are now being gathered more systematically. The prevalence varies dramatically. Belman *et al.* (1988) found 34% of their sample showed some signs of neurological impairment. Epstein *et al.* (1986) showed higher proportions. What is important from these studies is a need to understand the implications of the findings and to examine the sampling methods which may include an over-representa-tion of affected children. Tardieu *et al.* (1987) reflect lower rates of neuro-logical impairment. In the European Collaborative Study, neurological manifestations were restricted to children who had been diagnosed as having ARC or AIDS with a lack of observation in asymptomatic well children.

Neurological problems may result directly as a result of HIV penetra-tion of the brain and spinal cord. It may be an indirect effect or a co-factor in association with recreational drugs used by many of the mothers in the European and American studies. Neurological mani-festations may result from the opportunistic infections associated with AIDS or there may be developmental difficulties, accounted for, in part, by disruptions to early stimulation and parenting interactions either directly as a result of ill health and hospitalization, or indirectly as the result of illness and absence of the mother/father.

Hopkins *et al.* (New York, 1989) presented alarming data. They note that the total number of HIV-infected paediatric cases is in the region of 1700 (probably an underestimate). Depending on the extent of neuro-logical impairment, HIV could become one of the leading causes of 'mental retardation and developmental disability in children'.

Gibb (1990) summarizes the presentation of central nervous system infection by:

- Developmental delay;
- Acquired microcephally;
- Pyramidal signs;
- Cognitive deficits;
- Sensory impairment (notably hearing and vision);
- Seizures;
- Loss of developmental milestones;
- Ataxia;
- Extrapyramidal signs.

Hittleman (1990) studied a group of children in a prospective study in New York (n = 110). She compared children who were born to HIV-positive mothers but who sero-reverted and were HIV-negative themselves, control children born to HIV-negative mothers and experimental children who were HIV-positive. She found significant group effects on overall developmental indices. Furthermore, she documented persistent findings of developmental delay in the infected children. Wherever delay was apparent, it was of the motor system, at times confounded with cognitive deficits. She concluded that there was an increasing and urgent need for special educational facilities for such children.

Kabagabo *et al.* (1990) examined development in children in Kinshasa. They too found clear motor impairment with their sample. Deo Gratias *et al.* (1990) examined the psychomotor development of 218 children from HIV-positive mothers and a control group of similar size born to HIV-negative mothers. Developmental delay was more frequent in the former group at both 6 and 9 months of age. Similar findings were reported from Swales *et al.* (1990) using the Fagan visual recognition memory test.

Koch *et al.* (1990) examined the progress of uninfected infants born to HIV-positive mothers and found a risk of early neurodevelopmental abnormalities and cautioned that there may be hazards to the developing nervous system for uninfected infants.

Whitt *et al.* (1990) studied 25 children with haemophilia and HIV infection and compared them with uninfected haemophiliac children. They found more frequent neuropsychological impairments for the HIV infected group – most notably in the psychomotor domain.

Chase *et al.* (1990) confirmed these findings in a longitudinal study of eight infants using the Bayley Scales of Development.

Drug treatments

The drug AZT (zidovudine) has been used in children with AIDS. Pizzo *et al.* (1988) report improvements in a range of neurodevelopmental measures after dosage. However, widespread use is limited and good data are not yet to hand. Furthermore, toxic side effects seen in adults may affect a developing child. These need to be documented.

In adults, AZT has been shown to have a marked efficacy in delaying onset of health deterioration. More recent studies have shown that the doses of AZT can be reduced with good effect. This has the advantage, in adults, of reducing some of the many unpleasant side effects of AZT while still maintaining efficacy. A dosage comparison (high 180 mg/m^2 four times daily vs low 90mg/m^2 four times daily) is currently under way, but results are not to hand.

Despite the fact that studies are under way to examine dose effects, virus identification and classification of problems, the child with neurological problems will still present for care and be a client in need of help.

Parents and carers may face dilemmas about drug treatments. They may be uncertain about giving consent for the drugs to be used but worried about withholding them. They may be confused about research and trial protocols for drugs. They may agree to drug treatments in the first instance but over the longer term experience unforeseen problems whilst subjecting the child to a drug regimen which may be painful and difficult to withstand. They may find behavioural problems for children who resist treatments. Children with HIV may become ill as a result of opportunistic infections. Grosch Worner (1989) lists common opportunistic infecting agents as:

- Atypical mycobacteria;
- Candida and cryptococcal fungii;
- Herpes viruses;
- Protozoans, e.g. pneumocystis carinii; toxoplasma gondii;
- Cryptosporidium.

The age of the child, and the extent to which their primary immune response has developed, may determine the type and severity of infection. There is a paucity of published data on the treatment of opportunistic infections in children, the side effects of drugs, and the optimum paediatric doses. Workers need to be vigilant in scanning the literature reports concerning treatment and work hand in hand with medical practitioners.

Immunization

Early concerns were expressed about the safety and advisability of immunization of children with HIV. Given that true infection status cannot be established for up to two years in some cases, the option of abandoning immunization may leave a group of children who are already vulnerable open to the ravages of other life-threatening illnesses. Clearly, advice and action on this subject will change with the growing data base. Current data suggests that live vaccines (oral polio, measles and BCG) should be avoided in children who are showing signs of illness as their immune systems may be functioning inadequately. Children who appear well and symptom free should be treated routinely. Indeed, the WHO has stressed that these children need particular protection from natural disease. Some researchers recommend the use of killed (inactivated) polio vaccine for all children, whereas others recommend it only for those children whose carers are themselves ill with AIDS or ARC. As with all immunizations, at the time of immunizing the child it is often helpful to check the vaccination history of the parent. As data are gathered, recommendations may alter. Health care workers need to have up-to-date guidance for immunization policy.

Complications with HIV-infected children

Over 70% of paediatric HIV infection is acquired perinatally. Thus one can assume that in the majority of cases an infected child also indicates at least an infected mother, and possibly an extension to an infected father and sibling(s). Furthermore, there is evidence that the majority of such cases are confined to groups of the world population who are themselves already disadvantaged, such as drug users, immigrant or minority groups or third world (notably African) populations where resources for medical care and social intervention are limited and where general budget provision *per capita* is less than other sectors of society.

Hopkins (1989) examined 42 families in New York with an infected child aged between 10 months and 10 years. They found that half their sample were with foster families and in total 76% were not living with their natural parents.

They also identified an excessive presence of hearing impairment (50% conductive hearing loss, 5% severe–profound sensorineural hearing loss; 19% questionable hearing loss). With regard to developmental and neurological findings, they note that 24% showed borderline intellectual function, 14% were recorded as mild mental retardation, 10% showed language disorder, 10% with attention deficit disorder and only 12% had no abnormalities requiring intervention. These workers do not give details about overlap of problems and it may well be that many children have multiple rather than single problems requiring many interventions and overlap of problems.

This study may be biased in that the children may have been gathered from the severe end of the spectrum to receive such care and attention as the family unit was able to provide. However, until population based studies are conducted, it must be concluded that a proportion of children with AIDS- or HIV-related disorder will require an extensive service input.

Kletter *et al.* (1989) studied a small cohort of 35 children prospectively. They compared children born to HIV-negative mothers with HIV-positive children and HIV-negative children born to HIV-positive women. They found that mental and motor development of HIV-infected children declined over time and furthermore that the mental and motor development of infants exposed to HIV but not infected lagged behind that of unexposed control children. The numbers in this study were very small, but this clearly marks out the need to continue to monitor all children affected by HIV and not only those who become HIV-positive. The reasons for delay may be environmentally linked to an ill mother rather than direct effects of HIV. More studies are needed.

Care of the child with AIDS in hospital

Psychological care of children with AIDS is of great importance. These children are suffering from a terminal illness, compounded by the fact that they may have a mother or father (or both) who are similarly infected. In some families infection may extend to siblings and thus multiple problems are possible. The treatment of the child may involve constant hospitalization, painful medical procedures plus the added assault of opportunistic infections.

Anxiety

When faced with an unfamiliar or potentially threatening environment, many children may react adversely. Reactions differ widely and can be seen as manifestations of anxiety. Any anxiety management programme or approach which can reduce the stressful nature of the child's experience has obvious benefits for both the child and those who are caring for the child. Not only may anxiety interventions reduce the traumatic nature of the experience for the child, but it may actively assist in encouraging co-operation by the child in treatment and medical procedures.

There are no studies which examine psychological progress and effects of children with AIDS in hospital. However, there is a wide literature on other children, and on some with comparable conditions, which may be of help.

Wolfer and Visintainer (1975) found that an intervention programme utilizing parental and nursing input, together with prior psychological preparation, showed many positive benefits. These included reduced heart rates after unpleasant blood tests and reduced resistance to procedures such as anaesthesia.

Preparing a child for hospitalization

Studies have shown that children can be beneficially prepared for hospitalization. Time scales are different for younger children and preparation should be done close to the admission time. The child should have a clear idea of what to anticipate and expect. Very often children can become fearful of the trappings of a hospital. Preparation can allow for the child to familiarize him or herself with these which can diffuse anticipatory anxiety. Some suggestions include:

(1) Visits to the hospital.
(2) Introduction to the staff.
(3) Reassurance for the child.
(4) Utilization of hospital paraphernalia in play (such as empty syringes for painting, hospital dishes for water or for making collages).
(5) Incorporating scenes into play. Here, children can be provided with toys which will allow them to practise coping in game form.
(6) Children can be given clear continuity from home to hospital environment. This can be achieved by allowing them to choose some favourite items to accompany them to hospital. Such items can be reassuring for the child.
(7) Plans for discharge. A child can plan something special for discharge which can help to look beyond the time of hospitalization.
(8) Preparing a child for painful procedures. Children can be taught relaxation techniques. Studies on children attending dental clinics have shown that where the child can have some control over pain, their tolerance levels are much higher. Such findings can be incorporated into preparations for painful procedures with children in hospital generally.
(9) Ensure that the child does not suffer from undue separations. Allow a parent or caretaker to be with the child whenever possible; involve the caretaker in procedures which require the co-operation of the child and provide facilities for the caretaker to accompany the child.

Appraisal

In adults, stressor appraisal may affect coping. The cognitive facilities of children may differ and this may limit their ability to cope. Eland and Anderson (1977) and Poster (1983) note that younger children are particularly distressed by highly visual short-term painful procedures. It may be that they focus on the visual aspects of the encounter and on the high pain intensity. Peterson (1989) warns that younger children can be particularly prone to cognitive distortions in the absence of mature cognitive skills. For example, she cites that they are more likely to see illness or surgery as punishment or attribute spurious origins. Furthermore, inaccurate or incomplete understanding of bodily functioning, structure and purpose may predispose children to unpleasant misconceptions about medical procedures (Petrillo & Sanger 1972; Sheridan 1975).

Resources

The child needs to develop coping resources either directly or indirectly. Indirect resources emanate from their caregiver who can act as a support system or mediator (Bryant 1985). This needs to be acknowledged and incorporated into the care plan by including such people at all times and not removing them at times of greatest stress for the dependent child. If, in the case of HIV, the parent who normally plays this role is ill, then a designated person should be appointed (or self-appointed) to take over the role. This requires time and dedication in order to become attuned to the child's needs and communications for help and to become responsive. In older children, peers can be helpfully incorporated (Hengeller 1986), but this may be problematic if AIDS and HIV are secret and have a stigma attached. In such cases their contribution could be counterproductive.

Internally, the child acquires skill with age and experience. Some coping behaviours are age-specific and may not be adaptive at a later age. Children's coping often mirrors adult styles. In understanding the literature, as well as its application, one must bear in mind that situations differ, children and their personalities differ, and repeated exposure may alter coping styles which were useful in one-off situations.

The literature describes active versus avoidant coping. A number of studies have pointed to the benefits of active coping styles (Peterson & Toler 1986; Melamed 1982). Based on these studies many workers have set up programmes to prepare children with HIV. However, Peterson points out some of the problems related to providing preparation to children who are coping via defensive repressive styles. The literature at present has not shown that preparation can 'harm' children, and it seems that the optimum situation is to tailor preparation to the coping style of the child.

Schwartz (1989) identified a range of problems experienced by children with HIV- and AIDS-related problems in hospital. They interviewed 25 parents of hospitalized children in order to examine the most common stressors experienced. They found:

- Fear of progressive illness (76%);
- Fear of the child dying (76%);
- Worry about the child experiencing pain and suffering (72%);
- Loss of normality (60%);
- Negative reaction of others (52%);
- Parental illness (48%);
- Guilt (48%);
- Loss of control (44%);
- Change in family structure (40%).

From this study, a set of guidelines can be gathered. Essentially interference with the parenting role was found to be problematic. Multiple care-givers may also make it difficult to provide optimum emotional support for parents.

Schooling

Schooling becomes an issue for older children. The provision of education is compulsory in most countries. The rule of thumb should be that no child should be excluded from education on the basis of HIV or AIDS. The problems to be encountered in a school situation centre around:

- Who to tell on the staff (if anyone)?
- Who needs to know and why?
- What facilities does the child need?
- Feedback loops;
- Infection control;
- Behaviours that arouse problems;
- Constant absence;

- Parental illness;
- Biting;
- Fighting;
- Nose bleeds;
- Illness;
- Body fluids (e.g. excretions or secretions);
- Specific help;
- Special needs;
- Special education;
- Continuity;
- Variety;
- Dedicated personnel;
- Specialized or integrated approach;
- Social stigma;
- Peers and teachers;
- Staff training.

The list is endless. Programmes should be set up to deal with these problems in advance of the child's admittance to the school. The child can only suffer if these issues are debated and unresolved in his/her presence. In the face of these overwhelming difficulties and much prejudice, many parents opt not to inform the school at all. Until times change and society is more accepting, the way forward must be for general education for all schools and staff who may well have an HIV-positive child. In all other areas, acquaintance and work with people with HIV has been the single most effective way of reducing anxiety and overcoming prejudice.

Rogers *et al.* (1990) have examined evidence against casual transmission. As the body of literature on this subject grows, there are large numbers of cases to support the conclusion that this virus has not been transmitted from children in schools, care centres, or to their family members. In the absence of such casual transmission, the need to inform school staff dissipates. Thus schools should ensure that they have the confidence of parents and the best interests of the child at heart if they expect parents to confide in them.

Confidentiality

Confidentiality and secrets still form a major theme in this illness. Social stigma and social withdrawal have been the hallmark of reaction in countries all around the globe. Mok (1990) found confidentiality to be a major issue with her subjects. Many parents do not tell the child the diagnosis. Many do not find comfort or solace from friends or relations. Society at large has a poor track record in this instance and stigma abounds. Indeed, in a study in Kinshasa, Kanenga (1990) found that 23% of children orphaned were also abandoned by their wider family as a result of AIDS and HIV diagnosis.

Within school settings there is a clear dilemma about informing. The parent who needs understanding and help may need to inform the educational authorities. The child who needs special attention and help may need to be identified. Yet stigma and ostracization of such children lead to a (justified) reluctance on the part of the parents to divulge HIV status – a rather sad indictment of society. Indeed, a study by Hinton (1977) showed that dying patients most commonly mentioned pain as their feared item. Yet HIV patients (Sherr & George 1988) were noted in fearing 'telling others' most. This is true for adults and children alike.

The counselling approach to this problem must be multi-pronged. In the first instance, educational establishments need to receive education so that fear and ignorance are replaced with insight and knowledge. Sensible action (such as good infection control and good policies for handling blood, ill children, matters of confidence) should precede exposure to a vulnerable and sensitive child with HIV.

Parents should think clearly about who they are going to tell, how they are going to tell them, and what would happen if their confidentiality is breached. Support for the school staff who are told may limit the possibility of such breaches in confidentiality. Essentially, it is the behaviour of the schools in their response to the children that may well determine whether they are informed. A reassured parent will feel much happier about telling a school which has shown itself to be responsible, caring and discrete.

In the US experience, many of these children have special educational needs. The question of specialized versus integrated education must be addressed.

Forms of care

All parents have the right to choose, while able, the kind of care they would like for their child. There is a grey area where society and the law may intervene. From a psychological point of view, clearly, the interests of the child should be paramount, while the interests of the parent should never be overlooked. It is rare that a compromise cannot be worked out if all parties involved are willing to try.

Care may be difficult in the presence of an ill parent or parents. Future care arrangements need to be made for children. Parental ill health or death may necessitate the involvement of other agencies. In the UK, adoption and fostering are options. In Africa, the social service system seem to rely heavily on the extended family. Clearly the resources to hand need to be used. They may well become strained and require assistance, support and respite.

Skinner (1989) has provided an excellent outline of methods of preparation for potential care agencies. She also cautions about the detrimental effect of overinvolvement of multiple outside agencies.

Mok (1990) underlines the need to create adequate management training and placement practices for foster care. She describes the experience in Edinburgh where placement for children was needed in a background of both staff and foster family anxiety and reticence. They proceeded by approaching potential families individually and supplying them with information. Subsequently they laid groundwork for all potential families (self-selected) by training and information input. They have successfully placed 36 children. The outcome to date has been that a majority have returned to their families of birth. Seven children have been adopted. Factors of note in this experience was the need to provide back-up and support for the foster carers. This took the form of short break placements and a mutual self support group for foster families. Innovations have allowed this system to progress with the provision of potential foster families to help during illness. This allows the natural mother to have respite care while she is ill, and also accustoms the child to familiar carers who may take over care in the advent of parental death. In this study, 25% of the children had utilized this overlap system.

AIDS and the family

HIV can affect many of the normal family interactions and parenting skills. An ill child may be overprotected and thus play can be limited. Thus life experience may differ and the child may have a self-image of fragility. The chain reaction of ill health in the child may lead to a downward turn in the family as a whole. The demands made on a mother from an ill child may be overwhelming for a mother who may become ill herself.

The loss of attention, however it comes about, can affect the development of both the infected and non-infected children in a family. The concern and worry for the ill members of the family can be an ever-present pressure on all family members. Death and illness may be experiences the family members have to deal with. Besides the emotional impact of this, there are practical effects such as the loss of playmates. School performance can be dramatically altered. If the diagnosis of AIDS is known, the stigma may result in a child being isolated. In some countries, fees for medical expenses may limit the family budget and schooling may become a luxury which cannot be afforded. This will mark the downhill slip of affected families. Teenage siblings may have to leave school if a parent is too ill or has died in order to act as the primary caretaker.

Parents as carers and helpers

All psychological models point to the benefits of involving parents as carers. There is also a need to understand the difficulties parents may face while they undertake the role of carer.

Parents can be used to supplement professionals. Professionals must ensure that help is given where needed. If a parent copes well that does not mean that they should not have good respite and assistance.

Most fear and distress is made worse when a person feels out of control and useless. To counteract such feelings, staff can usefully incorporate parents into the caring regimen and respond to their needs and their ideas and solicit their advice. Always remember that it is their child and they probably know him or her best.

No parent can cope with an overwhelming situation without supplementary care and some relief. Staff should always assist parents and ascertain that they have clear limits and goals.

Stigma, social isolation and confidentiality

It must never be forgotten that AIDS carries with it a social stigma unparalleled in childhood illness. Harris (1990) found that 23% of orphaned children were abandoned by their wider families when the diagnosis of AIDS in the mother was known.

Mok (1990) documented how her cohort of mothers in Edinburgh relied almost exclusively on a small group of medical experts as they maintained a veil of secrecy around their HIV and AIDS diagnosis.

None had divulged their predicament to wider family and there was great reluctance to actually meet others in similar predicaments.

In New York there have been reports of helpful groups held for parents or carers of children with AIDS. These were particularly beneficial for parents who had maintained secrecy and were thus not able to discuss their problems and share the worries with the channels that are normally available.

Mutual support groups have been set up in some centres (Positively Women, for example, in the UK). In the USA, a day camp centre has been set up to provide vacations for children with HIV and AIDS. Although it is not necessary to isolate these children, some parents find it relieving to have a centre to turn to where they do not feel the pressure of social stigma.

The social stigma may extend within the family. Some parents are reluctant to inform their child of an HIV diagnosis for fear that the child will either tell others in all innocence or that they will react with tremendous shock. This presents many obstacles in the ongoing care of a child who may have to face up to illness and lifestyle adjustments as they grow older.

Maximizing input for children with limitations

If a child faces possible limitations, understanding and input that can be provided to ameliorate or minimize this. Much of this knowledge needs to be gleaned from other areas of handicap. However, it is important that the advent of AIDS- and HIV-related problems does not result in attempts to re-invent the wheel. Workers should glean and adapt areas of knowledge in the first instance and systematic monitoring should allow for assessment of efficacy and adjustment where necessary.

In order to understand the impact that limitations have on the development, it is a pre-requisite to understand the processes underlying child development (Lewis 1987). If workers can anticipate the effects that developmental obstacles may have on the process of development, they may anticipate problems and provide additional input for these children.

Despite the cause of developmental obstacles, the expression may bear resemblance to other difficulties. It is to this literature that one must turn. As motor difficulties have been recorded for children with HIV, this may result in restrictions in the extent to which they can interact with their environment. Such physical barriers may be enhanced when the child is removed from his or her natural environment into hospital, and when the range of caretakers fluctuates or diminishes due to an ill mother or father. The variety of theories which attempt to explain how development unfolds lead to different predictions about the impact of motor deficits on a child. Some views (Bower *et al.* 1974) contend the structures and knowledge are present at birth. Others such as Watson (1919), discussing early behaviourism or empiricism, hold an opposite view where all knowledge is learned or acquired via life experience.

Perhaps the theorists with the most appealling view take a more active central position whereby they underline the necessity for the child to interact with an environment. This would allow the child to construct an understanding of the world and of the child within that world (e.g. Piaget 1963). Thus a child with motor or exposure problems would have limited experience and would thereby be affected. The kinds of difficulties which have been monitored in other areas include hand/eye co-ordination (Decarie 1969), perceptual development (Anderson & Spain 1977) and writing skills (Anderson & Spain 1977). Spatial design copying was found to be difficult in a study by Abercrombie (1964) but what was of note was that not all children affected by different motor handicaps exhibited these problems (Pringle & Fiddes 1970).

Cognitive development in children with motor handicaps is often difficult to measure as brain damage may often go hand in hand with motor handicaps. Hittleman (1990) showed that all children with mental retardation in her sample of children with HIV/AIDS had also had motor deficits. Intelligence Quotients (IQs) are often used to measure intelligence. However, there is an extended debate about the adequacy, fairness, cultural bias, and accuracy of these tools. The consensus view seems to indicate that such tests are helpful when they provide an objective assessment, when they assist in highlighting areas for future input, and for gross decision making. One needs to exercise caution when interpreting IQ data. Another area of interest is one which examines the level of understanding a child may generate and develop about objects in the presence of motor handicaps which may limit, alter or affect their interaction with physical objects in their world. Décarie (1969), and Kopp and Shaperman (1973), have both found that motor handicaps did not necessarily limit the child's understanding of object permanence.

Studies have looked at what physically handicapped children understand about people (Lewis 1987). In an overview, she concludes that there is great variability within the group of children but also points out that there is evidence that some children with motor handicaps do exhibit delays (Décarie 1969; O'Neill & Décarie 1973) but there is little evidence to suggest that understanding differs dramatically from non-handicapped children. She further points out that some understanding of social relationships may interact with language skill.

With particular regard to education, motor speed may be an obstacle which has unexpected ramifications for the child; for example, arithmetic may pose a problem. Often early learning skills (reading, writing and arithmetic) rely on repetition, and hospitalization may represent a disruption which can be an added impediment (Pringle & Fiddes 1970). Linguistic and social development may be affected either by the intellectual impairment, the problems with physical apparatus, and the social interference and feedback that these may elicit. Lewis points out that physical handicap alone is not a prescription for mental handicap.

Children may need continuous and early exposure to learning material. They may require specific input, with a good staff/child ratio to maximize their learning. Patience may be needed to help a child with fine motor skills. A hospitalized child should be exposed to as much continuity of education as is possible. Parents can be involved in educational supplement whenever possible. This not only provides them with a positive role, but may serve to increase the child's opportunities to learn.

Children with HIV need to be treated as individuals. This may necessitate creative approaches to assessment and intervention. Any developmental delays or handicaps which a child with HIV or AIDS suffers from ought to be taken into account when planning input and education. Workers must draw a distinction between problems resulting from HIV itself and those which arise indirectly such as from social stigma, an ill mother, drug side effects, constant hospitalization, and so on. Handicaps may mask the abilities of a child. In some circumstances, a compromised child may be presumed to have more abilities than they actually have and input may be overlooked. Workers need to have particular awareness of the limitations imposed by motor handicaps. They need to look to the literature for other motor handicapped children in order to equip themselves for potential delays in this group of children. The points to remember are:

(1) Handicaps are not a unifying factor. Children will differ in the range and extent of their limitations, their social surroundings, their support, and their personal qualities.
(2) Handicaps are often multiple. The full picture for children with

AIDS is unclear, but if a child has a developmental problem, the possibility of additional problems needs to be assessed.

(3)   Motor deficits often limit the child's ability to interact with the environment; this is seen as a key factor in developmental theories. Input should be expanded to ensure that the child has maximum exposure and experience of the environment.

(4)   Practical help, support and supplementing for families is a key factor.

(5)   Parents and family may play a key role in the development of the child and should be included in decision making and help.

(6)   If a child has multiple hospital stays, day-to-day development may be disrupted and the child may be doubly disadvantaged. Hospital schemes which improve the stimulation and experience of children in hospital should be encouraged (Woodburn 1973).

(7)   Cognitive developmental theories such as those of Piaget place much emphasis on the role of action in cognitive development. Studies have shown that children with limited abilities to interact with their environment still develop cognitively. Lewis (1987) notes that a variety of different types of action seem to give such children a way into cognition. The role of the carer is to promote opportunities for such interaction.

(8)   Families who are supporting a child with additional input may need consistent encouragement and back-up.

Siblings

Dunn (1989) has provided comprehensive psychological studies of siblings charting the effects of siblings on each other, psychological hurdles, and implications for future growth and development. These data can be adjusted to examine the problems that siblings may face in the light of HIV. There are a variety of situations in which siblings find themselves:

- Siblings who are HIV-positive as well;
- Siblings who are HIV-negative in the presence of another HIV-positive (or AIDS-diagnosed) child;
- Siblings who are well with HIV-positive or AIDS-diagnosed parent/s;
- Orphaned siblings.

In all such cases, the growth, well being and welfare of the siblings should not be overlooked.

Harris (1990) carried out an early stage descriptive study on siblings of HIV-positive children in New York City. One of the limitations of this study was that, despite wide ranges of problems described, there was no control group which would highlight the particular problems associated with HIV, and some of the tools used may need population standardization. However, in this study, 112 HIV-positive children and their siblings were involved. Of these, 44 lived with their mothers, 23 were fostered by a family member, and a further 25 were in foster placement. From this group a sample who were residing with their biological mother (14 out of 44) had a sibling aged two years or over and these were assessed according to the Achenbach Schedule. Overall, the findings revealed that 43% had behavioural problems. The occurrence of behavioural problems were more likely in larger families (not an uncommon finding in behavioural problems generally). Furthermore, boys were less likely to show problems than girls. This may be a spurious finding as acting out may be more socially acceptable in boys and thus not deemed as 'problem behaviour'. Generally, the problems recorded included sleep disturbance, somatic complaints, social withdrawal, obesity, depression, hyperactivity, aggression and obsessive difficulties.

This study highlights some of the problems that these siblings may experience. However, it is unclear to what extent these were created, promoted or enhanced by the presence of a sibling with HIV. It can be postulated that constant hospitalization, hospital visits, medical procedures, stress and emotional problems, uncertainty, stigma and fear may all be ingredients contributing to such problems. However, it may well be that this is simply descriptive of the range of behavioural problems experienced by inner city children of single parent, drugusing, HIV-infected mothers where economic hardship and social isolation is taking its toll. Although this study does not address these factors, it does raise the issue and whatever the aetiology of the problem, some input could be helpful to such children.

Delaporte (1990) studied the siblings of HIV-infected children and found that 18.8% of siblings were themselves infected. Thus HIV can become a disease which affects not only the parents and the child with HIV, but perhaps one or more siblings or indeed the whole family.

Twins

There is little data that relates to twins. Incidental information gleaned from studies has shown that in one study, one twin born to an HIV positive mother proceeded to become infected whilst the other remained HIV-negative.

Wiznia *et al.* (1990) noted a high rate of twins in a cohort of 80 children born to HIV-infected drug-using mothers. The reasons for twinning are essentially unknown and it is unclear whether this is a drug-related phenomenon, an HIV-related phenomenon, or a chance finding.

AIDS orphans

One of the more dramatic statistics concerning AIDS is the impact it has on orphaned children. This not only affects the children directly, but causes extreme hardship and trauma for parents who have to take on board the fact that they may not see their children grow up, and for grandparents and extended families who may be overburdened with the care of orphans. In countries where there are limited or no health and welfare agencies, the welfare care relies heavily on extended families. AIDS orphans may strain such systems heavily, even to disintegration. This may mark the emergence of children who do not have traditional care venues to lean upon.

A study by Kamenga in Kinshasa (1990) tried to identify the numbers of AIDS orphans and to track social and psychological consequences for the children concerned. This study compared the children of 468 HIV-positive mothers with those of 572 HIV-negative mothers. They found that the percentage death at follow-up was 33.4% in the former compared with 8.5% in the latter group. Of the children born to HIV-positive mothers, 6.7% were orphaned compared to 0.2% of those born to HIV-negative mothers.

Further data revealed that some of these children were orphaned at young ages (mean 18.7 months). Follow-up interviews found all the control children at home whereas over a quarter (28%) of the other group were not at home. Further obstacles to health and well being were monitored in clinic absences (for immunizations and check-ups). Over a fifth of the index children had not reported or been brought to the clinic, unlike all of the control children who had attended. Further hardship may have been experienced by these children as one in two had a sibling dispersed. None of the control children were separated from their siblings. This may represent a double deprivation for children. Children were often abandoned by families on hearing that AIDS or HIV infection was implicated (n = 23%).

Cheek (1990) examined the incidence of orphans as a result of AIDS in sub-Saharan Africa and noted that the number of uninfected AIDS-related orphans below the age of ten years could rise to over 250 000 by 1990 in this region alone.

Hunter *et al.* (1989) studied orphans in Uganda and examined ways in which policy could be adapted to meet the growing needs of this population.

Lwegaba and Twatwa reported on AIDS in Uganda where over 6772 cases of AIDS have been reported with a 1:1 male female ratio. Antenatal infection reaches as much as 14% in some centres and for every adult AIDS couple there are seven orphans.

Child abuse

Sexual abuse of children is always a possibility that must be borne in mind. As HIV is sexually transmitted, there is a theoretical risk of infection via this route. To date only one reported study attempts to document cases of this sort. Di John (1990) recorded two case histories where sexual abuse may have been implicated in HIV transmission. Furthermore, these workers set out pointers which may indicate sexual abuse – namely the presence of other sexually transmitted diseases in young children or the presence of HIV in a young child when maternal infection is unlikely.

Caselli (1989) reports on a similar route of infection. An Italian child (aged 4) was found to be seropositive with no risk factors acknowledged in the parents. On examination, the family revealed an HIV-positive sibling (18 months) and the mother was HIV-positive with the father HIV-negative. The mother reported a single incident of sexual abuse at the age of 15 during a stay in Zaire in 1974. Caselli claims that it is possible that this episode of sexual abuse accounted for HIV infection and the ramifications only came to light 14 years later.

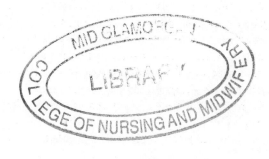

Chapter 11

Bereavement and Death

The literature on dying and bereavement in children is expanding. Much of this can be applied to the HIV area. The limitations result from the paucity of literature on AIDS and children. The special needs of these children can be conjectured but only the unfolding of time, insightful research, and perhaps (sadly) mistakes, misjudgements and errors, will highlight the special problems and the optimum ways of handling these.

The special problems of AIDS relate, at present, to the social stigma of the condition, the fact that it may affect more than one member of the family, and the fact that it may leave a child both bereaved and dying simultaneously and in this case there is a dearth of helpful literature. The only comparable data come from disaster situations where multiple losses are experienced. We need to sift through and learn from this literature. However, the extent to which cases are comparable is unclear, and this is compounded by the lack of insight into children and the focus on adults.

The bereaved child

The death of a parent, sibling or close relative leaves a bereaved child. The age of the child often has implications for the input the child needs, the optimum coping mechanisms, and the way the bereavement is handled. Although it is unrealistic to impose rigid age divisions, children differ markedly as their development progresses. Under six months of age, it is difficult to know the extent to which a child grasps the meaning and impact of a bereavement. There are probably emotional feelings which may well comprise the precursors to mourning and grief. Given that dialogue is not possible with such a child, the level of interaction should be matched to the child's needs.

If the death that a baby experiences is that of the mother then there is a dramatic effect on the mothering relationship which becomes disrupted and is difficult to replace. Although the tasks of mothering can be replaced by many people it is important to bear in mind that the child's needs extend beyond gratification and feeding. The practical advice must be to allow for a key individual to take over mothering of the infant. Ideally such an individual should be someone who can have sustained input over considerable time so that the child does not have to experience a loss of mothering on more than one occasion.

One of the problems with AIDS and HIV is that the virus may well cross over from father to mother and child. Thus an ill father may be providing subsequent mothering. This should be supplemented with a slow handover to a set of key individuals.

In Africa, it has been estimated that there will be 20 000 orphans by the year 2000. The mothering needs of these children must be addressed by the community. Some reports have shown the new role of grandparents who have been brought back into child rearing at a time of retirement. The stresses and strains of this new role, together with the costs, should form the basis of input for this group.

With young babies, it is difficult to understand their responses and reactions and interpret them as bereavement reactions. They may show distress but this may be as a result of a lost reaction to their needs or to a lost individual. As it is hard to differentiate on the data that are known, in order to minimize hurt experienced by children, reactions to their needs should be paramount.

The longer term effects of bereavement on very young children are unknown. Studies which have attempted to examine these often have many methodological flaws. Retrospective studies reveal little concrete data, but are most useful in steering subsequent research. Prospective studies suffer from flaws where it is impossible to tease out the incidental effects of a loss (such as changed socio-economic circumstances, changed psychological mood and state of a care-giver and changed responses to needs), and the absence of the index loved one. The overwhelming message from the literature focusses on quality of subsequent mothering as an important key factor in life adjustment. As such when young babies are faced with a loss, this ought to be a primary goal in care planning and resource input.

For bereaved older children, the level of meaning will vary. This will depend on family factors, developmental and cognitive abilities of the child, individual circumstances, and subsequent life circumstances. Again the loss may be typified by a pining and despair reaction. The hardest part for the child to deal with is the fact that there will be no return of the loved one. Again, irrespective of the age of the child, it seems that the level of care offered in its place is crucial in determining the psychological and life adjustment of the bereaved child.

Raphael (1977) points out that bereavement must be viewed in the context of the family and goes on to describe different family patterns which may affect the impact and reactions surrounding a bereavement. The different families include families in which:

- Death is a taboo;
- Someone is to blame;
- Relationships are avoided;
- Things must go on as before;
- Openness and sharing of real feelings take place.

Such family adaptation to the loss determines the level of discussion, understanding, explanation and help that a child can receive around a bereavement. It directly affects the amount of information the child will have about the illness, will understand about the patterns of emotional adjustment and responses of family members and him/herself, and how far he/she will respond to crisis situations, will accommodate and adjust to new roles, and will be able to resolve the loss.

HIV has been associated with increased suicide risk and it is known (Shepherd & Barraclough 1976) that there may be some particular bereavement issues surrounding suicide. This may be exacerbated if the suicide was associated with HIV. The above workers found that over half of their subjects failed to inform the child of the suicide and the remainder provided varying amounts of information. Children were told at a mean age of 10 years. Younger children (8 years) were given some information and the mean age for children who were told nothing was 4. This is in sharp contrast to the finding by Lansdown (1990) that children at this age can hold a meaningful discourse on death and have quite some concept of the notions involved in death and loss. One difficulty with the Shepherd and Barraclough data emerges from the fact that parental reports were used as the source of the data. A similar study with data gathered directly from children may give a clearer understanding into their insights, needs and ability to understand the impact of the death.

There is some literature which suggests that children whose parents commit suicide may have an increased tendency to attempt suicide themselves. Thus counselling should be used to help children avoid resorting to suicidal thoughts (and acts) as solutions to their problems. Suicide may also carry with it a social stigma. This is a double stigma in the presence of HIV infection. If there is an attempt to cover up the causes of death the child may have an interrupted mourning. Furthermore, the adults may also have interrupted mourning and these are the very adults who may well be responsible for the care and emotional support of these children.

The major theme here seems to be the willingness to talk to children in the first place and the subsequent detail given. Complicating factors in the prognosis of the child do seem to be the extent of mourning and adjustment in the surviving parent.

One area of parental loss that has given way to systematic insight does not apply to death but to divorce. Such literature may be applicable as from the child's point of view there is still a loss, and hence any learning from this literature may be useful in the absence of direct source material. Overall, the studies have attempted to equate later disorders or behavioural problems to earlier loss. It is difficult to draw cast iron conclusions from these studies as they do not give prospective data and thus one cannot conclude that all children suffering from loss will have subsequent problems. Furthermore, it is unclear which factors contribute to the problems if the relationship is true. This is a key component as any preventive work must be focussed on the right remedy. Studies have shown anti-social behaviour (Newman & Denman 1971, Douglas 1970).

Psychological effects of bereavement

Van Eerdewegh *et al.* (1982), in a study of bereaved children, found an increase in general symptomatology. This included mood changes, bouts of sadness, crying and irritability, many reports of sleep difficulties, reductions in appetite, withdrawn social behaviour, temper episodes, and bedwetting. In a similar prospective study by Raphael (1977), parental reports plus child assessments revealed high levels of behavioural symptoms in the period directly after the loss, lasting for weeks and sometimes months. A fifth of the sample experienced at least two symptoms which included withdrawal, bouts of aggression (where previously this had not been noted), clinging to adults and severe separation fussing, sleep and appetite disturbances, and alterations in habits.

Other workers have gone further to relate bereavements and losses to more physical problems. Although much of the evidence is weak, it may be that an immune-compromised child is particularly vulnerable. If there is a link between medical conditions and psychological distress, these studies should be noted with care. For example, Morillo and Gardener (1980) found links with thyrotoxicosis; Herioch, Batson and Baum (1978) found links with juvenile rheumatoid arthritis.

Some children suffer from adjustment disorders after bereavement and these need specific attention and are neither simple nor transient.

Future psychological problems have been tracked. Felner *et al.* (1981) recorded school problems in bereaved children and difficulties in adaptation. School refusal and disinterest was also recorded by Black (1974) and Van Eerdewegh *et al.* 1982). With older children, bereavement is often linked closely to the event whereas with younger children there may well be a delay. Generally, children as they get older start to exhibit a range of bereavement reactions similar to those of adults. The important thing is to bear in mind that many minor and major problems in later life have been documented ranging from transient school refusal to more severe problems such as psychiatric disorder, depression, disrupted or difficult relationship patterns, increased sensitivity to losses, and increased trauma at anniversary times (similarly to adults), and sometimes individual life crises occurring at the age-anniversary point of the experienced loss.

At the time of the bereavement these points should be noted as they may affect decisions made for a child which, in turn, may ameliorate or eradicate the possibility of future problems. In general, the factors which seem to contribute to the course of bereavement reaction include the quality and level of pre-existing relationships, the individual circumstances of the death, the availability and quality of support both immediately after the death and in the longer term, and the presence of additional stresses. Birtchnell (1971) noted a protective effect of older siblings and hence family break-up ought to be resisted or only considered when alternatives are non-existent. This is a point of note given that many studies in Africa report the dispersion of siblings in cohorts of children orphaned through AIDS (Kanenga 1990).

Thus, workers should take into account both the developmental age of the child and their life experience in determining how children perceive death. Although there are no prescriptive theories of loss, it is often useful to know the kinds of psychological reaction that children may face. This will allow carers to anticipate reactions and help the child face the reaction. They must bear in mind that children do not necessarily have to feel these emotions or go through stages. Such reactions may include:

Shock.   This is found amongst children and adults alike. It can be short lived, transitory or long lasting.

Denial. The reality of a loss may be overwhelming and a child may need to deny it. Such a child will need gentle help to grasp the reality and permanence of the loss.

Guilt. It is not uncommon for people to experience guilt feelings after a loss. These may be rationally or irrationally based. Children may feel that they were somehow responsible for a death. They may blame others such as a surviving parent, a sibling, or hospital staff.

Anger. Children, like adults, may feel extreme anger. This can be as a result of their own loss and their inability to grasp or understand the events that surround them.

Physical Symptoms. Extreme grief may bring about physical symptoms such as pains, breathlessness, headaches or weaknesses.

Depression. Although childhood depression is seen as rare, it may be seen in a recently bereaved child. It is more common for a child to feel a deep sadness. Emotional intensity often has shorter durations with children than with adults. It is not that children's feelings are any less sensitive; perhaps they are less able to cope, and the feelings are overwhelming at times. Most children tend to cope with grief by exhibiting mood swings.

Anxiety. When death confronts a child there are rarely rational explanations. In such circumstances children can become overly fearful for their lives. They may fear that death will strike at another family member. They may suddenly feel out of control. Their world may be unpredictable and this can fill them with panic. They need to have some of their faith in the world restored.

Curiosity. Many children do not acknowledge the social niceties that adults use to avoid death talk. Their intrigue about the unknown and unexplained leads them to ask straightforward perplexing questions. Their curiosity is natural and not 'unhealthy'. Such curiosity can become obsessive when the child is not given satisfactory answers. If a child asks many questions that the carer finds difficult to answer, it is often helpful to explain to the child that there are some things which cannot be understood, for example:

CHILD: Where do you go when you die?
CARER: Really, people do not know. Some people believe in heaven, but others do not. Some people believe your spirit lives on, but others do not. What do you believe?

Here the carer allows the child to have some understanding, but also probes into the child's concern.

Copying.   A child may try to recreate the lost person by copying small mannerisms or characteristics of the dead relative.

Children and trauma

The major finding from psychology which needs to be applied here is the recognition that children are different from adults. Children are not simply 'little adults' or 'miniature versions'. The key to understanding appropriate reactions to children must lie in an understanding of these differences and the reactions of children.

Essentially, children may not manifest the same signs and outward behaviours as adults. Thus, at times of grief, for example, a child may continue to play, smile and laugh whereas an adult may maintain a sombre mood for extended periods. It would be inaccurate to assume that the child does not feel the same pain, hurt, anguish or grief. The younger child simply cannot sustain a sad mood to the same extent as an adult, yet they may well be grief stricken. Any reactions to the child should not be based purely on outward manifestations of mood.

Often a younger child may not fully understand the impact or importance of an event. Thus trauma will have a reduced effect. At times they may be reacting to a different set of events. For example, a young child may not understand what the implications of HIV are, but may well pick up a clear feeling of fear, panic and desolation from a parent.

For younger children, attachment anxiety is more common than in older children. Thus children in traumatic circumstances should be handled with care. They should be seen sooner rather than later. Workers should not assume that they do not experience grief simply by outward manifestations of play and elevated mood. Workers should take great pains not to separate child from parent and to ensure that the child is accompanied by someone close whenever possible.

Telling a child about HIV

Telling anyone about HIV is always difficult. No less so for children. There are always questions about whether a child should be told, when a child should be told, who should do the telling, and how should it be done.

There are no easy answers and no rules for all. Rather there are a series of factors that should be taken into account when facing HIV infection and children.

For a start, telling the child should always be kept in mind. If a child is not told, the counsellor should have a clear insight into why the child is not told – who this is protecting, when this will change, what has to happen in order for this to change, who knows, and so on.

Raise the subject by checking out with the child what they know and understand:

COUNSELLOR: 'How do people die?'
CHILD: 'By guns and war'
COUNSELLOR: 'Are there any other ways?'
CHILD: 'I do not know'

Clearly, here the child has a notion of death, but sees it as some far removed idea, using information gained from stories or television. The counsellor can probe further:

COUNSELLOR: 'Who can die?'
CHILD: 'Old people, and dogs when they get run over'
COUNSELLOR: 'Can children die?'
CHILD: 'I think so, but I do not know anyone who has died. Does it hurt?'

Here, the counsellor can raise the subject, allow the child to think through, and also provide an opening for questions. Children are often direct and ask clear questions. Replies should be at their level and a balance struck between accurate and informative answers with limitations on copious and inappropriate detail.

There is a distinction between a child who has HIV and one who is affected when a parent or sibling has HIV. All children have the need to know, but the impact, pacing and sequelae may differ.

Talking about death with children

In order to understand how one should talk to children about death, be it their own from illness, that of a sibling, or the death of a parent, it is a prerequisite to have some understanding of children's concepts of death and how they accommodate these.

Essentially, the older a child grows, the closer their ideas about death tally with those of adults. It is arbitrary to have a cut-off age for any child and each individual child should be treated according to their individual developmental insight and progress. Perceptions of death are closely allied to perceptions of illness. Great care should be taken to understand what children know and do not know, what they believe, what they expect, and how they explain certain phenomena to themselves.

Reilly *et al.* (1983) examined children's understanding of death. They looked particularly at notions of permanence and the extent to which the child took on this idea. They found dramatic changes across age groups with only half the 5-year-olds stating that they would die, just under three-quarters of 6-year-olds and over 80% of 7-year-olds. Thus, in the short space of three years a marked change occurs for the majority of children in grasping the fact of their own mortality. Another study by Kane (1979) looked at specific notions associated with death and measured the extent to which children of different age groups had grasped such components. These were presented as increasing with age and included the notions of: Realization, separation, immobility, irrevocability, causality, dysfunctionality, universality, insensitivity, appearance and personification.

Such studies are often helpful in pointing out the way in which dealing with death for children can be focussed. However, they are limited in that they do not tell us about individual children and their needs. Nor do they tell us about the views of sick children who may differ markedly from healthy children. Exposure to learning about death may rapidly increase a child's insight. These studies do not tell us that children cannot comprehend these notions, just simply that a large proportion of children at given ages do not appear to have grasped them when questioned.

Death of a child

There are varying groups of children who may die from AIDS. Their differences are vast and this may affect the way they are handled, the way they approach their illness, and the way their parents react and cope. These include children who have acquired HIV from different sources, children with different support available, infected and non-infected children.

Mode of infection

Some children are infected via contaminated blood products. This often signals the co-existence of other conditions such as haemophilia, thalassaemia or malaria. There may be profound parental guilt associated with genetically transmitted illnesses which necessitated the child's exposure to contaminated blood in the first place. Such guilt may extend to the health care team who previously were the providers of care but who may, unknowingly, have injected the child with HIV.

Other children are infected transplacentally. This may be known at the time of pregnancy or only come to light when a child is ill and a mother is tested retrospectively. Such children may well be considerably younger and have very different needs. For a start these children may have lived in a twilight zone since birth. While HIV tests are unable to tell whether antibody is maternal (passively transmitted) or produced by the infant, it is unclear if the infant is infected. Such a child can continue in a state of uncertainty until 24 months (Peckham 1989). By the age of two, children have much insight. Here it is not a case of telling or not telling, but of handling uncertainty. Is it fair to burden such a young child with possible bad news if it may in fact prove untrue? Yet on the other hand how does one explain to the child the constant hospital visits, blood tests and painful procedures? Clearly a protocol must be worked out for each child so that the child is given explanations which are consistent and helpful. Denial and lies are not helpful especially since the child will certainly have one, if not two parents, and in some cases a sibling or two, who are affected by HIV.

Care and support
Some children will be cared for by the family, one parent or two, by an extended family, by foster parents, adoptive parents or they may be under the care of institutions. For any child to cope with important life events, there must be a clear supportive and caring environment with named dedicated individuals responsible for individual child welfare.

Background medical care
The availability of medical facilities may vary considerably. Some parents may want to contain their child at home and others may have no option.

Facing the death

Children have (or should have) the same rights as adults. This includes the right to know, to be given time to understand the concept and its implications, and time to plan. The counselling objective is concerned with optimum time and method of telling and continuing support after the child has been told.

In these circumstances, individual factors will play a decisive role and the first step in the process must be an open and honest fact-gathering exercise where the child is approached on his/her level, in the presence of people s/he trusts, and the child's understanding is gauged. This not only allows the counsellor or health care worker to form a starting point. It also gives necessary insight to allow for appropriate pacing, for understanding of misconceptions, and the ability to understand and dispel fantasy ideas which are sometimes horrific or frightening and can cause unnecessary distress and suffering.

The child's age and the support surrounding the child are two key elements in pacing.

Children may have much clear insight, but their sense of time may have an individual focus. This means that a child is better able to deal with events in the more immediate future and may find events in the distant future harder to grasp and take on board. In such circumstances information should be given to children in a paced way. Children are often very good at determining how much they can take on board at any given point. Let the child be the monitor and listen carefully to questioning. Give the child whatever s/he can take and maintain an ongoing open dialogue. There is thus no situation of pretence and lying, but rather an unfolding to match the child's understanding.

Silence, denial and pretence are three factors that are often present when a child is dying. This can emanate either from the family or from doctors. Such defences may be the props that are keeping the child together and it is important not to destroy these without careful thought and the provision of alternatives. If there are no alternatives, perhaps the pretence is not harmful. What is important is that the counsellor understands why there are such things as denial, lack of discussion, and pretence, and whose interest they serve. Sometimes it is done for mutual protection. The child may have much more insight into the reality of a situation but holds back to protect a parent. At other times, and perhaps simultaneously, a parent is trying to protect the child.

Counselling is not only linked to informing a child about death, but is extended to cover the multiple questions that a child may have. These may surface at different times and must be met. As with adults, honesty is always the best policy. Do not underestimate a child's understanding. Jargon-free simplistic explanations go a long way. At the same time, ensure that the child has a clear understanding of your explanations by checking back. Duggan (1990) describes a case where a child misunderstood an explanation of internal tissue to refer to Kleenex (paper towels) and had a vision of his insides filled with paper. Another example was one where a child was given an explanation of lung function by way of an example of a balloon. The child was frightened as she was aware that balloons burst and was worried that her lungs would do likewise.

The counsellor may be trained and practised in talking about death, but it may well be the choice of the family that they themselves hold the discussion. In such circumstances the counsellor can be of enormous assistance. The counsellor can practise with the parent how they will tell the child. They can anticipate difficult and awkward questions and plan responses. A counsellor can also serve as a source to whom the parent can turn after the discussion to debrief, to understand, to discuss, or simply to reassure.

Facing death for adults may be easier if they can plan. Children, too, have such needs. They may plan differently, but planning may afford them both a sense of reassurance and of finished business which will help them. Adults write wills. Children do not. Yet the meaning of a will is simply the disposal of assets with token gestures of meaningful items to meaningful others. This is easily within a child's domain (Kuykendall 1989). It not only allows the child to express its wishes, but also gives a child some control which may be lost in many other spheres of existence.

The first hurdle a child needs to cross concerns the crisis of discovery (Buckingham 1989). For children who are newly infected, this may occur suddenly. For those with transplacental exposure the discovery may be an ever-present possibility. The final confirmation, however, may still be traumatic. The child may be overindulged or overprotected as an initial reaction. Children are also very sensitive to emotional messages they receive from the carers and this may directly or indirectly affect their behaviour.

Children are no different from adults in their need for information and to have their questions asked and answered. Sometimes children ask questions to which there is no answer. Fictitious or vague answers, however, are not helpful here. There is a commonly recorded reluctance among doctors to tell patients (be they adult or child) of the terminal nature of illness despite the fact that many patients express a desire to know (Ley 1989). The child who is dying will in all probability have anxieties and worries about the dying process. Frank and open discussion may afford much relief to them. They need to be treated in an environment that allows them to ask their questions and allows them to trust that the response is honest. Conversely, their fears can often be enhanced if they are excluded from the discussion.

Glaser and Straus (1965) point out that the behaviour of a dying person is affected by the awareness he/she has. This may well hold true for children and may be affected by how much they know. Knowing and telling can become part of an ornate strategy. Bluebond-Langer (1978) describes 'mutual pretence' for leukaemic children where information is kept secret amongst groups of carers. She presents an interesting analysis of children's understanding of their world in the presence of terminal illness, how they interpret knowledge about hospitals showing a deep understanding of both the written and unwritten rules. Based on this analysis, she claims that terminally ill children know that they are dying before death is imminent. Pretence and avoidance are often invoked to facilitate tasks and maintain illusions of normalcy. This may help pace families but may deny them an opportunity for open discussion and frank expression of emotion.

This mutual pretence is in contrast to an open awareness strategy which allows for dialogue and acknowledgement of the child's prognosis.

The trappings of illness bring with it many fearful and perhaps painful procedures. If this cannot be helped the child should be prepared for these and paced through them. Johnson (1971) found that in terms of reducing anxiety and increasing coping behaviour in adults information about sensations was superior to information about medical procedures. This may well be true for children.

When a child finally enters the terminal phase this can last for weeks or months. A child with AIDS may suffer from debilitating opportunistic infections, but may recover and have bouts of symptom-free time. This may be a difficult time for the family who have lived through the illness episode with the child, and then have to face a seemingly well child while knowing that another opportunistic infection may strike. Furthermore, some children exhibit developmental delays and milestone regressions. This may be particularly hard for parents and for the child who may regress visibly during this period.

The child may need much encouragement to face up to life with enthusiasm.

The terminal period marks the time when the death is imminent and seen as inevitable. Decision making and farewells are necessary at this point. When death is immediate, requests for information and explanations may differ. A child may have a need to say farewell, either overtly or symbolically. This can be easily facilitated. Family decisions about place of death can be acknowledged. Wish and dream fulfilment are often strived for. This allows the family to 'give' the child one final, memorable experience. Some families do not want this. Some families start to withdraw from the child. Such mourning may be helpful to them, but often staff feel angry at such parents.

There are advantages and disadvantages to children dying at home. In some countries there are no choices. In others, where choice exists, the parents need to be involved fully. Other facilities such as hospice or hospital settings will need to be able to receive such a child without adding social stigma to the burden of the death.

The death itself will vary according to the child, the age, the circumstances. It may also be compounded by all the trappings of death such as hospitals, rituals, health care workers, medical paraphernalia and numbness.

The bereaved adult

For an adult, losses occur at time of death, their own, or that of a loved one. Yet there are multiple losses with AIDS that may trigger bereavement and grieving of a sort usually reserved for death. For counsellors, death and bereavement have to be faced and loss reactions ought to be recognized.

Despite the existence of theories which describe stages of grieving, counsellors must be wary of imposing these onto a client and thereby suffocating their emotional expression. Theories are helpful in forewarning both counsellors and clients about the intensity and range of reactions, but grief always remains an individual experience, free to vary.

Bereavement in the face of multiple loss is rarely described. A few writers examining human disasters (such as multiple accidents, war or mass murder) may have touched upon the differences found in multiple death. AIDS and HIV are somewhere between the two. The nature of the HIV virus may mean that an adult is infected, and their sexual partner is infected, as are their children. Some individuals may suffer multiple bereavements as societies and friendship networks become ill or die. The literature has pointed out that coping, in the face of multiple stressors, is usually impaired.

An adult with HIV will be faced with multiple losses. These include:

(1)   Loss of a future or the future they had previously anticipated. Loss of good health and concomitant strains resulting from reduced energy, multiple illness, hospitalization, becoming a medical novelty, drug taking regimens, and medical interventions.
(2)   The loss of children can be an enormous burden. This may occur

either through the actual death of a child, loss through termination or coming to terms with childlessness if there is an active decision to avoid pregnancy in the first place.

(3) Loss of control can often leave an individual feeling helpless, panic stricken and passive. Dependence and inactivity can follow. Counselling intervention should aim to maximize control and involve individuals at all points in decision making. This will allow someone to take responsibility for their own decisions and may ameliorate the effects of reduced control.

(4) Loss of sex in that HIV may mark a dramatic change in sexual relationships. Some individuals refrain from sex after diagnosis and this may represent an acute loss. Others adopt safer sex practices which may mark a considerable change in their lifestyle and sexual expression. Many people feel that non-penetrative sex is no substitute and is not 'real' sex. Death of a sexual partner may also mean that someone with HIV will have limited opportunities to find another sexual partner. Avenues that were previously open may now be in-accessible and new strategies may need to be learned. This can pose considerable difficulty.

(5) Practical losses which can affect people deeply. These include economic hardship if a job is lost, loneliness if friends are lost, and isolation if the cumulative effect of losses leave them with low energy, poor resources, and limited social support.

In adults, death can be seen as timely or untimely. Although some individuals would propose that death is never timely, untimely death somehow involves the notion of unfinished business, or a death too early. AIDS usually takes its toll in young adults who have not spent much time thinking about death or preparing themselves.

Hinton (1977) examined fears of the dying and found that many people feared pain. With HIV this may be a factor as well and workers should reassure clients about pain management and pain control. In a study of HIV clients (Sherr & George 1987), it was found that they feared the reaction of others more than pain. This is somewhat of an indictment of our society and great strides could be made if social stigma were to be removed.

Counsellors who are working with the dying adult need to appreciate that there are often fears associated with dying rather than with death. Clients can benefit from open and frank discussion. They may want to adjust their life goals, review some of their life achievements, or carry out tasks to ensure that their lives are left with some form of order. Counsellors can facilitate this process either by providing time and opportunity for the client to talk, or by helping with practical features such as wills. Some clients have strong views about their own death and may want to plan for it. This may include where they would like to die, how they would like to be buried or even features of their own funeral. On the other hand, some clients do not want to dwell on death and find it an onerous burden to discuss death with every health care worker who approaches them. There is a fine balance between allowing a client the opportunity to discuss death and imposing such a discussion on them.

Death for a parent is difficult when younger children are involved. Parents may feel an overwhelming sense of loss at the prospect of not seeing their child grow older. They may want to have a clear idea of future care for their child and have such plans in order.

Chapter 12

Education and Training

Education and training form a basic tool in the fight against HIV and AIDS. Training is a wide reaching concept. It covers direct staff training, patient education and health education. Prior to exposure to HIV-related problems, staff should ideally have some training. However, it may well happen that this is not available. In a study on health education, Sherr (1987) found that high- and low-risk subjects were most likely to turn to medical sources for their information about AIDS and HIV. This adds a burden to the requirements of all staff (whether directly involved in AIDS and HIV or not) to have a basic minimum training in order to respond appropriately to the needs of their patients.

Training falls into two broad categories – direct training within the discipline on AIDS and HIV infection, and the cross discipline need to train staff on psychological aspects of care and counselling. In the absence of a cure for HIV, counselling forms a major input tool. Furthermore, as containment of spread is reliant to a certain extent on behaviour change, counselling and psychological knowledge can maximize the efficacy of this. Staff should remember that although there is a specialized body of knowledge, many of the lessons can be borrowed from other good practice systems and in this respect there is nothing very special about AIDS and HIV infection. Training of course will depend on the area of work.

Those who are likely to benefit from training include:

Counsellors. All counsellors working with those infected with HIV, those testing for HIV and those at possible risk.

Midwifery staff. Antenatal, postnatal delivery, Special Care units, community care.

Nursing staff. Across the board covering obstetric and paediatric input, community work, and especially specialities such as health advising.

General practitioners. Doctors form a front line access to medical input and much of the patients' experience may hinge on the abilities and expertise of their GP together with the GP's willingness to treat them, to give them insightful care, and to either provide front line counselling or refer them on.

Health advisers. These include all front line workers involved in advice and help around issues of sexually transmitted diseases.

Other agencies. There are a wide range of agencies who may need training and who may, at any given point, be involved in contact or care of women or babies affected by HIV.

For all carers, there are a set of common principles which permeate all disciplines:

(a) Basic information. Accurate factual information is a pre-requisite for work and should be the minimum requirement for anyone offering care.
(b) Decision making and behaviour change are the key elements of a counselling approach.
(c) When there is a knowledge limitation this must be conveyed to the client.

Staff training

Although there are many studies on training, few have been directed specifically at obstetric staff. There have been numerous studies which have shown that the advent of AIDS may affect recruitment into hospital units and training schemes (Strunin 1989) and that knowledge and attitudes play a part in willingness to treat and career decision making (Feingold 1988).

Counselling training for health care staff is a specialized field and is seen as a crucial component for AIDS and HIV (Miller & Pinching 1989). Psychological aspects include risk assessment, risk adjustment, behaviour change, decision making, anxiety and stress management, life crisis, relationship problems, death, dying and bereavement. Counselling training also allows for a reduction in anxiety in health care staff about such encounters (Sherr & McCreaner 1989).

An accurate factual knowledge base is a pre-requisite for good quality health care for women and children affected by AIDS and HIV. Often there are considerable knowledge gaps (Sherr 1987; 1988) and sometimes these are not significantly altered over time (Sherr 1989). Public health education campaigns often permeate into the health worker knowledge base. More sophisticated knowledge and the ability to apply this and convey it to an uninformed patient is a skill which needs training and refining.

In a study on obstetric and gynaecology staff training (Sherr 1987), a group of obstetric staff were monitored before and after intervention. Training comprised specialized teaching in HIV screening, AIDS and obstetrics, counselling interventions and infection control. A group of obstetric staff who were exposed to a non-relevant training intervention were similarly monitored for comparison. It was shown that training significantly increased knowledge and reduced anxiety about dealing with HIV-positive patients. Input also resulted in a shift away from HIV testing in cases of uncertainty. Simply raising the issue of HIV with staff in the absence of input (control group) resulted in increased anxiety.

This same study monitored the benefits of staff training and highlighted how short-term training could go a long way in preparing staff on how to care for HIV-positive patients, allowing them to examine their policy and procedure on HIV-testing and encouraging them to appreciate the psychological cost of screening to women. Counselling skills can be markedly improved if such training is successful.

Staff training packages will depend on a number of factors. These include:

- Facilities available;
- Background infection;
- Patient group;
- Pre-existing skills;
- Motivation;
- Policy.

Numerous staff training packages now exist and these can be adapted and incorporated into most settings. The key element of good training should be to ensure that it is relevant and applicable locally (Sherr & McCreaner 1989).

Staff training can occur at numerous career phases, geared to an individual's qualifications and experience:

(1) Prior to qualification. Ideally, new staff training programmes should include HIV and AIDS training. This will ensure that in the

future specialized work is incorporated into standard training and minimum standards can be ensured.

(2) During qualification. New problems, such as AIDS and HIV, may necessitate training. It is important not to de-skill staff in the face of new challenges, but to incorporate new knowledge into their knowledge base. It is also important that training comes early on, is ongoing, and precedes policy making and patient referral.

(3) On exposure. Once exposed to patients with HIV and AIDS, staff may need specified training. This should be adjusted to meet their individual needs, focus on their deficits, and supplement their skills. This can take various forms.

(4) After exposure. It is often not possible for all staff to be trained prior to exposure. However, there is much to be learned from debriefing and follow-up. It is especially important for this to occur with a new and sometimes frightening illness where staff are faced with multiple concerns, uncertainty, and life threatening illness. In the absence of such educational input, staff may withdraw, put up barriers, and provide a reduced service in the future.

Counselling skills form a special area. Most health care workers are confronted with counselling situations. Much learning is centred around experience and observation. However, counselling is a skill which must be practised in order to be perfected. Thus theoretical learning from books is not sufficient. In other professions the tools of the trade may be novel, even alien, to begin with; formal training is required in order to understand how to use them. The sheer familiarity in everyday life with communication skills such as listening and talking may lead to a tendency to undervalue the training process. Staff education in counselling is central to ensure that staff do not presume skills where none exist. Indeed, other studies in obstetric care have shown that the simple motivation to 'try harder' does not affect outcome. This was shown in an early study in doctor–patient communication in obstetric care by Houghton (1967) who found that there were no discernible differences in the group who agreed to 'try harder'.

Rutter and Maguire (1977) have shown how medical students have limitations in their interviewing and communication skills. They further showed that short-term training significantly enhanced such skills. Sherr and Sherr (1981) showed that professionals could be trained in communication skills and those who were trained were perceived as more proficient by clients.

Sherr, Davey and Strong (1990) have shown that specialized training in areas of anxiety, depression and suicide is necessary and helpful, but short training may be ineffective in removing deeply ingrained myths (particularly with regard to suicide) and, in the absence of such skills, counsellors often resort to their lay beliefs on aetiology and treatment of psychological conditions.

Training in HIV should contain the following elements:

- Setting up a training course;
- Aims and goals;
- Participants;
- Evaluation;
- Content;
- Follow-up.

Short training courses may not lead directly to skilled counsellors. However, it is still possible to attune them to counselling issues and increase their awareness of counselling approaches. Sherr and McCreaner summarize seven guiding points:

(1) The majority of carers are usually already in possession of skills which, for various reasons, they do not use in their clinic situation;
(2) Basic information is the foundation stone of all good counselling. Mere possession of the facts is not the total requirement. Workers also need to have the skills to convey these facts accurately and clearly to patients.
(3) Many professionals have not developed good listening skills.
(4) Counselling practice with constructive feedback is an important component of any training scheme.
(5) AIDS and HIV have wide-reaching ramifications. Training can be extended to incorporate these (such as dealing with sexuality, death, voluntary service, suicide and so on).
(6) There are many ways of learning and teaching. Training programmes should be innovative and should try multiple ways to maximize their efficacy for the majority of trainees.
(7) Training needs follow-up.

Counselling skills are active rather than passive. They need to be practised. It is difficult to incorporate theory and theoretical learning from books into an active skill without practising and, ideally, receiving feedback with a subsequent opportunity to practise. The forms of feedback that are effective may vary. Some workers have shown beneficial effects from peer review, good use of audio-visual technology, role modelling, and role play.

Essentially, there are cognitive and behavioural aspects to counselling, and training should incorporate both.

In some circumstances, staff will be called upon to carry out a counselling task without direct training. The key items to cover should include:

Basic facts. All staff working with AIDS and HIV must have an accurate and up-to-date working knowledge of the subject. This includes a clear understanding both of what is known and what is not known. They need to know where their knowledge ends, and where to turn (or where their patients can turn) for full facts.

Recall. Staff need to understand that counselling is not simply imparting knowledge to patients. Even with this task there are problems related to communication skills and the limits that people have on their ability to recall multiple items. This limit is often reduced in the presence of stress.

Enhance recall. There are numerous tactics which can enhance recall and all workers who are involved in imparting information should be familiar with these. They include simplification of content, clarity, structuring, pacing, and dividing and supplementing with tools such as written material, repetition, notes or follow-up.

Jargon can stand in the way of good communication and should be avoided or explained.

Questioning forms a key element in all encounters and counsellors must be trained to use questioning helpfully and to facilitate questioning in their clients.

Listening skills can be learned and form a key element to any counselling encounter.

Anxiety may be a major factor throughout. It may affect all interaction, it may limit recall, it may affect behaviour and may cause extensive distress to clients.

Coping is one of the major goals of counselling. It is never easy to help people with coping. Simply telling them what to do is rarely helpful. One needs to explore the options the client feels able to entertain, the obstacles which may hinder such options, and ways of overcoming such obstacles.

Counselling is not necessarily passive. Other active skills such as relaxation may usefully supplement counselling knowledge. Counsellors should have an understanding of different avenues of input which may be helpful such as individual work, couples work, family work, group work, feedback and individual participation.

Counsellors should be familiar with pain management and decision making skills. Sexuality is often a difficult and touchy subject for staff to handle. Dodd and Parsons (1984) outline factors, including information and full training, which may be useful to help with the insightful assessment of patients and discussions on sexuality.

Examples of training courses available

Many institutions have initiated widespread training for AIDS and HIV. The WHO has set up numerous packages and in other centres either local or national initiatives have been launched (Sherr 1989).

Experience with such training courses has shown that long-term requirements change with the passage of time. In the early days, there was a great demand for straightforward factual information. With the passage of time there is a need for more skill-based learning together with updating.

Courses need to have clear strategies and goals. Evaluation is vital to facilitate insight and to point out change and future direction. Sherr (1988) found that the provision of training often created a new need rather than satisfying old needs. Sherr and McCreaner (1989) described the impact of training workshops on a group of 100 health care workers. They were questioned prior to attendance, immediately after attendance, and at six months follow-up. The data revealed a high demand for education, specifically for counselling skills. Workshop participants comprised those who had patient exposure and those who had none. Workshops reduced anxiety about contact, procedures, and counselling. This reduction was maintained at six-month follow-up. Work with AIDS and HIV infection brings with it some levels of stress, but one must not underestimate the level of reward that it brings as well. Anticipated demand for training in this study was high given poor local facilities and high demand.

Sherr and McCreaner (1989) examined the training needs and sources for high and low stressed workers. They found that educational input was a significant factor associated with reduced stress level. Essentially, staff were poor at turning to venues outside of the institution and education was often used as a stress reduction mechanism.

Finally, trainers need to be flexible. At some point staff reach saturation and find it difficult to take on new training ideas.

Some staff use education as a support channel and continuous updating may be vital in an ever-changing field. Sherr and Hedge (1990) found that training for obstetric staff was highly rated and significantly reduced anxiety about contact with HIV patients, taking blood, and delivery.

Staff support

Staff support is an insurance policy for continued high level input. Unsupported staff soon reach breaking point and cannot be expected to provide high level input over extended periods of time. Some staff feel no need for support. However, this does not mean they do not have needs. A good staff training system will ensure that input can be tailored to staff needs. For example, Sherr and George (1988) found that staff in the UK preferred educational meetings to support groups. It was possible that such staff gained beneficial input from the content of such meetings as well as deriving benefit from the informal contacts made around such meetings. Thus the provision of educational updates and seminars may play a vital role in informing staff and supporting them.

Pasacreta and Jacobsen (1989) identify the problems that nursing staff may face and urge the need to contrast this with the challenges and rewards which are also part of the care package. These involve the ability to make a meaningful contribution to a new frontier, of providing care for a group of patients who may suffer from discrimination, and the ability to become involved in research and clinical care. They identify differences between nurses who have limited or no previous exposure to patients and those who, on the other hand, specialize in AIDS care. The underexposed group may have concerns about contagion which can manifest in behaviours which will remove them from the wards. They may have rational or irrational fears which need accurate current information in order to be managed. The experienced group have often come to terms with fears of contagion but these can often be reawakened. Yet their main problem is with the symptoms of 'burnout' (overwork, stress, feeling undervalued, and becoming distanced from the emotional pain of the work) (Pines & Maslach 1978). These workers set up a staff support group. Although they claim benefit, no empirical data was gathered.

Provision of information (patient education and health education)

Information is often seen as a major antidote for anxiety, panic and fear. AIDS is no different. Health education in the light of AIDS and

HIV is a necessity and not a luxury. Information and health education have been the major offensive weapons against this virus. Everyone agrees that health education is necessary, but few agree on why this is so. Indeed, many campaigns have fallen short because there has not been a clear aim. Health education campaigns serve many purposes. They need to inform the public at large. They need to educate the public about protection from infection. They need to educate the public about compassionate and appropriate reactions to the infected. They may also have hidden agendas such as that of a government which needs to be seen to be reacting to AIDS. Thus the many roles of public information and health education make it difficult to assess the world-wide AIDS information explosion. The net effect has been a global increase in knowledge. From being an obscure term ten years ago, AIDS and HIV have now become household words. It is now important not to ask the question 'do health education campaigns work?' but rather to understand the way in which they work, how they affect people, who they affect, in what way the effect is noted, and the mechanisms involved. This would allow for a greater insight and assist planning and prediction.

Health education programmes have been mounted to inform the infected, inform those at high risk, and inform the general public. Aims include: to prevent the spread of AIDS, to reduce anxiety, to ensure appropriate reaction to people with HIV or AIDS, and to update those involved in care provision.

Health education has used many modes including mass media, traditional educational input, theatre, and active and passive learning, to mention only a few.

The content has been either for general consumption or aimed at particular audiences. Targeted information packages have been compiled for the needs of particular groups. Women in general may have their own needs. Pregnant women may desire information or may want full factual knowledge prior to HIV screening. The advent of HIV screening may necessitate such leaflets where verbal input cannot be provided because of the sheer volume of patients. An example of this is the UK government information campaign which preceded and paralleled the seroprevalence study in obstetric clinics, accident and emergency, and STD clinics.

Sherr and Hedge (1990) examined the impact of an information leaflet on antenatal clinic attenders. They found that there was no effect in terms of anxiety reduction, reassurance, or attitude towards HIV-testing in pregnancy. However, they also found that the leaflet in question had many limitations and this may have accounted for the findings. Based on this study an improved leaflet was utilized. One can thus conclude that for written material clear aims are necessary. In addition, optimum results are obtained when written material is pre-tested.

A study by Sherr and Hedge (1990) examined the use of written material as an alternative for counselling input in antenatal clinics. They found that in a large London centre there were only three leaflets in common use. Readability varied across the leaflets. In depth group discussion highlighted some of the limitations of such leaflets. Essentially, groups of women felt that the leaflets themselves might rouse anxiety. The leaflets would be at their most useful if they were distributed with care. Simply leaving them out in clinics for self-selection was found to be useless as all women agreed that the social stigma of taking such a leaflet in a public place would intimidate them. They were worried if leaflets were posted to them as this might imply reason for concern by health care staff. They thought such leaflets should be backed up by a question and answer session. In conclusion, it was felt that such material, if of high standard and relevant to the recipient population, was useful but limited. It was good as an adjunct to counselling but not seen as sufficient to stand in its stead. The leaflets already in existence were shown to a group of raters the majority of whom felt there was a bias (although direction differed). This finding points to the fact that it is difficult to construct an adequate leaflet, yet alone a bias-free one.

In conclusion, the advantages of written material are:

- It can be targeted at a particular audience and encompass particular needs;
- It can convey a substantial amount of information;
- It can be taken home and kept for future reference;
- It may serve as a useful conversation opener in a quest for further information;
- It may go some way towards ensuring that patients (especially pregnant women) are giving informed consent to testing;
- Without adequate information choice is limited or even effectively denied. The provision of information may serve to enhance choice;
- It may be helpful if a policy of risk identification is used in a centre.

The disadvantages of written material are:

- It needs to be readable, understood, and recalled before it can be of any practical use. This is often difficult to attain with a written document;

- It may not reach all clients – especially those who do not share the language of the leaflet, the culture of the leaflet, or who are unable to read;
- It cannot be seen as a substitute for counselling;
- It may raise more anxiety than it resolves;
- It may never reach the target audience, and staff, unaware of this, may fail to discuss HIV and AIDS with patients in the false belief that the leaflet or written material has already done this;
- It may reflect a biased point of view.

Leaflet construction is difficult and the following pointers should be remembered:

- Presentation is important. A leaflet which is not read is impotent;
- Simple clear messages are the easiest to recall and understand;
- Leaflets should be jargon-free. If jargon is necessary then it ought to be explained;
- Contrast is useful. This assists attention, recall and understanding. Use of colour, graphics, pictures and symbols are good;
- Breakdown enhances readability. The use of subheadings, flow charts, tables and graphs can assist in breaking down complex information;
- Readability is a key factor. All leaflets should be subjected to some of the readability scales to ensure that they will be understood by the population for whom they are written;
- Follow-up must be included in a leaflet. If leaflets do not address all needs, then this should be anticipated. Follow-up strategies, telephone numbers, addresses, contact people or action should be clearly outlined;
- Leaflet construction should take into account factors which receive the attention of the audience as well as factors which facilitate the message. As such, fear arousal may be effective to gain attention, but may be useless in altering behaviour. Other methods should be tried, such as humour, intrigue, compassion and so on.

Impact of health education

Health education may have differing impacts. Miller (1987) noted that work load in STD clinics was greatly increased when the UK government mounted its initial health education campaigns. Such effects ought to be anticipated and general health education campaigns should be preceded by staff training. Funding for campaigns should include counsellors to react to panic responses, requests for information and testing.

There may be a need for specialized training where children are concerned.

Policy should be preceded by training. In the UK, it was intended to use antenatal clinics for HIV sero-prevalence screening in a project in 1990. The first announcements for this policy were made through the press. Thus midwifery and medical staff at the clinics concerned were not informed or well-prepared prior to notification of the public. This left them potentially ill-equipped to respond accurately and with reassurance to public enquiries. A survey of midwifery staff at that time (Sherr & Brierly in preparation) found that a high proportion of staff had heard about the study through the press. Many respondents would have welcomed more training or resources to provide training for a wider range of staff.

Conclusion

Training is a key element in the battle against AIDS and the provision of care. Although the immediate results are sometimes not very obvious, it is important that accurate knowledge is used to combat fears and anxieties and to engender behaviour change. Some examples have been outlined here. Yet there are many more possible avenues for health education which can be explored. Evaluation is vital at all levels. This should not only highlight success and failure, but should document why approaches work, how they work and who they work for.

Chapter 13

What the Future Holds

It is hard to be optimistic in the presence of the preceding chapters. Yet gloom and doom do not help positively and the future needs to be faced in a practical and sensible manner.

Research

Only with ongoing research will workers have a full understanding of the nature of the problems they face, the optimum modes of intervention, and the efficacy of treatment programmes. Research should not be done at the expense of clinical care. AIDS presents a challenge where many workers are faced with overwhelming and immediate problems and research may be seen as a luxury which can be ill afforded. In such circumstances workers simply proceed in the way they feel most appropriate. It is perfectly possible to incorporate research into such strategies. A simple and systematic monitoring of progress can still provide feedback on the efficacy of such interventions, highlight pitfalls which perhaps could not have been anticipated, and point the way for the future.

There are many urgent questions that need to be answered by research. Is there a preferred organ of manifestation of HIV in fetal tissue? When and how does HIV cross the placenta? Is there a difference in postnatal outcome (for mother and baby) according to time of infection? Are there different virus strains and what are their effects? What are the interactive effects of other medical factors with HIV such as malnutrition, disease, drug effects, STDs. What are the effects of counselling? Do they increase condom uptake, decrease anal intercourse, affect termination, affect pregnancy rate, quality of life and adjustment? What are the parenting demands and challenges in the presence of HIV? Are children over-protected – are they told of HIV? If not, what are the reasons and are they based in fact or myth? Long-term follow-up of children who sero-revert or who were never HIV-positive but were born to HIV-positive mothers needs to be carried out. The list of challenges is seemingly endless.

Planning

When an epidemic is in its early stages, planners can either face the problems to come and attempt to create a strategy or they can shrug it off, hope it will go away and fail to prepare adequately. The global statistics on AIDS and HIV infection cannot be ignored. Networks must be set up early in the day. If there are resource limitations or indeed a total lack of resources, workers need to think through how their available resources will be best adapted.

Studies on the future special needs of children with HIV infection and AIDS clearly point to the need to provide special educational input for children in the future. In the West, the numbers are now small but growing. The full extent of the problem has not yet been documented in the developing countries.

Specific problems

There are numerous specific problems which have been identified in relation to mothers and babies. AIDS orphans are a phenomena which will require close monitoring and the input of resources. Preparation should ensure that children are not dispersed from their siblings and that support is given to overburdened relatives who take on much of the burden. Planning and preparation will be the antidote to disaster. When relatives and extended family members are not available to care for the child, systems of fostering should be examined. Previous models may be inadequate to contain the problems associated with AIDS and HIV. The literature on adoption generally must be consulted when children with AIDS or HIV infection, or those born to parents afffected by HIV, are to be adopted. Adoption may be generally affected by HIV screening and workers need to ensure that the rights of children are not overlooked.

Extended families carry much of the burden, especially in countries where there are limited resources. These include not only wider family members, but particularly grandparents, who may carry a heavy burden. They may have to face the loss of their own children and the need to become primary caretakers for their grandchildren. This may be at the very time when they were giving up work and in need of some care themselves. Thus the loss of income and support from their children adds to the strain. Furthermore, future generations may be affected. When these children grow up and have their own children, there will be no grandparents for them to turn to. The generation who lose their parents now will give birth to a generation who will never know the love and affection of grandparents.

Treatment, care and understanding must go hand in hand with prevention strategies. Although the focus of this text has been on the psychological aspects of HIV and AIDS, workers need to have a comprehensive understanding of the medical background and clinical factors associated with HIV. Those workers who are not conversant with these need to foster close multi-disciplinary co-operation. One of the skills of a good counsellor must be to understand where individual limitations lie whilst at the same time having good access to channels or sources which can address such limitations.

Innovative strategies for coping with AIDS and HIV must be explored. There are considerable obstacles to progress. AIDS work has constantly been hampered by the marginalization of some individuals within affected groups. This must be avoided in a joint effort to combat the devastating effects of HIV on the community at large and mothers and babies in particular.

The particular role of women in society has much bearing on the way in which this epidemic will unfold. There are no texts on HIV that are particularly dedicated to men. Why should women be different? Is it that they are different or that the fact that they are overlooked highlights their need and necessitates specialized attention? It may well be a combination of the two.

As HIV affects women and babies, early intervention must be a priority. Workers should examine avenues which are already utilized and interject counselling and education at these points. Such venues may include family planning centres. Family planning advice may vary with the advent of HIV and the use of condoms may need particular promotion.

As data unfold workers need to track whether any of the affected children are exhibiting developmental delays. As treatment for the opportunistic infections becomes more sophisticated and effective, survival of these children will increase. This will necessitate specialized input for these children to maximize their skills and their life opportunity. It may also place an enormous burden of care onto the shoulders of caretakers and respite care should be seen as a necessity. This should be provided before the strain is noted and not when families reach breaking point.

One of the greatest difficulties with AIDS and HIV is the concept of multiple illness and multiple infections. This means that a family may be in the constant shadow of illness.

All the above are made more problematic by the demands for strict confidentiality and the level of secrecy and stigma associated with HIV infection. The urgent agenda must be to ensure acceptance and demystification of this virus so that the burden of secrecy and stigma can be removed for those who are already overburdened. Until such time, confidentiality must be taken with great seriousness.

In the light of the above, the challenges for the future are clear. They set an agenda for humanity to lower its petty borders and to provide humane care. Wherever possible, suffering should be alleviated and pain should be minimized. When previous models of care prove inadequate to accommodate the wide range of needs, workers may have to involve other approaches which allow for decision making and control wherever this is possible or practical. Workers have to take care not to judge.

For children, especially young infants, the challenges for workers are to provide continuity of care. This care needs to be of high quality and should address both their physical and emotional requirements.

Pregnancy, with all its promise, usually signifies emotions of joy and hope. HIV represents a contradiction which may overshadow much of the experience. But whatever the hurdles, pregnant women, babies, families and workers are vibrant and living, touched by hope, happiness, fears, uncertainty, laughter and tears. In the face of all this, it is essential to maintain optimism and hope. Workers can only hope to provide high quality care if they are able to give of themselves and that means ensuring that their own stress levels are minimized and that they are fully supported.

References

Abercrombie M.L.J. (1964) *Perceptual and Visuo-Motor Disorders in Cerebral Palsy*, Spastics Society/Heinemann.

Adam K.S. (1982) Loss suicide and attachment. In *The place of attachment in human behaviour*, (Ed. by C.M. Parkes & J. Stevenson Hinde). Basic Books, New York.

Aguero G., Wignall F.S., Alexander W. et al. (1987) *HIV infections in Peru*. III Int. Cont. on AIDS, 5087.

Anderson E.M. & Spain B. (1977) *The Child with Spina Bifida*, Methuen, London.

Araneta M.R., Thomas P.A., Cedeno S. et al. (1987) *Seroprevalence of HIV 1 among pregnant women at time of birth and abortion in NYC-87*. III Int. Conf. on AIDS, 4037.

Areskog-Wijma B. (1987) The gynaecological examination – women's experiences and preferences and the role of the gynaecologist. *Jnl. of Psychosomatic Obstet. and Gynec.*, **6**, 59–69.

Armson B.A. Mennuti T.D. & Talbog G.H. (1987) *Seroprevalence of HIV in an obstetric population*. III Int. Conf. on AIDS, 4629.

Astbury J. (1980) Labour pain – the role of childbirth education information expectation. In *Problems in Pain* (Ed. by C. Peck & M. Wallace). Pergamon Press, Oxford.

Barbacci M. (1989) *Identification of HIV seropositivity during pregnancy and its effect on future pregnancy decisions*. E6, WHO Paris Conference.

Barbacci M. (1990) Paper presented at VI Int. Conf. on AIDS, San Francisco, THC 41.

Barbacci M., Chaisson R., Anderson J. et al. (1989) *Knowledge of HIV serostatus and pregnancy decisions*. V Int. Conf. on AIDS, Montreal, ABS MBP 10.

Barbacci M., Quinn T., Kline R. et al. (1989) *Failure of targetted screening to identify HIV-positive pregnant women*. V Int. Conf. on AIDS, Montreal, ABS MBP 5.

Barbour R., Macintyre S., McIlwaine G. & Wilson E. (1989) Uptake of AIDS counselling and testing at a Scottish family planning clinic. *B. Jnl. of Family Planning 1989*, **15**, 61–2.

Barreto J., Araujo T., Bergstrom S. et al. (1987) *Comparative study on HIV in pregnant women, Maputo Mozambique 82/83 & 88*. III Int. Conf. on AIDS, 4035.

Barton J., O'Connor T., Cannon M.J. & Weldon Linne C.M., (1989) Prevalence of human immunodeficiency virus in a general prenatal population. *Am. Jnl. of Obstet. and Gynec.*, Vol 160, **6**, 1316–24.

Beck A., Rush A., Shaw B. & Emery C. (1979) *Cognitive Therapy of Depression*. Wiley, Chichester.

Beck A.T. (1976) *Cognitive Therapy and Emotional Disorders*. Int. Univ. Press, New York.

Beck E., Donegan C., Cohen C.S. et al. (1989) Risk factors for HIV 1 infection in a British Population: Lessons from a London STD Clinic. *AIDS*, **3**, 533–8.

Belman A. (1989) *Neurologic manifestations of human immunodeficiency virus infection in infants and children*. WHO Mother and Babies AIDS Conference, Paris.

Belman A.L., Lantos G., Horoupian D. & Novick B.E. (1986) AIDS calcification of the basal ganglia in infants and children. *Neurology*, **36**, 1192–9.

Belman A.L., Diamond G.W., Dickson D., Horoupian D., Llena J., Lantos G. & Rubinstein A. (1988) Pediatric acquired immunodeficiency syndrome neurologic symptoms. *A Jnl of Diseases of Children*, **142**, p. 29.

Berrebi A. (1990) Paper presented at VI Int. Conf. on AIDS, San Francisco, THC 651.

Berthaud M., Marcel A., Sunderland A. et al. (1987) *HIV infection in pregnant Haitian women*. III Int. Conf. on AIDS 9547.

Bird A.G. & Snow M.H. (1988) HIV monitoring of pregnant women. *The Lancet*, March 26, p. 713.

Birtchnell J. (1971) Early parent death in relation to size and constitution of sibship in psychiatric patients and general population controls. *Acta Psychiatrica Scandinavica*, **47**, 250–70.

Birtchnell J. (1975) Psychiatric breakdown following recent parent death. *B. Jnl. of Med. Psy.*, **48**, 379–90.

Black D. (1974) *What happens to bereaved children*. Proceedings of Royal Society of Medicine, **69**, 38–40.

Blanche S., Rouzioux C., Guhard M. et al. (1989) A prospective study of infants born to women seropositive for human immunodeficiency virus type 1. *New Engl. J. Med.*, **320**, 1643–8.

Bledsoe K.L. et al. (1990) Paper presented at VI Int. Conf. on AIDS, San Francisco, THC 652.

Bluebond-Langer M. (1978) *The private worlds of dying children*. Princeton University Press, Princeton.

Bohlin A.B. et al. (1990) Paper presented at VI Int. Conf. on AIDS, San Francisco, PB 442.

Boulos R. (1989) Papers presented at V Int. Conf. on AIDS, Montreal.

Boulos R. (1990) Paper presented at VI Int. Conf. on AIDS, San Francisco.

Boulos R., Hasley N., Brutus J. et al. (1987) *Risk factors for HIV 1 infection in pregnant Haitian women*. III Int. Conf. on AIDS 5119.

Boulos R., Halsey N., Holt E., Brutus J.R., Quinn T. et al. (1989) *Factors associated with HIV 1 in pregnant Haitian Women*, WHO Paris Conference, E5.

Bower, T.G.R. (1974) *Development in Infancy*, Freeman, San Francisco.

Braddick M., Datta P., Embree J. et al. (1987) *Progression of HIV following pregnancy*. III Int. Conf. on AIDS, 5121.

Braddick M., Kreiss J., Quinn T. et al. (1988) *Congenital transmission of HIV in Nairobi, Kenya*. IV Int. Conf. on AIDS, TH 75.

Brandt T. et al. (1990) Paper presented at VI Int. Conf. on AIDS, San Francisco.

Brattebo G. & Wiseborg T. (1988) HIV monitoring of pregnant women. *The Lancet*, March 26, 713–14.

Braverman J. & Roux F.J.L. (1978) Screening for the patient at risk for postpartum depression. *Obstetrics and Gynaecology*, **52**, 731.

Brierly J. (1987) Human immunodeficiency virus: The challenge of a lifetime. *Midwives Chronicle and Nursing Notes*, II, sup x–xiii.

Brierly J. (1989) AIDS and Midwifery.

British Birth Survey (1988) HMSO London.

Brossard Y., Goudeau A., Larsen M. et al. (1987) *A Sero Ep Study of HIV in 15,646 pregnant women in Paris Feb–Oct 1987*. III Int. Conf. on AIDS, 4632.

Brown L.K. & Fritz K. (1988) Children's knowledge and attitudes about AIDS. *Jnl. of Am. Ac. of Ch. & Adolesc. Psychiatry*, 27, 4, 501–508.

Brown G.W. & Harris J.O. (1978) *Social Origins of Depression*, Tavistock, London.

Brunet J.B. (1989) Paper presented at the WHO Paris Conference.

Bucceri A. et al. (1989) Paper presented at the WHO Paris Conference.

Bucherl, Heiner, Frosner C.G. (1987) *Low prevalence of HIV 1 Infection in a rural area of Kenya*. III Int. Conf. on AIDS 5051.

Buckett W.M., Conlon M.H., Luesley D.M. & Lawton F.G. (1988) Attitudes of a multiracial antenatal population to HIV screening

B.M.J. Feb 28, 296, 6622, p. 643.

Buckingham R.W. (1989) *Care of the dying child – a practical guide for those who help others.* Continuum, New York.

Burnard P. (1990) Counselling skills for health professionals. *Therapy in Practice 9.* Chapman Hall, London.

Carroll J.F.K. (1979) Staff burnout as a form of ecological dysfunction. *Contemporary Drug Problems 8,* 207–227.

Caselli D. (1989) *Uncommon source for HIV: vertical transmission in Italy.* WHO Paris Conference, B29.

Caspe W.L. et al. (1990) Paper presented at VI Int. Conf. on AIDS, San Francisco, SC 667.

CDC (1990) *The new faces of AIDS. A maternal and pediatric epidemic.* US Dept of Health and Human Services Report, June 1990.

CDSC Communicable Disease Report 1989 89/27: 3–4.

Centers for Disease Control, CDC Surveillance Supplements MMWR 1989.

Chalmers I., Enkin M. & Keirse M.J. (1989) *Effective care in pregnancy and childbirth.* Oxford University Press, Oxford.

Chase E. et al. (1990) Paper presented at VI Int. Conf. on AIDS, San Francisco.

Cheek J. (1990) Paper presented at VI Int. Conf. on AIDS, San Francisco, FC221.

Chin J. (1989) *The economic and demographic aspects of HIV infection in women and children.* WHO Conference, Paris, 259.

Chin J. (1989) *Estimates and projections of perinatal transmission of HIV V.* Int. Conf. on AIDS, Montreal, TBO 18.

Chin J., Sankaran G. & Mann J. (1989) Mother to infant transmission of HIV: an increasing global problem. In *Maternal and Child Health Care in Developing Countries,* Ed. by E. Kessel and A. Awan, 299–306, WHO, Switzerland.

Chiphangwi J., Keller M., Ndovi E. et al. (1987) *Prevalence of HIV 1 infection in pregnant women in Malawi.* III Int. Conf. on AIDS, 5037.

Chiphangwi J. (1989) *Transmission of HIV infection from mother to child in developing countries.* WHO Conference, Paris.

Cirara N. (1990) Paper presented at VI Int. Conf. on AIDS, San Francisco.

Ciraru-Vigneron N. Nguyen R. Tan Ung. et al. (1987) *Prospective study for HIV infection among high risk pregnant women.* III Int. Conf. on AIDS, 4627.

Coden M. (1989) Paper presented at WHO Conference, Paris.

Connor E., Thomas D., Goode L. et al. (1989) *Seroprealence of HIV 1 and HTLV 1 among pregnant women in Newark NJ.* V Int. Conf. on AIDS,

Montreal, ABS MBP19.

Corey G. (1982) *Theory and practice of counselling and psychotherapy.* Brooks/Cole, Monterey CA.

Cowan J.E. et al. (1990) Paper presented at VI Int. Conf. on AIDS, San Francisco, SC 708.

Crandon A.J. (1979) Maternal anxiety and obstetric complications. *Jnl. of Psychosomatic Research*, **23**, 109–11.

Crombleholme W. (1990) Paper presented at VI Int. Conf. on AIDS, San Francisco, THC 605.

Dalton K. (1971) *Depression after childbirth*. Oxford University Press, Oxford.

Dalton K. (1971) Prospective study into puerperal depression. *Brit. J. Psychiat.*, **118**, 689.

Dalton K. (1982) *Premenstrual syndrome and progesterone therapy*, Heinemann, London.

Datla P. (1990) VI Int. Conf. on AIDS, San Francisco, THC 611.

Davids A. (1961) Anxiety, pregnancy and childbirth abnormalities. *Jnl. of Consulting Psychology*, **25**, 76–77.

Davison C.F., Hudson C.N., Ades A.E., Peckham C.S. (1989) Antenatal testing for human immunodeficiency virus. *The Lancet*, Dec 16, 1442–4.

Decarie T.G. (1969) A study of the mental and emotional development of the thalidomide child, in *Determinants of Infant Behaviour, Vol IV*, ed. by B.M. Foss. Methuen, London.

Delaporte E. (1990) Paper presented at VI Int. Conf. on AIDS, San Francisco, THC 618.

Delaporte E., Dazza M.C., Wain Hobson S. et al. (1988) *HIV related viruses in pregnant women in Gabon.* IV Int. Conf. on AIDS, WP32.

De Menezes Succi R. (1989) *Latin America and the Caribbean.* WHO AIDS Conference, Paris.

De Rossi A., Giaquantio C., Zacchello F. et al. (1987) *Is HIV testing of unselected pregnant women high priority in Italy?* III Int. Conf. on AIDS, 4633.

De Rossi A., Chieco Bianchi L., Giaquinto C. & Zacchello F. (1988) Letter to *The Lancet*, March 26, p. 714.

Denayer M., Jonckheer T., Piot P. & Stroobrant A. (1990) Antental testing for HIV *The Lancet*, Feb 3, p. 292.

Des Jarlais D.C. & Friedman S.R. (1988) Gender differences in response to HIV infection. In *Psychological, neuropsychiatric and substance abuse aspects of AIDS*. (Ed. by T.P. Bridge), Raven Press, New York.

Des Jarlais D.C. & Friedman S.K. (1989) AIDS and IV drug use. *Science* 245 (4918), 578.

Di John D. (1990) Paper presented at VI Int. Conf. on AIDS, San Francisco, THC 565.

Dodd B.G. & Parsons A.D. (1984) Psychological problems. In *Psychology and gynaecological problems* (Ed. by A. Broome & L. Wallace), 189–210, Tavistock Publications, London.

Donegan S.P., Edelin K.C. & Craven D.E. (1987) *Prevalence of antibodies to HIV in fetal cord blood*. III Int. Conf. on AIDS, 4629.

Donnai P., Charles N. & Harris R. (1981) Attitudes of patients after genetic termination of pregnancy. *BMJ*, **282**, 621–2

Douglas J.W.B. (1970) Broken families and child behaviour. *Jnl. Royal Coll. of Physicians of London*, **8**, 203–210.

Dowd E.T. (Ed) (1981) Leisure counselling. Special Issue, *Counselling Psychologist*, **9**, (3).

Duerr A.C. (1990) Paper presented at VI Int. Conf. on AIDS, San Francisco, THC 575/6.

Duggan C. (1990) Paper presented at Institute of Child Health AIDS and Women/Children Study Day.

Dunlop J.Z. (1978) Counselling patients requesting an abortion. *Practitioner*, **220**, 847–5.

Dunn J. (1984) *Sisters and Brothers*. Fontana, London.

Eland J.M. & Anderson J.E. (1977) The experience of pain in children. In *Pain a source book for nurses and other professionals* (Ed. by A. Jacox), 453–473, Little Brown, Boston.

Elliott S.A. (1984) Pregnancy and after. In *Contributions to Medical Psychology*, vol 3, (Ed. by S. Rachman), Pergamon Press, Oxford.

Elliott S.A., Rugg A.J., Watson J.P. & Brough D.I. (1983) Mood change during pregnancy and after the birth of a child. *Brit. Jnl. of Clinical Psychology*, 1983.

Ellis A. (1979) *New developments in R.E.T.*, Brooks Cole, Monterey, Cal.

Enkin M. (1982) Antenatal classes. In *Effectiveness and satisfaction in antenatal care*, Ed. by M. Enkin & I. Chalmers, Spastics International Medical Books, London.

Epstein L.G., Sharer L.R., Oleske J.M., Connor E.M., Goudsmit J., Bagdon L., Robert Guroff M. & Koenigsberger M.R. (1986) Neurologic manifestations of human immunodeficiency virus infection in children. *Pediatrics*, **78**, 678–87.

European Collaborative Study (1988) Mother to child transmission of HIV infection. *The Lancet*, ii, 1039–42.

European Collaborative Study (1991) Children born to women with HIV 1 infection: natural history and risk of transmission. *The Lancet*, Feb 2, 8736, vol 337, 253–60.

Evatt B. (1989) *The first and second epidemics*. Abst V. Int. Conf. on

AIDS, Montreal, THB 031.

Farrant W. (1979) *Amniocentesis procedures and correlated stress experience for mothers.* Human Relations in Obstetrics Workshop, Warwick.

Farrant W. (1980) Stress after amniocentesis for high serum alphafeto-protein concentrates. *BMJ*, **2**, 452.

Feingold A. (1988) Paper presented at the Int. Conf. on AIDS, Washington.

Felner R.D., Genter M.A., Bocke M.F. & Cowen E.L. (1981) Parental death or divorce and the school adjustment of young children. *Am. Jnl. of Com. Psy.* 9, 2, 181–91.

Ferris S. et al. (1990) Paper presented at VI Int. Conf. on AIDS, San Francisco, THC 546.

Forbes P.B. (1986) The significance of AIDS in obstetric practice. *Brit. Jnl. Hosp. Med.* **36**, 342–6.

Fortuny Guasch C., Jimenez R., Roca A., Ercilla M.G. & Barrera J.M. (1989) *Clinical and serologic prospective study in 90 infants of HIV sero-positive mothers.* WHO Conference, Paris, B32.

Freudenberger H. J. (1974) Staff burnout: *Jnl. of Social Issues* 30, 159–165.

Fuller S.S., Endress M.P. & Johnson J.E. (1978) The effects of cognitive and behavioral control in coping with an aversive health examination. *Jnl. of Human Stress*, **4**, 18–25.

Garcia J. (198) Women's views of antenatal care. In *Effectiveness and satisfaction in antenatal care*, (Ed. by M. Enkin & I. Chalmers), 81–92. Spastics International Medical Publications/Heinemann Medical Books, London.

Gayle H., Jnaore E., Adjorlolo G. et al. (1989) *HIV Infection in children: Abidjan, Cote d'Ivoire.* WHO Conference, Paris.

Giaquinto C., de Rossi A., Mazza A. et al. (1989) *Natural history of perinatal HIV transmission.* WHO Conference, Paris.

Gillet J.H., Garraggo R., Abrar D., Bongain A., Lapalus P. & Dellamonica P. (1989) Fetoplacental passage of zidovudine. *The Lancet*, ii, July 29, 269–70.

Glaser B.G. & Strauss A.L. (1965) *Awareness of dying.* Aldine Press, Chicago.

Goedert J., Mendez H. & Drummond J. (1989) Mother to infant transmission of HIV type 1. *The Lancet*, Dec 9, 1334.

Greer H.S., Lal S., Lewis S.C. et al. (1976) Psychosocial consequences of therapeutic abortion; Kings termination Study II. *B.J. Psychiatry*, **128**, 74–9.

Grimm R.H. (1961) Psychological tension in pregnancy. *Psychosomatic*

Medicine, **23**, 520–7.

Grimm R.H., Shimoni K., Harlan W.R. & Estes E.H. (1975) Evaluation of patient care: protocol use by various providers. *New Eng. Jnl. of Medicine*, **302**, 900–2.

Griscelli C. (1989) *Diagnosis or HIV in infants.* V Int. Conf. on AIDS, Montreal, TB 020.

Griscelli C. (1990) Paper presented at VI Int. Conf. on AIDS, San Francisco, TB 020.

Grosch Worner I., Koch S., Vocks M. et al. (1989) *Outcome of children born to HIV infected mothers – a four year experience.* WHO Conference, Paris, B7.

Hall M. & Chng P.K. (1982) Antenatal care in practice. In *Effectiveness and satisfaction in antenatal care*, (Ed. by M. Enkin & I. Chalmers), op cit.

Halsey N.A., Boulos R., Holt E. et al. (1989) *Maternal infant HIV 1 infections in a Haitian slum population.* WHO Conference on Mothers and Babies, Paris, B5.

Halsey N.A., Townsend T., Coberly J. et al. (1987) *Seroprevalence of HIV infection in an obstetric population.* III Int. Conf. on AIDS, 4036.

Halsey N.A. et al. (1990) Paper presented at VI Int. Conf. on AIDS, San Francisco, THC 609/555.

Harris A. (1990) *Treating the non-infected sibling – an AIDS dilemma.* VI Int. Conf. on AIDS, THD 123.

Harrison W.O. & More T.A.L. (1987) *Perinatal HIV screening in a low risk population.* III Int. Conf. on AIDS, 4630.

Hauer L.B., Dattell B.J. & Sweet R.L. (1987) *HIV in pregnant women in San Francisco.* III Int. Conf. on AIDS, 4034.

Herioch, M.J., Batson J.W. & Baum J. (1978) Psychosocial factors in juvenile rheumatoid arthritis. *Arthritis & Rheumatism*, **21**, 2, 229–237.

Henrion R. (1989) AIDS and fetus. *Bulletin de l'Ac. Nat. de Med.*, **173**, (3), 333–7.

Henrion R. et al. (1990) Paper presented at VI Int. Conf. on AIDS, San Francisco, THC 545.

Heron J. (1977) *Behaviour analysis in education and training.* Human Potential Research Project, University of Surrey, Guildford, Surrey.

Hershenson D.B. & Power P.W. (1987) *Mental health counselling: Theory and Practice.* Pergamon Press, Oxford.

Henry K., Maki M. & Crossley K. (1988) Analysis of the use of HIV antibody (74% uptake). Testing in a Minnesota Hospital. *JAMA*, **259**, 229–32.

Hinton J. (1977) *Dying.* Penguin Books, London.

Hira S. (1990) Paper presented at VI Int. Conf. on AIDS, San Francisco, THC 612.

Hira S.K., Kamanga J., Bhat G.J., Mwale C., Tembo G., Luo N. & Perine P.L. (1989) Perinatal transmission of HIV I in Zambia. *BMJ*, vol 299, 1250–2.

Hittleman J. (1989) *Neurodevelopmental assessment of children with HIV Infection.* WHO Conference, Paris, C31.

Hittleman J. (1989) *Prospective neurodevelopmental outcome of infants with perinatally acquired HIV infection and their controls.* WHO Conference, Paris. C3.

Hittleman J. (1990) Paper presented at VI Int. Conf. on AIDS, San Francisco, SB 200.

Hoff R., Berardi V., Weiblen B.J. et al. (1987) *HIV seroprevalence in childbearing women.* III Int. Conf. on AIDS, 4626.

Hoff R., Beradi V.P., Weiblen B.J. et al. (1988) Seroprevalence of human immunodeficiency virus among childbearing women. *N. Engl. J. Med.* 318; 525.

Holman S., Sunderland A., Berthardt M. et al. (1989) Prenatal HIV counselling and testing. *Clin. Obstet. Gynec.*, Sept 1974, (3 pt. 1) p. 289, 294.

Holman S., Sunderland A., Moroso G. et al. (1987) *Multidisciplinary model for HIV testing of pregnant women in a drug treatment program.* III Int. Conf. on AIDS, 6604.

Holman S., Minkoff H., Hoegsberg B., Beller E. & Goldstein G. (1988) *A model program for routinely offered HIV antibody testing in pregnancy.* IV Int. Conf. on AIDS, Stockholm.

Holt E. (1990) Paper presented at VI Int. Conf. on AIDS, San Francisco, THC 617.

Hopkins K.M., Grosz J., Cohen H., Diamond G., Nozyce M. et al. (1989) The developmental and family services unit. A model AIDS project serving developmentally disabled children and their families. *AIDS Care*, vol 1, no 3, 281–5.

Houghton M. (196) Problems in hospital communication. In *Problems and progress in medical care*, Ed. G. McLachlan, Oxford University Press, Oxford.

Howard L.C., Hawkins D.A., Marwood R., Shanson D.C. & Gazzard B.G. (1989) Transmission of Human Immunodeficiency Virus by heterosexual contact with reference to antenatal screening. *Brit. Jnl. of Obstet. Gynec.* Vol 96, 135–9.

Hull H.F., Bettinger C.X.F., Gallaher M.M., Keller N.M., Wilson J. & Mertz G.J. (1988) Comparison of HIV antibody prevalence in patients consenting to and declining HIV antibody testing in an STD clinic.

JAMA, **260**, 935–8.

Hunter et al. (1989).

Illsley R. & Hall M.H. (1976) Psychosocial aspects of abortion. A review of issues and needed research. *WHO Bulletin*, **53**, 85–105.

Ippolito G., Stegagno M., Angeloni P. & Guzzanti E. (1990) Anonymous HIV testing on newborns. *JAMA*, vol 263, no 1, 36.

Ippolito G., Stegagno F., Costa P., Angeloni P. et al. (1989) *Detection of anti HIV antibodies in newborns a blind serosurvey in 92 Italian Hospitals.* WHO Conference, Paris, F10.

Irion O., (1989) Paper presented at WHO Conference, Paris, J1.

Irion O. et al. (1990) Paper presented at VI Int. Conf. on AIDS, San Francisco, SC 671.

Jakobs O. et al. (1990) Paper presented at VI Int. Conf. on AIDS, San Francisco, SD 819.

James M.E. (1988) HIV seropositivity diagnosed during pregnancy; psychosocial characterization of patients and their adaptation. *General Hospital Psychiatry*, **10**, 309–16.

Janis I. (1971) *Stress and Frustration.* Harcourt Brace and Jovanovich, New York.

Jenum P.A., Tjotta E.A. & Orstavik I. (1987) *Anti HIV screening of pregnant women in South Eastern Norway.* III Int. Conf. on AIDS, 4040.

Johnson J.E. & Leventhal H. (1974) Effects of accurate expectations and behavioural instructions on reactions during a noxious medical examination. *Jnl. of Personality and Social Psychology*, **29**, 5, 710–18.

Johnson J.P., Alger L., Nair P. et al. (1988) *HIV screening in the high risk obstetric population and infant serologic analysis.* IV Int. Conf. on AIDS, MP85.

Johnston M. (1980) Anxiety in surgical patients. *Psychological Medicine*, **10**, 145–52.

Johnston M. & Carpenter L. (1980) Relationship between pre-operative and post-operative state. *Psychological Medicine*, **10**, 361–70.

Johnston F., Brettle R., MacCallum L., Mok J., Peutherer J., Burns S. (1989) Women's knowledge of their HIV antibody state: its effect on their decision whether to continue the pregnancy. *BMJ*, Vol 300, 23–4.

Johnston F.D., MacCallum L.R., Brettle R.P. et al. (1988) Does infection with HIV affect the outcome of pregnancy? *BMJ*, 296–467.

Johnstone F.D., MacCallum L.R., Brettle R.P., Burns S.M. & Peutherer J.F. (1988) Testing for HIV in pregnancy; 3 years experience in Edinbugh city. *Scotl. Med. Jnl.* **34**, 561–563.

Joviasas E., Koch M.A. & Shafer, A. (1985) Letters to *The Lancet*, ii, 1129.

Kabagabo U. et al. (1990) Paper presented VI Int. Conf. on AIDS, San Francisco, Abst. SB 201.

Kamenga M. (1990) VI Int. Conf. on AIDS, San Francisco, THD 127.

Kane B. (1979) Children's concepts of death. *Jnl. of Genetic Psy.*, **134**, 11, 53.

Kantanen M.L., Cantell K., Aho K. et al. (1987) *Screening for HIV antibody during pregnancy in Finland.* III Int. Conf. on AIDS, 4631.

Kantanen M.L., Cantell K., Aho K., Brink A. & Ponka A. (1988) Screening for HIV antibody during pregnancy. *Serodiagnosis and Immunotherapy in Infectious Disease*, **2**, 113–15.

Kanti P., Ricard D., MBoup S. et al. (1987) *Perinatal transmission of HIV-2.* Paper presented at III Int. Conf. on AIDS, 6601.

Kaplan M., Farber B., Hall W.H. et al. (1989) *Pregnancy arising in HIV infected women while being repetitively counselled about safe sex.* V Int. Conf. on AIDS, Montreal, Abst MBP4.

Kaptue L., Durand J.P., Zekeng L. et al. (1987) *HIV Serosurvey in Cameroon.* III Int. Conf. on AIDS, 5536.

Kincey J. & Saltmore S. (1988) Stress and surgical treatments. In *Stress & Medical Procedures*, (Ed. M. Johnston & L. Wallace), Oxford University Press, Oxford.

Kletter R., Jeremy R.J., Rumsey C. et al. (1989) *A Prospective study of the mental and motor development of infants born to HIV infected intravenous drug using mothers.* V Int. Conf. on AIDS, Montreal, ABS MBP 24.

Koch T. et al. (1990) Paper presented at VI Int. Conf. on AIDS, San Francisco, SB203.

Kopp C.B. & Shaperman J. (1973) Cognitive development in the absence of object manipulation during infancy. *Developmental Psychology*, **9**, 430.

Kozlova A. (1990) *First cases of HIV 1 in Leningrad, USSR.* VI Int. Conf. on AIDS, San Francisco, FC 649.

Krasinski K., Borrowsky W., Bebenroth D. & Moore T. (1988) Failure of voluntary testing for human immunodeficiency virus to identify infected parturient women in a high risk population. *N. Engl. J. Med.*, **318**, 185.

Krener P. (1987) Impact of the diagnosis of AIDS on hospital care of an infant. *Neonatology Clin. Pediatr.*, (Philadelphia), Jan 26 (1), 30–34.

Kumar R. & Robson K. (1978) Neurotic disturbance during pregnancy and the puerperium. In *Mental Illness in Pregnancy and the Peurperium*, (Ed. M. Sandler), Oxford University Press, Oxford.

Kuykendall J. (1989) Death of a Child. In *Death, Dying and Bereavement*, Ed. by L. Sherr, Blackwell Scientific Publications, Oxford.

Kuznetsovo I.I. et al. (1990) VI Int. Conf. on AIDS, San Francisco, THC 48.

Lallemant M. (1989) Paper presented at WHO Conference, Paris, B11.

Lallemant M., Lallemant S., Cheyneir D. et al. (1987) *HIV I infection in an urban pop. of Congolese pregnant women*. III Int. Conf. on AIDS, 5028.

Lallemant M., Lallemant S., Cheynier D. et al. (1989) Mother child transmission of HIV 1 and infant survival in Brazzaville, Congo. *AIDS*, **3**, 643-6.

Landesman S., Holman S., McCalla S. et al. (1988) *HIV sero-survey of post partum women at a municipal hospital in NYC*. IV Int. Conf. on AIDS, TP78.

Landesman S., Minkoff H., Holman S. et al. (1987) Serosurvey of human immunodeficiency virus infection in parturients, *J.A.M.A.* 258; 2701.

Lansdown R. (1990) Paper presented at the Institute of Child Health Conference, London.

Larsson G., Bohlin A.B., Forsgren M. et al. (1987) *Experiences of screening for HIV in pregnant women*. Paper presented at the III Int. Conf. on AIDS, 6605.

Larsson G., Spangberg L., Lindgren S. & Bohlin A.B. (1990) Screening for HIV in pregnant women a study of maternal opinion. *AIDS Care*, vol 2, no 3, 223–8.

Larsson G., Lindgren S., Ottenblad C. et al. (1988) HIV Screening av gravida kvinnor ett ars resultat och erfarenheter, *Laekartidn*, **85**, 332–23.

Lasley-Bibbs V.A. (1990) VI Int. Conf. on AIDS, San Francisco, THC 655.

Lepage P. (1989) Paper presented at WHO Conference, Paris, C10.

Lepage P., van de Perre P., Carael M., Nsengumuremyi F., Njurunziza J. et al. (1987) Postnatal transmission of HIV from mother to child. *Lancet*, ii, 400.

Lepage P. et al. (1990) Paper presented at VI Int. Conf. on AIDS, San Francisco, THC 659.

Lewis V. (1987) *Development and Handicap*. Blackwell Scientific Publications, Oxford.

Ley P. (1982) Giving information to patients. In *Social Psychology and Behavioural Science* (Ed. J.R. Eiser) 339–73, John Wiley and Sons, New York.

Ley P. (1988) *Communicating with Patients*. Psychology and Medicine Series, Croom Helm, London.

Ley P. (1989) Improving patients' understanding: recall, satisfaction and compliance. In (Ed. A. Broome), *Health Psychology*, Chapman and Hall, London.

Lindgren S., Anzen B., Bohlin A.B. et al. (1987) *HIV infection in pregnant women and their children in Sweden*. Paper presented at III Int. Conf. on AIDS, 6608.

Lindsay M.K., Peterson H.B., Feng T.I., Slade B.A. et al. (1989) Routine antepartum human immunodeficiency virus infection screening in an inner city population. *Obstet Gynecol*, **74**, 3 pt. 1 289–94.

Lopita M. et al. (1990) VI Int. Conf. on AIDS, San Francisco, THC 653.

Lwegaba A.M.T. & Twatwa J. (1989) *The impact of AIDS on Ugandan mothers and children*. WHO Conference, Paris, D6.

McDonald R.L. (1963) The role of emotional factors in obstetric complications. *Psychosomatic Medicine*, **30**, 22–4.

MacIntyre S. (1977) The management of childbirth: A review of sociological issues. *Soc. Sci. and Med.*, **11**, 477–84.

MacIntyre S. (1979) *Findings from medical sociological research*. Paper given at the Scottish Home and Health Department Conference on Needs and Expectations in Obstetrics, Glasgow.

Magee J. (1975) The pelvic examination: a view from the other end of the table. *Annals Internal Medicine*, **83**, 563–7.

Makawa M., Miehakanda J., Silou I. et al. (1987) *Seroepidemiology of HIV 1 and HIV 2 infections in pregnant women*. III Int. Conf. on AIDS, 5117.

Mann J. (1989) *Women, children and the global AIDS strategy*. WHO Conference, Paris, Abst.

Manzila T., Baende E., Kabagabo U., Nsa W., Zola B. & Ryder R. (1989) *Perinatally acquired HIV infection: absence of an additional risk due to breast feeding in a cohort of 108 infants born to HIV-positive mothers*. WHO Conference, Paris, B2.

Marcus R.J. (1979) Evaluating abortion counselling. *Dimensions in Health Service*, Aug 16–18.

Marteau T.M. (1989) Psychological costs of screening. *BMJ*, vol 299, **26**, 527.

Martin J.M. (1988) Psychological consequences of AIDS-related bereavement. *Int. Jnl. Cons. and Clin. Psy.*, **6**, 856–62.

Martin J.M. & Sacks H.S. (1989) Do HIV infected children in foster care have access to clinical trials of new treatments? *AIDS and Public Policy Journal*, vol 5, **1**, 3–8.

Martin M.E. (1977) A maternity hospital study of psychiatric illness associated with childbirth. *Irish Jnl. of Med. Sci.*, **146**, 239.

Maslach C. (1981) *Burnout: the cost of caring*. Prentice Hall, Englewood, New Jersey.

Matthews A. & Ridgeway V. (1981) Personality and surgical recovery: a review. *B.J. of Clin. Psychol.*, **20**, 243–60.

Maynard E.L. (1989) HIV infection in pregnant women in Rhode Island. *N. Engl. J. of Med.*, **320**, (24), 1626.

Meadows J., Jenkinson S., Catalan J. & Gazzard B. (1990) Voluntary HIV testing in an antenatal clinic: differing uptake rakes for individual counselling midwives. *AIDS Care*, Vol II, 3, 229–234.

Medbo S., Lindemann R. (1989) *Infants born of HIV positive women in Norway*. WHO Conference, Paris, C38.

Melamed B.G. (1982) Reduction of medical fears: an information processing analysis. In *Learning theory approaches to psychiatry*, (Ed. by J. Boulougouris), 205–218, Wiley, New York.

Mendez H. (1989) *Natural history of infants born to HIV 1 seropositive mothers and their seronegative controls*. WHO Conference, Paris, C4.

Mendez H., Willoughby A., Hittleman J. et al. (1987) *Infants of HIV seropositive women and their seronegative controls*. III Int. Conf. on AIDS, 6594.

Miller D. & Pinching A.J. (1989) HIV tests and counselling current issues. *AIDS*, **3**, suppl 1, 3187–93.

Miller, D. (1987) Paper presented at III Int. Conf. on AIDS, Washington.

Miller D., Jeffries D.J., Green J., Harris J.R.W. & Pinching A.J. (1986) HTLV-III: Should testing ever be routine? *BMJ*, **292**, 941–3.

Miller S.M. & Mangan C.E. (1983) Interacting effects of information and coping style in adapting to gynaecological stress; should doctors tell all? *Jnl. of Personality and Social Psychology*, **45**, (1), 223–36.

Minkoff H. (1989) AIDS in Pregnancy. *Current Probl. Obstet. Gynecol. Fertil.*, November/December, 206–27.

Minkoff H.L. (1987) Care of pregnant women infected with HIV. *Jnl. of Med. Assoc.*, **258**, 2714–17.

Minkoff H.L., Holman S., Beller E., Delke I., Fishbone A. & Landesman S. (1988) SUNY Health Science Center; routinely offered prenatal HIV testing. *New Engl. J. Med.*, **319**, 1018.

Moatti J.P., Gales C., Seror V., Papiernik E. & Henrion R. (1990) Social acceptability of HIV screening among pregnant women. *AIDS Care*, vol II, (3), 213–22.

Mok J. (1987) HIV seropositive babies – implications for planning for their future. In *The implications of AIDS for children in care* (Ed. by D. Batty), BAAF, London.

Mok J. & O'Hara G. (1990) Placement of children from HIV affected families: The Edinburgh experience. *Pediatric AIDS and HIV Infection*, vol 1, 3, 20–22.

Mok J. (1990) Paper presented at VI Int. Conf. on AIDS, San Francisco,

THD 813.

Mok J., Hague R.A., Yap P.L. et al. (1989) Vertical transmission of HIV: A prospective study. *Archives of Disease in Childhood*, **64**, 1140–45.

Mok J.Y., Hague R.A., Taylor R.F. et al. (1989) The management of infants born to HIV seropositive women. *J. Infect.*, **18**, 119–24.

Mok, J. (1989) *Perinatal transmission of HIV*. V Int. Conf. on AIDS, Montreal, TBP 211.

Morbidity and Mortality Weekly Report MMWR (1987) Sep 11, **36**, (35), 593–595.

Morbidity and Mortality Weekly Report MMWR (1990).

Morgan B.M., Clifton P. & Lewis P.J. (1984) The consumer's attitude to obstetrics care. *B. Jnl. Obstet. and Gynec.*, **91**, (7), 624–28.

Morillo E.W. & Gardner L.I. (1980) Activation of latent graves disease in children. *Clinical Paediatrics*, **19**, (3), 16–63.

M'Pele P. (1989) *Africa implications of AIDS for mother and child*. WHO Conference, Paris.

Mucchilelli R. (1983) *Face to face in the counselling relationship*, Macmillan, London.

Mulleady G. (1989) Counselling and Drug Users. In *Counselling in HIV infection and AIDS*, Ed. by J. Green & A. McCreaner, Blackwell Scientific Publications, Oxford.

Mulleady G. & Sherr L. (1989) *Life style factors for drug users in relation to risks for HIV. AIDS Care*, vol 1, 1, 45–50.

Murai N. & Murai M. (1975) A study of moods in pregnant women. *Tohoku Psychologia Folia*, **34**, 10–16.

Mworozi E.A. & Kiguli S. (1989) *The relationship between the health status of HIV-positive mothers and that of their infants*, B6.

Naji S.A., Russell I.T., Foy C.J., Gallagher M., Rhodes T.J. & Moore M.P. (1989) HIV infection and Scottish general practice. *Journal of the Royal College of General Practitioners*, **39**, 234–8.

Nanda L. & Minkoff H. (1989) Paper presented at V Int. Conf. on AIDS, Montreal.

Ndugwa et al. (1990) Paper presented at VI Int. Conf. on AIDS, San Francisco, SC 668.

Nesheim S.R., Jones D.S., Sawyer M.K. & Nahmias A.J. (1989) *The natural history of HIV infection in a population based cohort of infants born to HIV positive women; the first two years*. WHO Conference, Paris, C6.

New York State Department of Health (1988) Epidemiology Notes, vol 3, no 7, July.

Newman G. & Denman S.B. (1971) Felony and paternal deprivation: a socio-psychiatric view. *Int. Jnl. of Soc. Psy.*, **17**, (1), 65–71.

NIH National Institute of Child Health (1989) *From Cells to Selves*, Pub 89-83.

Nisbett R. & Ross L. (1980) *Human inference*. Prentice Hall, Englewood, New Jersey.

Novick B.E. & Rubinstein A. (1987) AIDS – the paediatric perspective. *AIDS*, **1**, 3–7.

Novick L.F., Berns D., Stricof R. et al. (1989) HIV seroprevalence in newborns in New York State. *JAMA*, **261**, 1745–50.

Nsa W., Ryder R., Baende E. et al. (1987) *Mortality from perinatally acquired HIV infections in African children*. III Int. Conf. on AIDS, 4126.

Ntabab H.M., Liomba C.N., Schmidt H.J. et al. (1987) *HIV I Prevalence in hospital patients and pregnant women in Malawi*. III Int. Conf. on AIDS, 5036.

Nzilambi N., Ryder R.W., Behets F. et al. (1987) *Perinatal HIV transmission in two African hospitals*. III Int. Conf. on AIDS, Washington.

Nzilambi N., Ryder R., Behets F. et al. (1988) *Perinatal HIV transmission in two African hospitals*. IV Int. Conf. AIDS, TH 76.

Oakley A. (1979) *Becoming a Mother*. Martin Robertson, Oxford .

O'Brien M. & Smith C. (1981) Women's views and experience of antenatal care, *Practitioner*, **225**, 123–25.

Oleske J. et al. (1990). Paper presented at VI Int. Conf. on AIDS, San Francisco, THC 607.

Oleske J., Minnefor A., Cooper B. et al. (1984) Immune Deficiency Syndrome in Children. *JAMA*, **249**, 2345–9.

O'Neill M. & Décarie T.G. (1973) Quelques Aspects du développement cognitif d'enfants souffriant de malformations dués à la thalidomide. *Bull. de Psych.* **27**, 286–303.

Osokosky H.J. (1967) Women's reactions to pelvic examination. *Obstet. and Gynec.*, **30**, 146–9.

Pape J.W. & Johnson W. Jr (1989) Perinatal transmission of the human immunodeficiency virus. *Bull. Pan Am. Health Organ.*, **23**, (1–2), 50–61.

Pasacreta J.V. & Jacobsen P.B. (1989) Addressing the need for staff support among nurses caring for the AIDS population. *O.N.F.*, vol 16, no 5, 659–63.

Peckham C. & Senturia Y. (1987) Transmission of HIV infection: implications for fostering and adoption. In *The Implications of AIDS for children in care* (Ed. by D. Batty), BAAF, London.

Peckham C.S., Tedder R.S., Briggs M., Ades A., Hjelm M., Wilcox A.H., Parramjejia N. & O'Connor C. (1990) Prevalence of maternal HIV Infection based on unlinked anonymous testing of newborn babies. *The Lancet*, 335, 516–519.

Peckham C. et al. (1989) *Perinatal transmission in industrialized countries.* V Int. Conf. on AIDS, Montreal, TB 017.

Peckham L. (1989) Perinatally-acquired HIV infection. In *Aspects of Paediatric HIV Management,* (Ed. by I.V. Weller), Wellcome, UK.

Peterson L. (1989) Coping by children undergoing stressful medical procedures; some conceptual, methodological and therapeutic issues. *Jnl. of Cons. & Clin. Psychol.,* **57,** 3, 380–87.

Peterson L. & Toler S.M. (1986) An information seeking disposition in child surgery patients. *Health Psychology,* **5,** 343–58.

Petrillo M. & Sanger S. (1972) *Emotional care of hospitalized children.* Lippincott, Philadelphia.

Piaget J. (1963) *The origins of intelligence in children.* Norton, New York.

Pines O. & Maslach C. (1978) Characteristics of staff burnout. *Hosp. Community Psychiatry,* **29,** (4), 233–7.

Pista A. et al. (1990) *Prevalence of HIV 1 and 2: 3 year study.* VI Int. Conf. on AIDS, San Francisco, FC 641.

Pizzo P.A., Eddy J. & Falloon J. (1988) AIDS in children: current problems and therapeutic considerations. *Am. Jnl. Med.,* **85,** 195–202.

Pokrovsky, V. (1990) Paper presented at VI Int. Conf. on AIDS, San Francisco, FC 648.

Pons J.C., Brigaudiot V., Chambrin F., Dauphin J.F., Delfraissy E. & Papiernik A. (1989) *Pregnancy decision in HIV women.* WHO Conference, Paris.

Poster E.C. (1983) Stress immunization techniques to help children cope with hospitalization. *Maternal Child Nursing Journal,* **12,** 119-34.

Pringle M. & Fiddes D.O. (1970) *The Challenge of Thalidomide.* Nat. Bureau for Cooperation in Childcare, London.

Prazuck T. (1990) Paper presented at VI Int. Conf. on AIDS, San Francisco, THC 610.

Ramachandram P. (1989) Paper presented at WHO Conference, Paris.

Raphael B. (1977) *The anatomy of bereavement: a handbook for the caring profession.* Unwin Hyman, Boston.

Reading A. (1982) The management of fear related to vaginal examinations. *Journal of Psychosomatic Obstet. and Gynec.,* **1,** (3/4), 99–102.

Reading A. & Cox D. (1982) The effects of ultrasound examination on maternal anxiety levels. *J. Behavioural Medicine,* **5,** 237–247.

Reid M.E. & McIlwaine G.M. (1980) Consumer opinion of a hospital ante-natal clinic. *Social Science and Medicine,* **14a,** 363–8.

Reilly T.P. et al. (1983) Children's conception of death and personal mortality. *Journal of Paed. Psy.,* **8,** 21–31.

Rickard E. et al. (1990) Paper presented at VI Int. Conf. on AIDS, San Francisco, THC 608.

Ridgeway V. & Matthews A. (1982) Psychological preparation for surgery: a comparison of methods. *B. Jnl. of Clin. Psych.*, **21**, 271–80.

Rogers M.F., White C.R., Sanders R. et al. (1990) Lack of transmission of human immunodeficiency virus from infected children to their household contacts. *Pediatrics*, **85**, 210–14.

Rossi A.D., Chieco Bianchi L., Giaquinto C. & Zacchello F. (1988) HIV screening in pregnant women. *The Lancet*, March 26, 714.

Rothenberg R., Woelfel M., Stoneburner R., Milberg J., Parker R. & Truman B. (1987) Survival with the acquired immunodeficiency syndrome. *New Engl. Jnl. Med.*, **317**, (21), 1297–1302.

Rouzioux C. et al. (1989) *Prospective study of newborns to HIV seropositive mothers.* V Int. Conf. on AIDS, Montreal THCP 7.

Royal Commission on the National Health Services (1978) *Patients' Attitudes to the Hospital Service*, HMSO, London.

Rutter D. & Maguire P. (1976) History-taking for medical students. *The Lancet*, 558–60.

Ryder R.W. (1989) *Perinatal transmission of the HIV type 1 to infants of seropositive women in Zaire.* WHO Conference, Paris, B10.

Ryder R.W., Nsa W., Hassig S.E. et al. (1989) Perinatal transmission of HIV type 1 to infants of seropositive women in Zaire. *New Engl. Jnl. Med.*, **320**, 1637–1642.

Sangare L. et al. (1989) *Statut serologique population prostitutées au Burkino Fasso.* V Int. Conf. on AIDS, Montreal, THG 026.

Santana W. et al. (1990) Paper presented at VI Int. Conf. on AIDS, San Francisco, SC 66.

Schoellr M.C., Plebani A., Biolchini A. et al. (1989) *Paediatric HIV infection.* WHO Conference, Paris, C16.

Schoenbaum E.E., Davenny K. & Selwyn P.A. (1988) The impact of pregnancy on HIV related disease. *RCOG*, 65–75.

Schuerman L., de Vathaire F., Seynhaeve V. et al. (1989) *Prevalence of HIV1 and HIV2 in a semi-rural hospital in the Ivory Coast.* WHO Conference, Paris.

Schwartz T. (1989) *Caring for the HIV positive child: the identification of family stressors to target and improve the nursing interventions.* WHO Conference, Paris, D4.

Scott G. (1989) *Natural history of HIV in children.* V Int. Conf. on AIDS, Montreal, TB 021.

Scott G., Fischl M.A., Klimas N. et al. (1985) Mothers of infants with the acquired immunodeficiency syndrome. *JAMA*, **253**, 363–6.

Scott G., Hutto C. et al. (1987) *Probability of perinatal infections in infants of HIV 1-positive mothers.* III Int. Conf. on AIDS, 6583.

Scott G.B., Hutto C., Makuch R.W., Mastrucci M., O'Connor T.,

Mitchell C., Trapido E. & Parks W.P. (1989) Survival in children with perinatally acquired human immunodeficiency virus type 1 infection. *New Eng. Jnl. Med.*, **321**, (26), 1791–6.

Scrimgeour J.B., Gaudoin M., Hobson M., Neill R. & Papachrysostomou M. (1987) Screening for HIV during pregnancy. *The Lancet*, Mar 28, 753.

Selwyn P.A., Carter R.J., Schoenbaum E.E. et al. (1989) Knowledge of HIV antibody status and decision to continue or terminate pregnancy among intravenous drug users. *JAMA*, **261**, 3567–71.

Selwyn P.A., Schoenbaum E.E., Davenny K. et al. (1989) Prospective study of HIV infection and pregnancy outcomes in intravenous drug users. *JAMA*, **261**, 1289–94.

Shepherd and Barraclough (1976) The aftermath of parental suicide for children. *B.J. of Psychiatry*, **129**, 267–76.

Sheridan M.A. (1975) Talk time for hospitalized children. *Social Work*, **20**, 40–44.

Sherr L. & Sherr A. (1981) *The Quality of lawyering can be trained*. Paper to BPS London Conference.

Sherr L., Davey T. & Strong C. (1991) Counselling Psychology Quarterly (in press).

Sherr L. (1980) *Do doctors know what women know?* Paper presented to the Annual Conference of the British Psychological Society, Guildford.

Sherr L. (1981) *A smile is not enough. Doctor-patient communications in ante-natal care*. Paper present to the Annual Conference of the British Psychological Society, York.

Sherr L. (1982) *Role of information and feedback in antenatal care*. Paper presented to the London Conference of the British Psychological Society.

Sherr L. (1987) The impact of AIDS in obstetrics on obstetric staff. *Jnl. of Reproductive and Infant Psychology*, **5**, 87–96.

Sherr L. (1988) *AIDS in obstetrics*. IV Int. Conf. on AIDS, Stockholm.

Sherr L. (1989) HIV Infection. In *Death Dying and Bereavement* (Ed. by L. Sherr), Blackwell Scientific Publications, Oxford.

Sherr L. (1989) *The psychosocial cost of HIV screening in ante-natal clinics*. WHO Conference, Paris, D16.

Sherr L. (1989) *Changes in the impact of AIDS on obstetric staff*. WHO Conference, Paris, I18.

Sherr L. (1989) *To know or not to know: that is the question*. WHO Conference, Paris I17.

Sherr L. (1989) *Anxiety and communication in obstetric care*. Unpublished Ph.D. Thesis, University of Warwick.

Sherr L. & George H. (1988) *AIDS and Staff Stress*. Abstracts, Psychology and Health International, British Psychological Society.

Sherr L. & Hedge B. (1989) *On becoming a mother: counselling implications for mothers and fathers*. WHO Conference, Paris D17.

Sherr L. & Hedge B. (1990) The impact and use of written leaflets as a counselling alternative in mass antenatal HIV screening. *AIDS Care*, **2**, (3), 235–45.

Sherr L. & McCreaner A. (1989) Summary evaluation of the National AIDS Counselling Training Unit in the UK. *Counselling Psychology Quarterly*, **2**, (1), 21–32.

Shusterman L.R. (1979) Predicting the psychological consequences of abortion. *Social Science and Medicine*, **96**, 683.

Skinner K. (1990) Paper presented at the AIDS and Children Symposium of the London Conference, British Psychological Society.

Smith J.R., Reginald P.W. & Forster S.M. (1990) Safe sex and conception: a dilemma. *The Lancet*, **335**, 359.

Sperling R.S., Sacks H.S., Mayer L., Joyner M. & Berkowitz R.L. (1989) Umbilical cord blood serosurvey for HIV in parturient women in a voluntary hospital in New York City. *Obstet. Gynec.*, **73**, (2), 179–81.

Sprecher S., Soumenkoff C., Puissant F., Degueldre M. (1986) Vertical transmission of HIV in 15-week fetus. *The Lancet*, ii, 288–9.

Steptoe A. & O'Sullivan J. (1986) Monitoring and blunting: coping styles in women prior to surgery. *B. Jnl. of Clinical Psychology*, **25**, (2), 143–4.

Stevens A., Victor C. & Sherr L. (1990) Antenatal testing for HIV. *The Lancet*, Feb 3, 292.

Stevens A., Victor C., Sherr L. & Beard R. (1989) HIV testing in antenatal clinics: The impact on women. *AIDS Care*, **1**, (2), 165–71.

Stratton P. et al. (1990) Paper presented at VI Int. Conf. on AIDS, San Francisco, SC 665.

Strunin L. (1989) First year medical students' attitudes and knowledge about AIDS. *AIDS Care*, **1**, (1), 105.

Sunderland A., Moroso G., Holman S. et al. (1989) *Influence of HIV infection on pregnancy decisions*. V Int. Conf. on AIDS, Montreal, ABS WDP 58.

Sunderland A., Moroso G., Berthaud M., Holman S., Landesman S., Minkoff H. et al. (1988) *Influence of HIV infection on pregnancy decisions*. IV Int. Conf. on AIDS, Stockholm.

Swales T., Scott G. & Cohen D. (1990) *Neurocognitive functioning among infants exposed perinatally to HIV*. VI Int. Conf. on AIDS, San Francisco, TB 486.

Tardieu M., Blanche S., Duliege A.M. et al. (1987) *Neurologic involve-*

ment and prognostic factors after materno-fetal infection. V Int. Conf. on AIDS, Montreal MBO 39.

Temmerman M. (1989) *HIV infection as a risk factor for adverse obstetrical outcome.* WHO Conference, Paris, E3.

Temmerman M., Moses S., Kirau D., Fusallah S., Wamola I.A. & Piot P. (1990) Impact of single session post partum counselling of HIV infected women on their subsequent reproductive behaviour. *AIDS Care*, **2**, (3), 247–52.

Temoshok L. (1990) *Survival time in men with AIDS.* VI Int. Conf. on AIDS, San Francisco, 3133.

Thiry L., Sprecher Goldberger S., Jonckheer T. et al. (1985) Isolation of AIDS Virus from cell free breast milk of three virus carriers. *The Lancet*, ii, 891–92.

Toro A. (1989) *AIDS in Puerto Rico.* V Int. Conf. on AIDS, THE 67.

Tovo P.A. (1988) Epidemiology clinical features and prognostic factors of paediatric HIV infection. *The Lancet*, ii, Nov 5, 1043–1046.

Tovo P.A., de Martino M. (1987) Registor Italiono per AIDS. *Riv. Ital. Pediatr.*, **13**, 361–8.

Tovo P.A. & de Martino M. (1989) *The Italian register for HIV infection in children: epidemiological and clinical results.* WHO Conference, Paris.

Trezi A.H. (1989) Paper presented at WHO Conference, Paris.

Ultmann M.H., Belman A.L., Ruff H.A., Norvick B.E., Cone Wesson B., Cohen H.J. & Rubinstein A. (1985) Developmental abnormalities in infants and children with acquired immune deficiency syndrome (AIDS) and AIDS related complex: *Developmental Medicine and Child Neurology*, **27**, 563–71.

lUssher J. (1990) Cognitive behavioural couples therapy. *AIDS Care*, **2**, 1.

Van de Perre P. et al. (1990) Paper presented at the VI Int. Conf. on AIDS, San Francisco, THC 43.

Van Eerdewegh M.M., Bieri M.D., Parilla I.R.H. & Clayton P.J. (1982) The bereaved child. *B. Jnl. Psychiatry*, **14**, 23–9.

Van Lith J.M., Tijmstra T. & Uisser G. (1989) The attitudes of pregnant women towards HIV testing. *Nederlands Tijd. Gen.*, **133**, (25), 1273–7.

Vendrell P. et al. (1990) Paper presented at VI Int. Conf. on AIDS, San Francisco, THC 616.

Virnon D., Bernard N., Melchoir J. et al. (1987) *Anti HIV 1 Screening in pregnant women: a prospective study.* III Int. Conf. on AIDS, 6609.

Vogler M. (1989) *Changes in sexual and reproductive behaviour in heterosexual couples after HIV testing.* V Int. Conf. on AIDS, Montreal, TAP 101.

Vranx R., Alisjahbana A., Deville W. et al. (1987) *Anti-HIV prevalence in*

Indonesia. III Int. Conf. on AIDS, 5526.

Wallace L. (1984) Psychological preparation for gynaecological surgery. In *Psychology and Gynaecological Problems* (Ed. by A. Broome & L. Wallace), 161–88, Tavistock Publications, London.

Wang Q., Hardy W., Chein N. et al. (1987) *A preliminary serologic screening for retrovirus infection in Sichuan Province of the People's Republic of China*. III Int. Conf. on AIDS, 5528.

Weinbreck P., Loustaud V., Denis F. et al. (1988) Postnatal transmission of HIV. *Infection*, Feb 27, 482.

Weinman J. (1987) *An outline of Psychology as applied to Medicine*, 2nd edn. Wright, Bristol.

Weller I.D. & Peckham C. (1988) *Aspects of Paediatric HIV Management*. International Seminar Series, Wellcome, UK.

Wenstrom K.D. & Zuidema L.J. (1989) Determination of the seroprevalence of HIV infection in Gravidas by non-anonymous versus anonymous testing. *Obstet. and Gynec.*, **74**, (4), 558–61.

Whalen L. et al. (1990) Paper presented at VI Int. Conf. on AIDS, San Francisco, THD 85.

Whitt J.K. et al. (1990) Paper presented at VI Int. Conf. on AIDS, San Francisco, 3134.

WHO (1989) *AIDS Surveillance in Europe*. WHO Collaborating Centre on AIDS, quarterly report 22.

WHO (1990) *The Global AIDS Situation Updated*. Information Sheet no. 68.

Wilfert C. (1989) Paper presented at the WHO Conference, Paris.

Wiznia A., Bueti C., Douglas C. et al. (1989) *Factors influencing maternal decision making regarding pregnancy outcome in HIV infected women*. V Int. Conf. on AIDS, Montreal, MBP 7.

Wolfer J.A. & Visintainer M.A. (1975) Pediatric surgery patients' and parents' stress responses and adjustment. *Nursing Research*, **24**, 244–55.

Woodburn M. (1973) *Social implications of spina bifida – a study in SE Scotland*. Edinburgh Eastern Branch Scottish Spina Bifida Association.

Ziegler J.B., Cooper D.A., Johnson R.O. & Gold J. (1985) Post-natal transmission of AIDS-associated retrovirus from mother to infant. *The Lancet*, i, 896–897.

Ziegler J.B., Steward G.J., Penny R., Cooper D.A., Gold J., Stuckey A. & Good S. (1989) *Breast feeding and risk of transmission of HIV from mother to infant*. WHO Conference on Mothers and Babies, Paris, B3.

Zohoun I., Bigot A., Sankale J.L. et al. (1987) *Prevalence of HIV I and HIV 2 in Benin*. III Int. Conf. on AIDS, 5063.

Zuccolli G.V. et al. (1990) Paper presented at VI Int. Conf. on AIDS, San Francisco, THC 613.